The *Sams Teach Yourself in 24 Hours* S

 Y0-AAV-298

Sams Teach Yourself in 24 Hours books provide quick and easy answers in a proven step-by-step approach that works for you. In just 24 sessions, you will tackle every task you need to get the results you want. Let our experienced authors present the most accurate information to get you reliable answers—fast!

FILE MANAGEMENT KEYS

KEY COMBINATION	FUNCTION
Ctrl+O	Open a document
Ctrl+N	Start a new document
Ctrl+S	Save a document
Ctrl+P	Print a document
Ctrl+F4	Close a document

NAVIGATION KEYS

KEYBOARD TECHNIQUE	MOVES THE INSERTION POINT
↓	Down one line
↑	Up one line
→	One character to the right
←	One character to the left
Ctrl+→	One word to the right
Ctrl+←	One word to the left
Ctrl+↓	Down one paragraph
Ctrl+↑	Up one paragraph
End	To the end of the line
Home	To the beginning of the line
Page Down	Down one screen
Page Up	Up one screen
Ctrl+Page Down	To the top of the next page
Ctrl+Page Up	To the top of the previous page
Ctrl+End	End of document
Ctrl+Home	Beginning of document

SELECTION SHORTCUTS

TO SELECT	DO THIS
One word	Double-click the word.
One sentence	Ctrl+click the sentence.
One line	Click in the selection bar to the left of the line.
One paragraph	Double-click in the selection bar to the left of the paragraph. (You can also triple-click directly on the paragraph.)
Entire document	Triple-click or Ctrl+click anywhere in the selection bar, or press Ctrl+A.
Any amount of text	Click at the beginning of the text you want to select, and then Shift+click at the end of the text.

SAMS

Teach Yourself Microsoft® Word 2000

in 24 Hours

Editing Keys

Key Combination	Function
Ctrl+X	Cut
Ctrl+C	Copy
Ctrl+V	Paste
Ctrl+Z	Undo
Ctrl+Y	Redo
F4	Repeat the last action
Ctrl+F	Find
Ctrl+H	Replace
Delete key	Deletes character to the right of the insertion point
Backspace key	Deletes character to the left of the insertion point
Ctrl+Delete	Deletes word to the right of the insertion point
Ctrl+Backspace	Deletes word to the left of the insertion point
Select text and press the Delete key	Deletes selected text (can be any amount)
Select text and start typing	Deletes selected text (can be any amount) and replaces it with the text you type

Formatting Keys

Key Combination	Function
Ctrl+B	Bold
Ctrl+I	Italic
Ctrl+U	Underline
Ctrl+Shift+D	Double underline
Shift+F3	Change the case of text
Ctrl+L	Left-align
Ctrl+E	Center
Ctrl+R	Right-align
Ctrl+J	Justify
Ctrl+1	Single line spacing
Ctrl+2	Double line spacing
Ctrl+5	1.5 line spacing
Ctrl+M	Increase indent
Ctrl+Shift+M	Decrease indent
Ctrl+Spacebar	Remove character formatting
Ctrl+Q	Remove paragraph formatting

Keys for Inserting Special Characters

Key Combination	Function
Shift+Enter	Line break
Ctrl+Shift+Enter	Column break
Ctrl+Enter	Page break
Alt+Ctrl+C	Copyright symbol
Alt+Ctrl+R	Registered trademark symbol
Alt+Ctrl+T	Trademark symbol

Heidi Steele

SAMS Teach Yourself

Microsoft® Word 2000

in 24 Hours

SAMS

A Division of Macmillan Computer Publishing
201 West 103rd St., Indianapolis, Indiana 46290 USA

Sams Teach Yourself Microsoft® Word 2000 in 24 Hours

Copyright © 1999 by Sams Publishing

International Standard Book Number: 0-672-31442-8

Library of Congress Catalog Card Number: 98-86985

First Printing: April 1999

02   01   4   3

Interpretation of the printing code: The rightmost double-digit number is the year of the book's printing; the rightmost single digit, the number of the book's printing. For example, a printing code of 99-1 shows that the first printing of the book occurred in 1999.

Printed in the United States of America

Trademarks

EXECUTIVE EDITOR
Jim Minatel

DEVELOPMENT EDITOR
Susan Hobbs

ACQUISITIONS EDITOR
Renée Wilmeth

MANAGING EDITOR
Thomas F. Hayes

PROJECT EDITOR
Lori A. Lyons

COPY EDITORS
Julie McNamee
Victoria Elzey

TECHNICAL EDITOR
Debra Schnedler

INDEXER
Angie Bess

PROOFREADER
Maribeth Echard

LAYOUT TECHNICIAN
Louis Porter, Jr.

Overview

Table of Contents

Dedication

In memory of my father, Charles W. Steele.

About the Author

Heidi Steele is a freelance writer and software trainer. She specializes in demystifying computer concepts and making programs such as Word 2000 accessible to home users and professionals alike. Heidi Steele is the author of numerous other computer books, including *Easy Word 97, How to Use the Internet,* and *How to Use Word 97 for Windows.* She lives in Port Orchard, Washington.

Acknowledgments

Writing a book is an all-consuming task that would be impossible without the help of many people. My acquisitions editor, Renée Wilmeth, did a bang-up job as a one-woman cheerleading team. When I submitted a chapter a few days late, she did not, as one might expect, send email stressing the importance of deadlines. Rather, she fired off a typical Wilmeth-style one-liner: "You rock!" Renée can make you feel special for knowing how to tie your shoes, not to speak of writing a good book. Sadly, she has transferred to Macmillan's reference book division, and I miss her already. Jim Minatel stepped in when Renée stepped out, and I appreciate his friendly guidance, good humor, and plentiful tech support. My development editor, Susan Hobbs, pointed out areas of the book that needed clarification and made many helpful suggestions. Deb Schnedler, my technical editor, provided astute comments and corrections throughout the book.

Lisa Hochstein and Sol Katzman let me set up shop at their dining room table and finish the manuscript during a visit to Boston. And Deborah Craig generously allowed me to use her paper on Imogen Cunningham for many of the examples in this book. If you use a magnifying glass to read the text in these figures, you might learn a thing or two about Imogen in addition to Word.

Tell Us What You Think!

As the reader of this book, *you* are our most important critic and commentator. We value your opinion and want to know what we're doing right, what we could do better, what areas you'd like to see us publish in, and any other words of wisdom you're willing to pass our way.

As the Executive Editor for the General Desktop Applications team at Sams Publishing, I welcome your comments. You can fax, email, or write me directly to let me know what you did or didn't like about this book—as well as what we can do to make our books stronger.

Please note that I cannot help you with technical problems related to the topic of this book, and that due to the high volume of mail I receive, I might not be able to reply to every message.

When you write, please be sure to include this book's title and author as well as your name and phone or fax number. I will carefully review your comments and share them with the author and editors who worked on the book.

Fax: 317-581-4770

Email: office_sams@mcp.com

Mail: Executive Editor
            General Desktop Applications
            Sams Publishing
            201 West 103rd Street
            Indianapolis, IN 46290 USA

Introduction

Word is the most popular word processing program available. Its primary mission is to help you type and format text documents, but it also offers a host of other powerful features that let you create tables, work with graphics, create mass mailings, design Web pages, and more. This book teaches you to use the most recent incarnation of the program, Word 2000.

What This Book Will Do for You

If you rank learning new software right up there with trips to the dentist, you're not alone. Many people feel less than enthusiastic about exploring new programs because the "how-to" books they use are unclear or intimidating. This book aims to give you a much more positive learning experience. In it, you learn a good portion of the Word program—enough to create just about any type of document you need—in a thorough and systematic way.

Sams Teach Yourself Microsoft Word 2000 in 24 Hours is organized in 24 sessions that should take approximately one hour each to complete. Depending on your previous experience with Word and your areas of interest, some sessions may take less than an hour and others may take more. The exact amount of time is not important. After you've practiced and absorbed all the information in a session that is relevant to your work, you're ready to move on.

Conventions Used in This Book

Sams Teach Yourself Microsoft Word 2000 in 24 Hours uses a few conventions to present concepts and skills clearly:

- Menu commands are separated by commas. For example, if you need to select the Save command in the File menu, you will see instructions to choose File, Save.
- Tasks that require you to follow a series of steps appear in numbered To Do lists.
- Every hour ends with common questions and answers.

In addition to these conventions, each hour also includes three elements:

Notes provide additional information related to the topic of discussion.

Tips offer alternative or time-saving ways to do things.

Cautions warn you about potential pitfalls and tell you how to avoid them.

PART I
Getting Started

Hour

HOUR 1

Let's Start at the Beginning

Whether you use a computer at home or at the office, if you work with text documents of any sort, you will likely come to view Word 2000 as your "home base" on the computer. Word 2000 sets the standard for word processing programs. Word has an intuitive interface that lets you access commonly used commands, yet it is full of powerful features that enable you to create a wide assortment of specialized documents. In this hour, you get an overall idea of what Word 2000 can do, you learn a bit about installing it, and you find out how to start and exit Word.

Highlights of this hour include

- What can you do with Word
- What versions of Word came before Word 2000
- What new features come with Word 2000
- Pointers on installing Word 2000
- How to start Word
- How to exit Word

What Is Word Designed to Do?

Word's fundamental mission is simple: to help you type, revise, and format text. To this end, it offers a complete set of tools that enable you to create just about any type of document imaginable. You can produce anything from basic letters and memos to complex documents such as reports, papers, newsletters, brochures, résumés, mass mailings, envelopes, and mailing labels. You can even compose email messages and design Web pages in Word.

Each person who uses Word needs a slightly different combination of features. If you're an administrative assistant, you may need to use Word's mail merge feature to generate mass mailings. If you're a student, you'll want to learn about footnotes and endnotes for your term papers. If you're a marketing executive, you may want to use the table feature to present information in charts. Depending on the documents you create, you'll use some parts of Word constantly, and others you will never venture into. This is to be expected. Learn the areas of Word that you need, and don't feel compelled to explore every nook and cranny.

Word is part of Microsoft Office, a suite of business applications. The other key players in Office are Excel, a spreadsheet program, and PowerPoint, a presentation program. Depending on the edition of Office you have, you may also have a database program called Access, a personal information manager (PIM) and email application called Outlook, and possibly a few others. All the Office applications have a similar look, and they are tightly integrated to let you use them in combination with one another (see Hour 22, "Using Data from Other Office 2000 Applications in Your Word Documents").

What Came Before Word 2000?

Microsoft has been producing Word for years, so several versions of the program are floating around. To make things more confusing, there is more than one way to refer to some versions. Table 1.1 lists the most recent versions of Word to help you understand where Word 2000 fits in. You can run all these versions under Windows 95 or 98.

TABLE 1.1. THE RECENT INCARNATIONS OF MICROSOFT WORD

Version	Also Known As	Description
Word 6.0	Same	Word 6.0 was designed for Windows 3.1, but you can also run it with Windows 95 or 98.

Version	Also Known As	Description
Word 7.0	Word 95	Word 95 is the first version of Word that was designed specifically for Windows 95. It is sold separately and as part of Microsoft Office 95. Word 7.0 is very similar to Word 6.0.
Word 8.0	Word 97	Word 97 is sold separately and as part of Office 97.
Word 9.0	Word 2000	Word 2000 is sold separately and as part of Office 2000.

> You may work with people who haven't yet upgraded to Word 2000. If you do, you probably will have to open documents created in earlier versions of Word and save documents in a format that older versions of Word will be able to read. In Hour 21, "Collaborating on Documents," you learn how to cope with these situations.

What's New with Word 2000?

Word 2000 brings a host of enhancements that will help beginning and experienced users alike. Some changes are specific to Word, whereas others are Office-wide. The next four sections highlight the new behaviors and features that are the most obvious to users.

Each Document Is in Its Own Word Window

If you've used previous versions of Word, you'll immediately notice a change in how Word handles multiple open documents.

In earlier versions of Word, when you had more than one document open at the same time, they were all contained within a single Word window. To switch back and forth among them, you selected them from the bottom of the Window menu (or pressed Ctrl+F4). Regardless of the number of documents that were open, you had only one taskbar button for the Microsoft Word window. This type of arrangement is known as a *multiple document interface* (MDI) because you can have multiple documents open within a single Word interface.

Starting in Word 2000, Microsoft has shifted to a *single document interface* (SDI). Now the Word window can display only one document, so each document appears in its own Word window, complete with its own taskbar button. To switch among open documents, just click the documents' taskbar buttons, which are by default at the bottom of the screen (or use the Window menu of any Word window). Figure 1.1 shows three open Word documents.

Figure 1.1

Each document is in its own Word window.

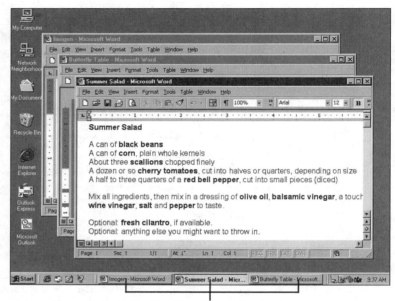

Each document has its own taskbar button.

This is a welcome change if you used to get confused about which documents you had open, or if you found it cumbersome to use the Window menu to switch among open documents.

In this book, the terms *file* and *document* are used interchangeably.

Personalized Menus and Toolbars

Previous versions of Word provided the same set of menus and toolbar buttons to everyone, regardless of which features you used most. This meant that your Word window was unnecessarily cluttered with menu commands and toolbar buttons that you never used.

Word 2000 introduces *personalized menus and toolbars* to give you a cleaner interface that reflects your own usage patterns. As you're working, Word monitors the commands you use and adapts your menus and toolbars to display only those commands and buttons that you use frequently. Commands and buttons that you don't use are hidden from view, although you can display them at any time with a click of the mouse. When you use a command or button that was hidden previously, Word makes it visible on the menu or toolbar. If you'd rather see the full versions of your menus and toolbars as in Word 97, you can easily do so.

Figure 1.2 shows the Word window when personalized menus and toolbars are turned on. The Standard and Formatting toolbars share the same row (they have room to do so because some of their buttons are hidden), and the menus show only frequently used commands. In this figure, the Tools menu is displayed.

FIGURE 1.2

The Word window with personalized menus and toolbars turned on.

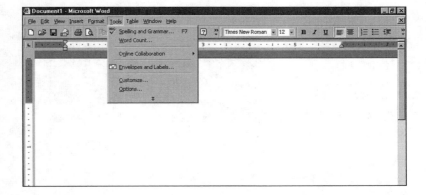

In Figure 1.3, personalized menus and toolbars are turned off. The full Standard and Formatting toolbars are displayed, each on their own row, and all the commands in the Tools menu are visible. (You learn more about working with personalized menus and toolbars in the next hour.)

FIGURE 1.3

The Word window with personalized menus and toolbars turned off.

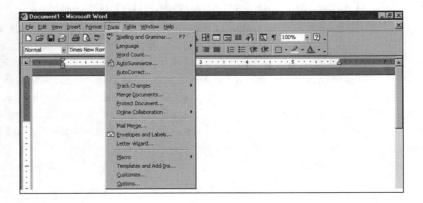

Typing Anywhere on the Page

Prior to Word 2000, you could move the insertion point only within areas of your document in which you'd already typed. Word 2000 removes this restriction with its new click-and-type feature. You double-click to move your insertion point into areas that don't yet contain text—in the middle of the page or below your last line of text, for example—and then start typing. When your mouse pointer is over an area where you can use click and type, the I-beam gains a small icon that indicates how the text will be aligned if you double-click and start typing. In Figure 1.4, the I-beam shows that the text will be left-aligned.

FIGURE 1.4

The click-and-type I-beam lets you type anywhere on the page.

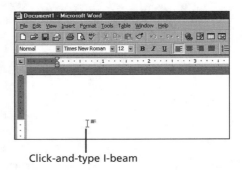

Click-and-type I-beam

Click and type is available only in Print Layout view. You learn much more about the click-and-type feature and typing in general in Hour 3.

Cutting and Copying Multiple Items

One cumbersome aspect of copying and moving text in the standard way—via the Windows Clipboard—is that you can copy or move only one selection at a time. For example, if you want to copy ten paragraphs from one document into another, and each paragraph is located on a different page in the source document, you have to copy and then paste them one at a time. The new Office Clipboard solves this problem by letting you "collect" multiple items that you've cut or copied and then paste them wherever you want, in whatever order you choose. Figure 1.5 shows the Office Clipboard with six items on it—three selections of Word text, a graphic image, some data from an Excel spreadsheet, and some text from a Web page. (You learn how to use this feature in Hour 6, "Revising Your Text.")

FIGURE 1.5

The Office Clipboard lets you move or copy multiple items from any Windows application into any Office application.

Installing Word 2000

If you are installing any edition of Office 2000, Word is included in the installation. To start the setup process, insert the Office CD in your CD-ROM drive, and follow the prompts to get to the Microsoft Office Setup dialog box. When it does, click the Install Now (or Upgrade Now) button to perform a standard installation.

If you purchased Word as a standalone program, insert the Word CD in your CD-ROM drive, and click the Install Now button when the Microsoft Word Setup dialog box appears.

If the setup dialog box for Office or Word doesn't appear automatically, you can start the installation process by displaying the contents of the Office or Word CD in Windows Explorer and double-clicking the file Setup.exe.

By default, the Office 2000 installation procedure does not install all features to your hard disk. Rather, it installs some features that aren't used as frequently on a "first use" basis. The first time you issue a command in an Office application that requires one of these features, the application displays a message box stating that the feature is not currently installed and asks whether you would like to install it now. If this happens when you're using Word, insert the Office CD and click the Yes button. Word will then copy the files that it needs for the feature from the CD. (Depending on how your CD-ROM drive is configured, it may automatically display the opening screen for the Office installation process. You don't need to see this screen when Word is copying files to install a new feature. To prevent this screen from displaying, press the Shift key for a few seconds while the CD is loading.)

Depending on your installation of Office, other features may be set to run from the Office CD or from a location on your network. If you issue a command that requires one of these features, you may receive a prompt to insert your Office CD or connect to the network location that contains the Office setup files.

For a detailed discussion of Office installation procedures, refer to Appendix A, "Modifying and Repairing Your Word Installation."

Starting Word

When you want to start a new Word document or continue working on an existing document, you need to open a Word window. You can do this in five ways. Experiment to see which method you like the best.

To Do: Use the Start Menu

The most basic way to start any Windows application, including Word, is from the Start menu:

1. Click the Start button at the left end of the taskbar.

2. Point to Programs in the Start menu.

▲ 3. In the Programs menu, click Microsoft Word, as shown in Figure 1.6.

FIGURE 1.6

Starting Word from the Start menu.

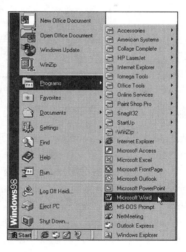

Using a Word Shortcut Icon

If you have a shortcut icon for Word on your Windows desktop, double-click it to start Word (see Figure 1.7).

FIGURE 1.7

Starting Word from a shortcut icon.

1

To Do: Create a Word Shortcut Icon

If you don't have a shortcut icon for Word and would like to create one, follow these steps:

1. Click the Start button.

2. Point to Programs to display the Programs menu.

3. Point to the Microsoft Word menu item.

4. Press and hold the Ctrl key as you drag the Microsoft Word menu item out onto the desktop. As you drag, an icon with a plus sign indicates that you're copying the menu item.

5. Release the mouse button and then the Ctrl key.

6. A shortcut to Word appears on your desktop.

> To delete a Word shortcut icon, right-click it and choose Delete in the context menu that appears. This deletes only the shortcut icon, not the Word application.

Using a Word Toolbar Button

Depending on your Office installation, you may see the Office Shortcut Bar on your Windows desktop. If you do, you can click the Word button in the Office Shortcut Bar to start the program (see Figure 1.8).

FIGURE **1.8**

*Starting Word from the
Office Shortcut Bar.*

In Windows 98 and in Word, whenever you point to a toolbar button, a
ScreenTip (a little bubble) appears to tell you the name of the button. In
Figure 1.8, you can see the ScreenTip that pops up when you point to the
Word button in the Office Shortcut Bar.

In addition, you or someone else may have added a Word shortcut to a Windows 98 toolbar. Figure 1.9 shows the Word button in the QuickLaunch toolbar, which Windows 98
displays by default next to the Start button. If you see the Word button in a toolbar, you
can click it to start the program.

FIGURE **1.9**

*Starting Word from the
QuickLaunch toolbar.*

To Do: Add a Word button to the Toolbar

If you would like to add the Word button to a Windows toolbar, follow these steps:

1. Click the Start button.
2. Point to Programs to display the Programs menu.

3. Point to the Microsoft Word menu item.

4. Press and hold the Ctrl key as you drag the Microsoft Word menu item from the Programs menu to the toolbar. As you drag, an icon with a plus sign indicates that you're copying the menu item.

5. Drag to the desired spot on the toolbar. A black I-beam indicates where on the toolbar the Word button will appear.

6. When the black I-beam is in the right spot, release the mouse button and then the Ctrl key.

7. The Word button appears on the toolbar.

> To delete the Word toolbar button, right-click it and choose Delete in the context menu that appears. This deletes only the toolbar button, not the Word program.

Clicking a Word Document Icon

You can click any Word document icon on your Windows desktop, in Windows Explorer, or in a My Computer folder window to start Word and open the document. Figure 1.10 shows a folder window that contains several Word document icons.

FIGURE 1.10

Starting Word from a Word document icon.

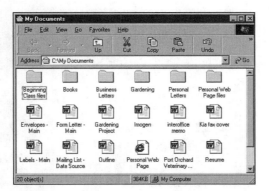

Starting a Word Document from a Word Window

If you already have a Word window open, you can start another Word document or open an existing document by issuing commands in the Word window. (You learn how to do this in Hour 4, "Managing Documents.")

Exiting Word

When you finish with the document that you're working on, you need to close its Word window.

To close a Word document, use one of these methods:

- Choose File, Exit, as shown in Figure 1.11.

FIGURE 1.11

Issue the File, Exit command to close a Word window.

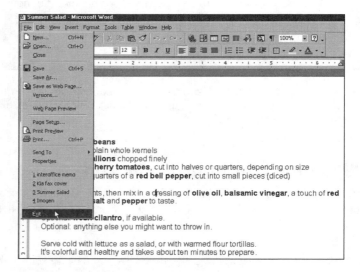

- Click the Close button in the upper-right corner of the window, as shown in Figure 1.12. (When you point to the button, the ScreenTip Close appears.)

Click to close Word.

FIGURE 1.12

Click the Close button to close a Word window.

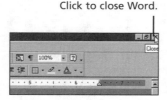

> If you have more than one Word document open, choosing File, Close has the same result as choosing File, Exit or clicking the Close button.

When you have only one Word window open, you can, if you like, close the document in the window but leave the Word window open. To do this, use either of these methods:

- Choose File, Close. (Choosing File, Exit would close the entire Word window, not just the document.)
- Click the lower of the two Close buttons in the upper-right corner of the Word window (see Figure 1.13). This second Close button appears only when you have one Word window open (note that its ScreenTip is Close Window, not Close).

Click to close only the document.

FIGURE 1.13

Close the document while leaving the Word window open.

The document closes, but the Word window stays open, as shown in Figure 1.14. From here, you can start a new document or open an existing one.

FIGURE 1.14

The Word window is open, but empty.

Summary

Word's mission is to help you create documents. It is rich enough in features to let you produce all manner of specialized documents, yet simple enough that you can type a basic letter or memo without having to remember an esoteric sequence of commands. Word 2000 adds new features that make the program even more approachable for beginners. In the next hour, you learn how to issue commands in the Word window, how to move and resize the Word window, and how to get help.

Q&A

Q If I already have Office 97, can I install Office 2000 without uninstalling Office 97?

A Yes. If you install Office 2000 on top of Office 97, Office 2000 will retain customized settings in Office 97 so that you don't have to redo them in Office 2000. Refer to Appendix A for more information.

Q I have Windows 98 and I'd like to single-click my Word shortcut icon instead of double-clicking it to start the program. How do I do that?

A Double-click the My Computer icon on your desktop, choose View, Folder Options in the My Computer window, mark the Web style option button, and click OK.

Q Should I close all Word windows before I shut down Windows?

A In general, it's a good idea to save and close your Word documents before shutting down Windows. However, if you do issue the command to shut down when you have open Word documents that have unsaved changes, Word will prompt you to save the documents before the computer shuts down.

HOUR 2

Getting Acquainted with Word

You are beginning a long-term relationship with Word, so it makes sense to spend a bit of time getting to know your surroundings. In this hour, you learn key terms and techniques for interacting with Word that you'll use every time you work on a document.

The highlights of this hour include

- Learning the parts of the Word window
- Issuing commands in Word using menus, toolbars, dialog boxes, and keyboard shortcuts
- Controlling the position and size of the Word window
- Getting help

Elements of the Word Window

Learning the names of the elements of the Word window may not be the most stimulating part of learning the program, but it's essential for understanding the instructions throughout the rest of this book, and in Word's help system. Figure 2.1 labels the most important parts of the Word window.

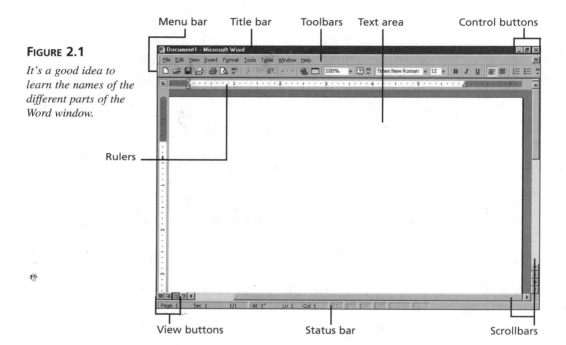

FIGURE 2.1

It's a good idea to learn the names of the different parts of the Word window.

Here is a description of these elements:

- *Title bar.* The title bar of any Windows application lists the name of the application—in this case, Microsoft Word. Word's title bar also contains the name of the open document. As you'll see in the section "Controlling the Word Window" later in this hour, you can use the title bar to move the Word window around the desktop, or to minimize or maximize the window. When the Word window is active, the title bar is colored. When another window is active, the title bar is gray.

- *Menu bar.* The menu bar contains a set of pull-down menus that you use to issue commands.

- *Toolbars.* The toolbars contain buttons that you can click to issue commands.

- *Rulers.* The vertical and horizontal rulers show you where your text is on the page. The gray sections at the ends of the rulers indicate the margin areas. You can use the rulers to change some formatting, including tabs, indents, and margins (see Hours 9, "Formatting Paragraphs," and 10, "Formatting Pages"). Depending on which *view* you're using, you may see only a horizontal ruler. (You'll learn about views in Hour 7, "Viewing and Printing Your Documents.") To hide the rulers, choose View, Ruler. To display them, choose View, Ruler again.

- *Text area*. This is the area in which you can type text.
- *View buttons*. You can use these buttons to switch views (see Hour 7).
- *Status bar*. The status bar tells you about the current status of your document. The left section tells you the current page number and the total number of pages. The middle section tells you the location of the insertion point (the cursor), and the right section tells you whether some special features are turned on.
- *Scrollbars*. The horizontal and vertical scrollbars let you bring different parts of a document into view. You'll learn how to use them in Hour 3, "Entering Text and Moving Around."
- *Control buttons*. These buttons let you control the Word window.

Issuing Commands

Word enables you to "talk" to it in a variety of ways. The exact methods that you use are a matter of personal preference. If you like reading text instead of deciphering tiny pictures on toolbar buttons, you probably prefer using the menus. If, on the other hand, you are visually oriented and like using a mouse, you may find yourself using toolbar buttons most of the time. Perhaps you're a fast typist and hate to take your hands away from the keyboard to reach for the mouse. If this is the case, you may come to rely almost completely on keyboard shortcuts. Experiment with all of the methods described here and see which ones you like best.

Working with Menus

The menu bar at the top of the Word window contains nine pull-down menus—File, Edit, View, and so on. You can issue all of the commands in Word via these menus. Chances are, you use toolbar buttons or keyboard shortcuts for many commands, but you can always fall back on the menus if you forget the alternate methods.

Menu Basics

To display a menu, click its name in the menu bar. For example, to display the Format menu, click *Format* in the menu bar, as shown in Figure 2.2. Then click a command in the menu to instruct Word to carry it out. If you want to close a menu without issuing a command, click anywhere outside the menu in the text area.

FIGURE 2.2

Click a menu name to display the menu.

Some menu commands, such as the ones shown in the Format menu in Figure 2.2, are followed by three dots (...). These commands lead to dialog boxes, which you use to give Word more information before it carries out a command. If a menu command is not followed by three dots, Word performs the command as soon as you click it.

Commands that are followed by three dots are safe to click when you're exploring Word on your own, because you can always back out of the resulting dialog box by clicking the Cancel button. And just looking over the options in a dialog box can give you a sense of what the command does. If you have an important document onscreen, it's a good idea to refrain from clicking a command that is not followed by three dots, unless you know what it does. (You can undo many actions, as you'll learn in Hour 6, but a few actions cannot be undone.)

If a menu command has a small triangle at its right, it leads to a submenu. To display the submenu, just point to the command. In Figure 2.3, the Insert, Picture submenu is displayed.

FIGURE 2.3

Menu commands with triangles lead to submenus.

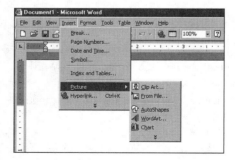

When a menu command is dim, it is not currently available. In Figure 2.4, the first four commands in the Edit menu are dim.

FIGURE 2.4

Dim commands are not currently available.

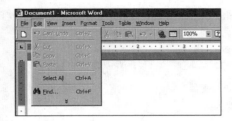

Many menu commands list keyboard shortcuts to their right. For example, in Figure 2.4, the keyboard shortcut Ctrl+A is listed to the right of the Select All command. You can use these keyboard shortcuts as an alternative to clicking the commands in the menus. See "Using Keyboard Shortcuts" later in this hour for more information.

Using the Keyboard to Issue Menu Commands

You can use the keyboard instead of the mouse to display menus and issue commands in them. To display a menu, press the Alt key, and then press the underlined letter in the menu name. For example, to display the Format menu, you press Alt+O. (It doesn't matter whether you type an upper- or lowercase letter.) After the menu is displayed, press the underlined letter in the command that you want to issue. For example, to issue the Paragraph command in the Format menu, press P. To close a menu without issuing any command, press the Alt key.

You can also use the keyboard to interact with dialog boxes. See "Working with Dialog Boxes" later in this hour for more information.

Using Personalized Menus

Word assumes that you want to use *personalized menus*. When this feature is enabled, clicking a menu name displays a *short menu* that contains only the commands you use frequently. This reduces clutter in your menus and makes it easier to find the commands you use all of the time.

If you want to use a command that is not visible in the short menu, use one of these methods to expand the menu and display all of its commands:

- Double-click the menu name.
- Click the down arrow at the bottom of the menu.
- Rest your mouse pointer over the menu for a few seconds.

Figure 2.5 shows the full Format menu (contrast it with the short menu shown previously in Figure 2.2).

FIGURE 2.5

When personalized menus are turned on, you can still display the full menus.

If you display the full menu and click one of the commands that was hidden in the short menu, Word adds it to the short menu. By the same token, if you don't use a command in the short menu for a period of time, Word may remove it from the short menu.

> If you want to restore the default set of commands in your short menus, choose Tools, Customize, click the Options tab, click the Reset My Usage Data button, click Yes, and click Close.

Turning Off Personalized Menus

For some of you, personalized menus may be the best thing since sliced bread. For others, they may be an irksome distraction.

To Do: Turn Off Personalized Menus

If you want to turn off personalized menus, follow these steps:

1. Choose Tools, Customize to display the Customize dialog box.
2. Click the Options tab.
3. Click the Menus Show Recently Used Commands First check box to clear its check mark.
 4. Click the Close button.

Now you can see the full menus all of the time. (If you need any help with these steps, see "Working with Dialog Boxes" later in this hour.) If you want to turn personalized menus back on at some point, follow these same steps, but mark the check box in step 3 instead of clearing it.

> To keep things simple, the remainder of this book assumes that personalized menus are turned off. If you prefer to keep this feature turned on, remember that some of the commands referred to in this book may not be included in your short menus; you might have to display the full menus to see them.

2

Right-Clicking to Display Menus On-the-Fly

In addition to using the pull-down menus at the top of the Word window, you can also use *context menus* (sometimes called *shortcut menus*). These are small menus that you display by clicking the right mouse button. The commands in a context menu vary depending on where you right-click. For example, if you right-click text, you get commands for editing and formatting text (see Figure 2.6), and if you right-click a toolbar, you get a list of available toolbars (see Figure 2.7).

FIGURE 2.6

Right-clicking text displays a context menu with commands for working with text.

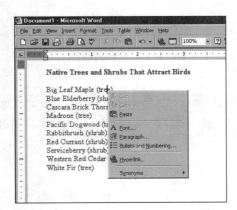

FIGURE 2.7

*Right-clicking a
toolbar displays a
context menu that lists
available toolbars.*

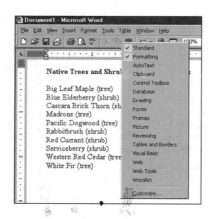

To choose a command in a context menu, use a left-click. To close a context menu
without choosing a command, click anywhere outside it.

Working with Toolbars

For many people, the fastest way to issue commands in Word is via the toolbars. Word
comes with 16 toolbars in all. By default, it displays two of them—the Standard and
Formatting toolbars, as shown in Figure 2.8. The Standard toolbar contains buttons for
performing file-management tasks, such as starting, saving, opening, and printing documents. The Formatting toolbar contains buttons for common formatting tasks, including
changing the font and font size, and adding boldface, italic, and underline to your text.

FIGURE 2.8

*The Standard and
Formatting toolbars
are displayed by
default.*

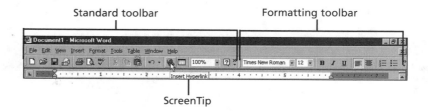

To see what a toolbar button does, rest your mouse pointer on it for a moment. A
ScreenTip appears with the button's name, as shown in Figure 2.8.

Displaying and Hiding Toolbars

The 14 toolbars that aren't displayed by default can help you with all kinds of tasks. For
example, the Tables and Borders toolbar has buttons for creating and formatting tables,
and the Reviewing toolbar contains buttons that are useful if you're editing someone
else's document. Some of these toolbars appear automatically when needed, but you can

also display any of them "manually" whenever you like. You may also want to hide toolbars that you never use to create more space in the Word window.

To display or hide a toolbar, choose View, Toolbars (see Figure 2.9). The toolbars that are currently displayed have check marks next to them. The ones that are currently hidden do not. Click the toolbar that you want to display or hide.

FIGURE 2.9

Use the Toolbars submenu to display or hide toolbars.

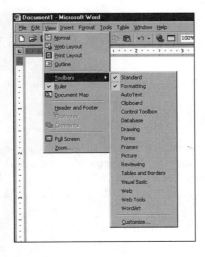

2

You can also display or hide a toolbar by right-clicking any toolbar that's currently displayed, and then clicking the desired toolbar in the context menu that appears (refer to Figure 2.7).

Accessing Hidden Toolbar Buttons

Depending on the size of your Word window, the number of toolbars that are sharing the same row, and so on, Word may not have room to display all of a toolbar's buttons. If you want to use a toolbar button that's currently hidden from view, click the More Buttons arrow at the right (or bottom) end of the toolbar. Word displays a list of all the hidden buttons (see Figure 2.10).

More Buttons arrow

FIGURE 2.10

Word puts any toolbar buttons that are currently hidden in the More Buttons list.

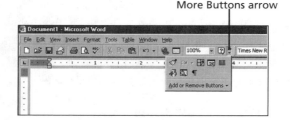

Click the button that you want to use. As soon as you click it, Word removes it from the More Buttons list and places it in a visible spot on the toolbar. (See "Moving Buttons Around a Toolbar" later in this hour if you want to adjust the button's position in the toolbar.)

> If you want to restore the default set of visible buttons in your toolbars, choose Tools, Customize, click the Options tab, click the Reset My Usage Data button, click Yes, and click Close.

Adding and Removing Toolbar Buttons

In addition to accessing hidden toolbar buttons, you can also use the More Buttons list to add new buttons to a toolbar, or to remove buttons that you never use. Click the More Buttons arrow at the right (or bottom) end of the toolbar, and then click Add or Remove Buttons (see Figure 2.11). Buttons that don't have check marks are not currently included in the toolbar; those that do have check marks are included. Click the button that you want to add or remove.

> If you've made a mess of a toolbar and want to reset it to the state it was in when you installed Word, click the More Buttons arrow, click Add or Remove Buttons, and then click Reset Toolbar.

Moving Toolbars Around the Word Window

You can position your toolbars anywhere you like in the Word window. One reason to move a toolbar is to make it easier to see. If you have several toolbars displayed at the top of the Word window, they may seem to merge into one jumbled clump of buttons. You can visually separate the toolbars by spreading them out in different parts of the Word window.

FIGURE 2.11

Click a button in the Add or Remove Buttons list that you want to add to or remove from the tool-bar.

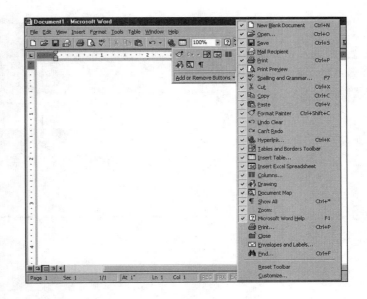

Another reason to move a toolbar is to bring all of its buttons into view. If a toolbar is sharing a row with other toolbars, some of its buttons are probably hidden. If you want to access all of the buttons without using the More Buttons list (see "Accessing Hidden Toolbar Buttons" earlier in this hour), you can move the toolbar onto its own row.

A quick way to put the Standard and Formatting toolbars on separate rows is to choose Tools, Customize, click the Options tab, clear the Standard And Formatting Toolbars Share One Row check box, and click the Close button.

The remaining hours in this book assume that the Formatting toolbar is positioned on its own row, directly beneath the Standard toolbar.

Word lets you *dock* toolbars on the top, left, right, and bottom edges of the window, or "float" them over the screen (see Figure 2.12).

Floating toolbar

FIGURE 2.12

*You can dock toolbars
or let them float.*

Docked toolbars

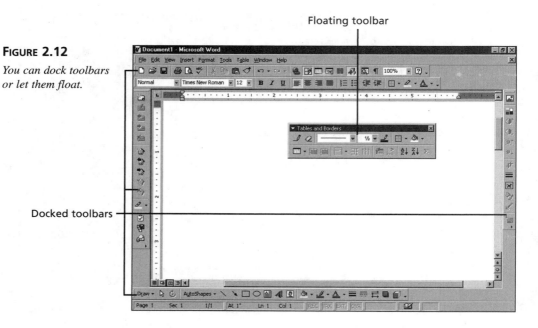

To move a docked toolbar, point to the line at the left (or top) end of the toolbar. The
mouse pointer becomes a four-headed arrow, as shown in Figure 2.13. If you want the
toolbar to float, drag it into the text area of the window, and release the mouse button.
(To *drag* something, you point to it and then press and hold down the left mouse
button as you move the mouse.) To move the toolbar after you've released the mouse
button, drag its title bar. (You can also change the shape of a floating toolbar by dragging
one of its borders.)

FIGURE 2.13

*Drag the line at the
top (or left) end of a
docked toolbar to
move it.*

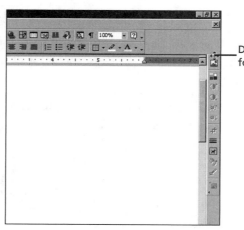

Drag when you see the
four-headed arrow.

If you want to dock a toolbar on an edge of the Word window, drag it toward that edge until its title bar disappears and it "flattens out," and then release the mouse button.

 If a toolbar is floating, you can quickly dock it on the edge of the window where it was most recently docked by double-clicking its title bar.

2

Moving Buttons Around a Toolbar

You can rearrange the order of the buttons on a toolbar if you like. To move a button, point to it and hold down your Alt key as you drag it to the desired position. As you drag, a black I-beam with a button icon attached to it shows where the toolbar button will end up. When the I-beam is in the right place, release the Alt key and your mouse button.

Working with Dialog Boxes

Dialog boxes let you specify exactly what you want Word to do before it carries out your command. There are a few standard elements in dialog boxes that you use to set options. The Print dialog box (choose File, Print), shown in Figure 2.14, contains most of these.

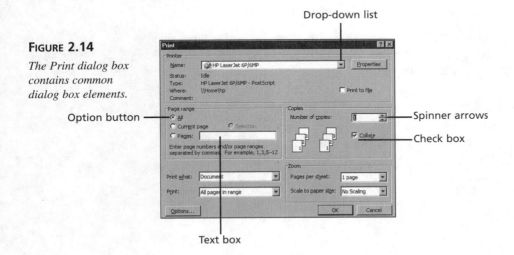

FIGURE 2.14

The Print dialog box contains common dialog box elements.

Here is a description of these elements:

- *Drop-down list.* Click the down arrow at the right end of a drop-down list to display a set of choices, and then click an item in the list. As soon as you click an item, the list closes. If you display a drop-down list and then decide not to change its current setting, click the down arrow again to close the list (or click anywhere else in the dialog box).
- *Option button.* To mark an option button, click it. A black dot appears in its center. To clear an option button, you have to click another option button in the same group. Only one option button in a group can be marked. (Option buttons are sometimes called *radio buttons.*)
- *Check box.* To mark a check box, click it. A check mark appears in the box. To clear the check mark, click the check box again. If you see a group of check boxes, you can mark as many of them as you like.
- *Text box.* A text box is a box in which you can type text. Click in a text box to place the insertion point in it, and then start typing. If there is already text in the box, you can replace it by dragging over it with the mouse to select it before you start typing.
- *Spinner arrows.* Some text boxes have spinner arrows. You can click the up and down arrows to increment the number in the text box up or down. Alternatively, you can just type the number in the box.

Some dialog boxes also contain *tabs* across the top of the dialog box. Each tab contains a separate set of options. Figure 2.15 shows the Options dialog box (Tools, Options), which contains 10 tabs. To bring a tab to the front, just click it.

FIGURE 2.15

In many dialog boxes, related sets of options are organized in tabs.

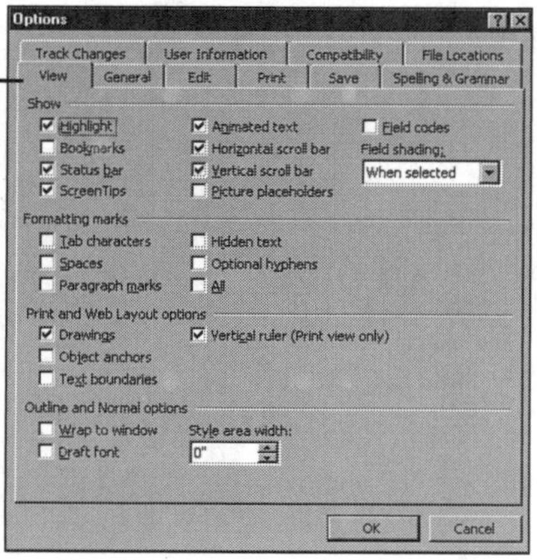

This dialog box has 10 tabs.

After you've made your selections in a dialog box, click the OK button to tell Word to carry out the command. (If a dialog box doesn't have an OK button, look for another likely candidate, such as a button labeled *Close* or *Insert*.) If you decide not to go ahead with a command, you can back out of the dialog box by clicking the Cancel button. Clicking the Close button (the X) in the upper-right corner of a dialog box is the same as clicking the Cancel button.

If you want, you can use the keyboard to make selections in a dialog box. To do so, first press the Tab key to move the *focus* to the option that you want to change. (To move in the reverse direction, press Shift+Tab.) When the option has the focus, it will be highlighted or have a dotted box around it. Then make your selection by using one of these methods:

- To choose an item in a drop-down list, bring the focus to the list, press the down-arrow key to display the list, use the up- and down-arrow keys to select the desired item, and then press Enter.
- To mark an option button, focus on the group of option buttons and then use the up- and down-arrow keys to mark the button.
- To mark or clear a check box, focus on it and press the Spacebar.
- To type in a text box, bring the focus to the text box (if the text box is currently empty, an insertion point appears in the box; if it contains text, the text will be selected) and then type your text.
- To choose a button in a dialog box, bring the focus to the button and then press Enter. If the button name has an underlined letter (or *hot key*), you can press the Alt key plus that letter to choose the button. For example, to choose the Properties button in the Print dialog box (refer to Figure 2.14), you can press Alt+P.

After you've made your selections, press Enter to choose the OK button. (If the OK button doesn't have a dark border around it, press the Tab key until it does, and then press Enter.) If you decide to back out of the dialog box without making any changes, press the Escape key. This is the equivalent of clicking the Cancel button.

Using Keyboard Shortcuts

Many common commands have keyboard shortcuts that you can use instead of the menus or toolbars. Some of these keyboard shortcuts are listed to the right of the commands in the menus. For example, the keyboard shortcut Ctrl+O appears to the right of the Open command in the File menu.

Make sure that you hold down the first key in a keyboard shortcut as you press the second key. For example, to issue the File, Open command with the keyboard, you press and hold down the Ctrl key as you press the letter O. If there are three keys in a keyboard shortcut, such as Shift+Ctrl+End, keep the first two held down as you press the third.

For a complete listing of keyboard shortcuts in Word's help system, ask the Office Assistant to search for *shortcut keys*. If you like, you can print the shortcuts and keep them next to your computer for reference. (See "Getting Help" later in this hour.)

Controlling the Word Window

You can change the appearance of the Word window in a variety of ways. You can make it disappear temporarily so that you can see what's behind it on the Windows desktop, or make it fill up the screen to give you more room to work. You can also move the Word window around on your desktop, or adjust its size.

Using the Control Buttons

The Control buttons appear in the upper-right corner of the Word window. The function of these buttons is the same for all Windows applications.

Click the Minimize button to temporarily hide the Word window, leaving only its taskbar button. To redisplay the Word window, click its taskbar button. If you want to make the Word window cover the entire desktop, click the Maximize button (see Figure 2.16).

FIGURE 2.16

The Minimize button shrinks the Word window to a taskbar button; the Maximize button enlarges it to cover the desktop.

Minimize

Maximize

As soon as the Word window is maximized, the Maximize button becomes a Restore button (see Figure 2.17). Click the Restore button to return (*restore*) the window to the size it was before you maximized it.

Restore

FIGURE 2.17

Click the Restore button to return the window to the size it was before it was maximized.

As you learned in the last hour, the Close button (the X) to the right of the Maximize/Restore button closes the Word window. If you have only one Word window open, a second Close button appears beneath the first one. Clicking this lower button closes only the document, leaving the Word window open.

Moving and Resizing the Window

If the Word window isn't maximized, you can move it around the Windows desktop or change its size.

To move the Word window, point to its title bar, drag the window to a different location, and release the mouse button.

To resize the Word window, point to the lower-right corner of the window. The mouse pointer becomes a diagonal black arrow, as shown in Figure 2.18. Drag in the desired direction to enlarge or shrink the window. (You can actually drag any edge or corner of the Word window to resize the window—the lower-right corner is just the most convenient spot.)

FIGURE 2.18

Drag a border or corner of the Word window to resize the window.

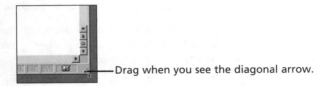

Drag when you see the diagonal arrow.

Getting Help

If you putter around in Word trying to figure things out on your own (which you are strongly encouraged to do!), you are bound to have some questions once in a while. Maybe a feature isn't working as you think it should, or you know that a particular task must be possible, but you don't know how to approach it. At these times, a solid familiarity with Word's help system can be of tremendous assistance. Not only can you often find the exact information you need, you can do it without pestering your coworkers or family members.

Using the Office Assistant

If you think of the help system as a huge library of information, the Office Assistant is the ever-polite but quirky librarian staffing the front desk. This animated critter (shown in Figure 2.19) helps you search for information, offers tips on how to type and format your documents more efficiently, and provides alerts about events that require your attention.

FIGURE 2.19

The Office Assistant helps you find the answers you need.

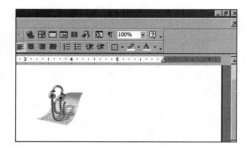

By default, the Office Assistant is a paper clip named Clippit. However, as you'll see in "Training the Office Assistant" later in this hour, you can easily switch to a different persona if Clippit doesn't do it for you. The Office Assistant tries to stay out of your way. If you do need to move it, just drag it to the desired location. You can even drag it outside the Word window.

If you don't see the Office Assistant, choose Help, Show the Office Assistant (or click the Microsoft Word Help button at the far-right end of the Standard toolbar). You can hide it at any time by choosing Help, Hide the Office Assistant.

If you see a light bulb next to the Office Assistant, it has a tip waiting for you. Click the light bulb to display the tip. When you're finished reading the tip, click anywhere outside of it to close it.

Starting in the next hour, the Office Assistant will be hidden in the examples shown in this book. If you keep yours visible, certain messages from Word may be delivered to you by the Office Assistant instead of the standard message boxes you see here.

Asking the Office Assistant Questions

When you have a question for the Office Assistant, type a word or phrase describing your topic in the yellow bubble attached to the Office Assistant (see Figure 2.20), and click the Search button. (If you don't see the yellow bubble, click the Office Assistant to display it.) In the list of topics that appears, click the one that relates most closely to your question.

FIGURE 2.20

Type your question and click the Search button.

2

The Microsoft Word Help window opens to the right of the Word window so that you can refer to it as you're working on your document (see Figure 2.21). When you've finished reading the topic, click the Close button (the X) in the upper-right corner of the window. If you want to explore other topics in the help system, see "Using the Microsoft Word Help Window" later in this hour.

FIGURE 2.21

The Microsoft Word Help window appears next to the Word window.

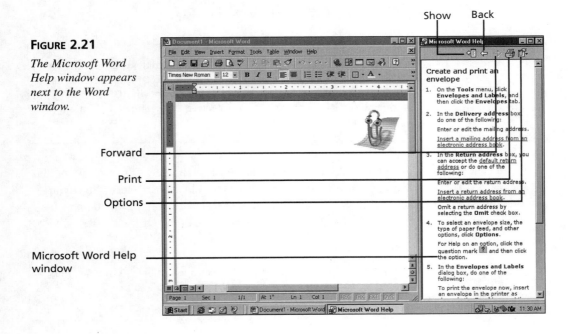

Training the Office Assistant

The Office Assistant tries its best to do your bidding, but you may want to give it a little guidance. For example, you can ask it to show you tips about keyboard shortcuts, or request that it refrain from making sounds. And if you're not particularly fond of your Office Assistant's current persona, you can ask it to switch to one that better suits your personality.

To train your Office Assistant, click it if necessary to display the yellow bubble, and click the Options button. In the Options tab of the Office Assistant dialog box (see Figure 2.22), mark or clear the check boxes to modify your Office Assistant's behavior, and click OK.

FIGURE 2.22

Mark or clear check boxes to tell your Office Assistant how to behave.

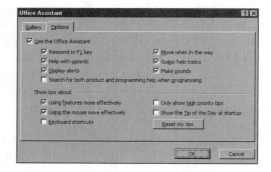

If frolicking puppies and bouncing balls are not your thing, you can turn off the Office Assistant entirely. To do so, clear the Use the Office Assistant check box (refer to Figure 2.22). If you do decide to fire your Office Assistant, you can still get to the Microsoft Word Help window by choosing Help, Microsoft Word Help.

To switch to a different Office Assistant, click the Gallery tab in the Office Assistant dialog box. Use the Next and Back buttons to browse the available characters. When you find one that you like, click OK. (Depending on your installation of Word, you may be prompted to insert your Office or Word CD to install some of the Office Assistants.)

The same Office Assistant appears in all Office applications, so changes you make to its behavior and appearance in Word also apply to Excel, PowerPoint, and so on.

Using the Microsoft Word Help Window

Whether the Office Assistant leads you to the Microsoft Word Help window or you get there on your own, you need to know how to sift through the resources Help offers.

The Word Help window is divided into two panes. When you access it through the Office Assistant, the window is "collapsed" to show only the right pane. To display the left pane, which lets you navigate through the help system, click the Show button in the upper-left corner of the right pane (refer to Figure 2.21). As soon as the window expands, the Show button becomes a Hide button. Click this button if you want to collapse the window to show only the right pane again.

Tabs at the top of the left pane let you access the Contents, Answer Wizard, and Index portions of the help system (see the next three sections). If you don't see these tabs, click the Options button at the top of the Microsoft Word Help window, and choose Show Tabs. As you explore topics in the help system, you can move back and forth among them by clicking the Back and Forward buttons at the top of the help window.

To print a help topic, click the Print button at the top of the window. In the Print dialog box that appears, click OK. (If you print from the Contents tab, described in the next section, you see two Print dialog boxes. Click OK in both of them.)

Using the Contents Tab

The Contents tab of the Microsoft Help Window organizes help topics into "books." Click the plus sign next to a book to display the topics, and possibly other books, that it contains. (The topics have icons that look like pages with question marks on them.) As soon as you expand a book, the plus sign changes to a minus sign, which you can click to collapse the view again. When you find a topic that you want to read, click it to display its contents in the right pane (see Figure 2.23).

Some help topics, such as the one about customizing toolbars shown in Figure 2.23, contain links (colored words) that you can click to jump to other help topics or Show Me buttons that you can click to have Word demonstrate the task at hand.

FIGURE 2.23

Expand a book in the Contents tab and then click a topic to display its contents in the right pane.

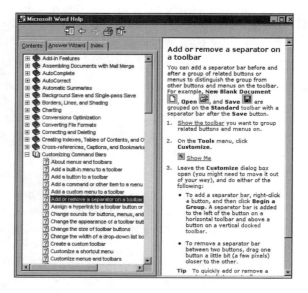

Using the Answer Wizard Tab

The Answer Wizard tab of the Microsoft Help Window works much like the Office Assistant. You can type a word or two describing your question in the What Would You Like to Do? box, and then click the Search button. In the topics that appear in the Select Topic to Display list, double-click the topic that you want to read about. Its contents appear in the right pane (see Figure 2.24).

FIGURE 2.24

The Answer Wizard searches for topics related to your question.

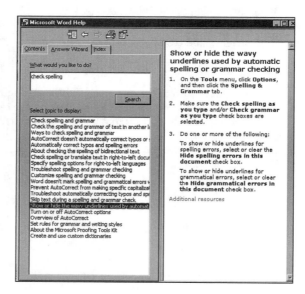

Using the Index Tab

The Index tab of the Microsoft Help Window provides a searchable index of keywords in the help system. To use it, type a word describing your question in the Type Keywords text box. As you type, the Or Choose Keywords list scrolls to keywords matching the letters you've typed. You can double-click any of these keywords to display a list of related topics in the Choose a Topic list. To display topics related to the exact word you've typed in the Type Keywords text box, click the Search button. Double-click any topic in the Choose a Topic list to display it in the right pane of the help window (see Figure 2.25).

2

FIGURE 2.25

The Index tab lets you search the index of the help system.

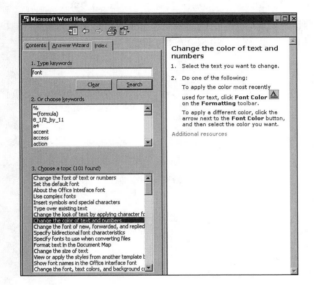

Summary

Getting familiar with the Word environment is the first step toward learning to use the program effectively. You now have a vocabulary to describe the Word window, you know how to issue commands, and you know how to find help. In the next hour, you go right to the heart of using Word: typing text.

Q&A

Q How much of what I learned in this hour applies to other Office applications, such as Excel and PowerPoint?

A Almost all of it. The basic techniques for interacting with menus, toolbars, and dialog boxes, and for controlling the size and position of the window are the same for all Office applications. You have to learn this stuff only once!

Q **Why does the Office Assistant always pop up when I choose Help, Microsoft Word Help? I want to go directly to the Microsoft Word Help window without using it.**

A The Help, Microsoft Word Help command makes the Office Assistant come running unless you disable the beast by clearing the Use the Office Assistant check box in the Options tab of the Office Assistant dialog box. After you disable the Office Assistant, this command takes you directly to the Microsoft Word Help window.

Q **If I disable the Office Assistant, can I get it back?**

A Yes. The Help, Show the Office Assistant command always displays the Office Assistant, even if you had disabled it.

PART II
Getting to Work

Hour

HOUR 3

Entering Text and Moving Around

Typing text is what word processing is all about. You can, in fact, create a perfectly respectable document by typing alone. Everything else—all of the formatting that you can apply—is icing on the cake. In this hour, you first learn the basic principles of typing in a word processing program. After you know how to get text onto the page, you then practice moving around the document so that you can edit the text and apply formatting.

The highlights of this hour include

- Starting new paragraphs
- Creating blank lines
- Starting a new page
- Moving the insertion point in a document
- Jumping to a particular page

Typing Text

When you start Word, it gives you a blank document to let you start typing right away. Word makes some assumptions about how the document will look, so you don't need to worry about formatting at all unless you want to change the default settings. Here are the most important ones:

- 8 1/2- by 11-inch paper
- 1-inch margins on the top and bottom of the page, and 1 1/4-inch margins on the left and right sides of the page
- Single spacing
- Times New Roman, 12-point font

Later in this book, you learn how to change all of these formatting options. For now, you can just focus on typing.

Typing Paragraphs and Creating Blank Lines

The key to having a happy typing experience is knowing when to press Enter. Follow these two rules for typing paragraphs of text:

- When your text reaches the right margin, just continue typing. When Word can't fit any more text on the line, it automatically wraps the text to the next line for you. You should not press Enter at the ends of the lines within a paragraph.
- When you reach the end of the paragraph, you do need to press Enter. This brings the insertion point (the cursor) down to the next line.

Figure 3.1 illustrates these two rules.

FIGURE 3.1

Do not press Enter within a paragraph. Do press Enter at the end of the paragraph.

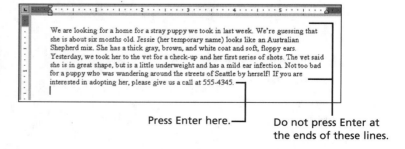

We are looking for a home for a stray puppy we took in last week. We're guessing that she is about six months old. Jessie (her temporary name) looks like an Australian Shepherd mix. She has a thick gray, brown, and white coat and soft, floppy ears. Yesterday, we took her to the vet for a check-up and her first series of shots. The vet said she is in great shape, but is a little underweight and has a mild ear infection. Not too bad for a puppy who was wandering around the streets of Seattle by herself! If you are interested in adopting her, please give us a call at 555-4345.

Press Enter here.

Do not press Enter at the ends of these lines.

If you do accidentally press Enter at the end of lines within a paragraph, your line breaks go haywire as soon as you add or delete any text. If your paragraph has some lines that are much shorter than they should be (a tell-tale sign that you pressed Enter within the paragraph), follow the instructions in "Seeing Your Paragraph, Tab, and Space Marks" later in this hour to hunt down the offending paragraph marks and delete them.

When you press Enter, you actually insert a hidden character called a *paragraph mark*, which tells Word to end the paragraph. Word's definition of a paragraph may be a little broader than yours. It considers a *paragraph* to be any amount of text that ends with a paragraph mark. So as far as Word is concerned, blank lines and short lines of text—such as headings or the lines in an address block—are separate paragraphs.

3

To create blank lines between your paragraphs, press Enter twice between each paragraph, once to end the paragraph you just typed and once to create the blank line. If you need several blank lines, just continue pressing Enter. If you press Enter too many times and need to delete a blank line, press the Backspace key. You'll learn much more about deleting in Hour 6, "Revising Your Text."

Figure 3.2 illustrates when to press Enter to create short lines of text and blank lines.

FIGURE 3.2

Press Enter to end short paragraphs and create blank lines.

Press Enter to end these short lines.

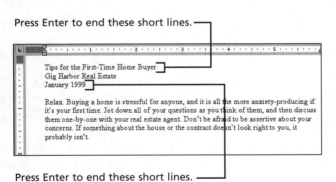

Press Enter to end these short lines.

In "Paragraph Spacing" in Hour 9, you'll learn how to automatically add a blank line after each paragraph without pressing Enter a second time.

As you type, you may see an occasional red or green wavy line under your text. These lines indicate possible spelling or grammatical errors. You'll learn how to use them (and hide them if they bother you) in Hour 13, "Checking Your Spelling and Grammar and Using the Thesaurus."

Inserting Tabs

Word gives you default tab stops every one-half inch across the horizontal ruler. (If you don't see your rulers, choose View, Ruler.) Each time you press the Tab key, the insertion point jumps out to the next tab stop. Any text to the right of the insertion point moves along with it. Figure 3.3 shows the beginning of a memo in which the Tab key was pressed after the labels To:, From:, Date: and Re: to line up the text at the half-inch mark on the horizontal ruler.

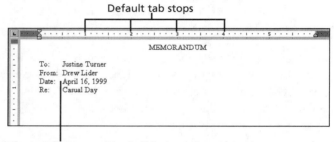

FIGURE 3.3

Press the Tab key to push text out to the next tab stop.

If you press the Tab key too many times, press the Backspace key to delete the extra tabs.

If you need to line up your text at precise locations along the horizontal ruler, you may want to replace the default tabs stops with *custom tab stops*. You'll learn how to do this in Hour 9, "Formatting Paragraphs."

You can also press the Tab key at the beginning of a paragraph to indent the first line by one-half inch. Figure 3.4 shows a document whose a paragraphs are indented in this way.

By default, when you press Tab at the beginning of a paragraph, Word sets a *first-line indent* for the paragraph. You'll learn much more about indentation in Hour 9. What's important to understand now is that if Word applies this formatting, then when you press Enter at the end of the paragraph, Word automatically indents the next paragraph for you. If this default behavior has been turned off, just press Tab at the beginning of each paragraph.

3

FIGURE 3.4

Press the Tab key at the beginning of each paragraph to indent the first line.

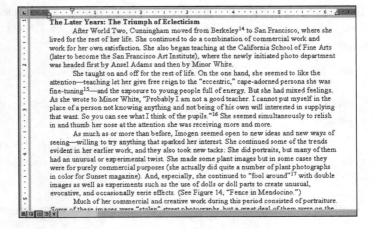

Seeing Your Paragraph, Tab, and Space Marks

As you're typing your document, you may occasionally want to check whether you accidentally pressed Enter at the end of a line within a paragraph, or pressed Enter too many times between paragraphs. Or, maybe you think you may have pressed the Tab key one time too many, or typed an extra space between two words. You can use Word's Show/Hide feature to solve these mysteries. To turn it on, click the Show/Hide button on the Formatting toolbar (or press Ctrl+Shift+*). This is a *toggle* button, meaning that you click it once to turn it on, and again when you want to turn it off (see Figure 3.5).

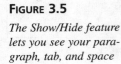

FIGURE 3.5

The Show/Hide feature lets you see your paragraph, tab, and space marks.

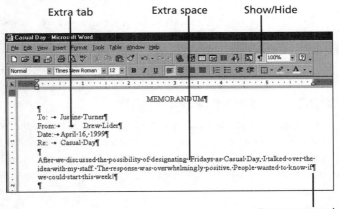

The Show/Hide feature uses the paragraph mark symbol to indicate you where you pressed Enter, a right arrow to show where you pressed the Tab key, and a dot to mark where you pressed the Spacebar.

Figure 3.5 shows a document that has an errant paragraph, tab, and space mark. The user accidentally pressed the Tab key a second time on the From: line, typed an extra space between the words *designating* and *Fridays,* and pressed Enter at the end of a line within a paragraph.

To delete any of these hidden characters, click immediately to the left of the character and press the Delete key. Figure 3.6 shows the same document after these three problems were fixed.

FIGURE 3.6

The extra paragraph, tab, and space marks have been deleted.

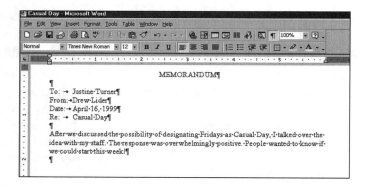

Your document looks cluttered when Show/Hide is enabled, so you may want to turn it on just long enough to investigate and fix a mistake relating to hidden characters, and then turn it off.

Typing onto the Next Page

As you're typing, Word calculates how many lines fit on a page. When the page you're on is full, Word automatically inserts a page break and starts another page. Figure 3.7 shows the break between two pages of text, as it appears in Print Layout view. (You'll learn about views in Hour 7, "Viewing and Printing Your Documents.")

FIGURE 3.7

Word breaks pages for you.

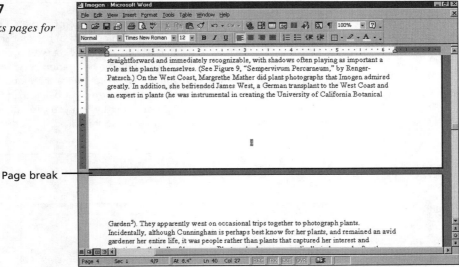

Page break ────

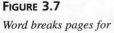

As you add or delete text, Word adjusts the page break so that it is always in the right place. This type of "adjustable" page break is called a *soft page break* (or *automatic page break*). There may be times when you need to break a page even though it is not yet full. For example, you might want to start the next section of a report on a new page, or create a title page. To do this, you have to insert a *hard page break* (or *manual page break*). You'll learn how to do this in Hour 10, "Formatting Pages."

Navigating Through Text

As you're typing a document, you will surely want to revise what you've written. Maybe you want to add a paragraph earlier in the document, change some wording, or delete a sentence or two. Before you can edit your text, however, you have to move the insertion point (*navigate*) to the location where you want to make the change. Word enables you to navigate with both the keyboard and the mouse. In the remainder of this hour, you practice both types of navigation techniques.

It's important to differentiate between the *insertion point* and the *I-beam* (see Figure 3.8). The insertion point is the flashing vertical bar that shows where text will be inserted or deleted. When you navigate with the keyboard, the insertion point moves as you press the navigation keys. The I-beam is the mouse pointer that appears when you move the mouse over text. It does not show you where text will be inserted or deleted. In fact, its sole mission in life is to move the insertion point when you click. (If you're using the click-and-type feature, you need to double-click. This is discussed in "Inserting Text" in Hour 6.)

FIGURE 3.8

The insertion point shows you where text will be inserted or deleted; the I-beam lets you move the insertion point.

I-beam

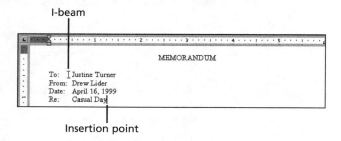

Insertion point

Navigating with the Mouse

To navigate with the mouse, simply point to the location where you want to place the insertion point and click. If the location is currently offscreen, you need to use the scrollbars or the Browse buttons to scroll the location into view, as described in the next two sections.

Using the Scrollbars

Word provides a vertical scrollbar on the right side of the Word window and a horizontal scrollbar across the bottom of the window. You will frequently use the vertical scrollbar to scroll up and down through your document. By default, the entire width of your document is visible in the Word window, so you rarely need to use the horizontal scrollbar.

 When you use the scrollbar to scroll a document, the insertion point doesn't move to the portion of the document that you've scrolled onscreen until you click.

You can click the up and down arrows at either end of the vertical scrollbar to scroll approximately one line at a time. To scroll more quickly, point to the up or down arrow and hold down the mouse button. To move longer distances, it's faster to drag the scroll box along the scrollbar. As you drag, a ScreenTip tells you what page you are on, and, if your document has headings, what section of the document you're in (see Figure 3.9).

FIGURE 3.9

Page 8 of this nine-page document is scrolled into view.

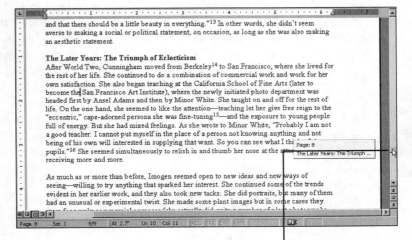

Drag the scroll box to travel longer distances.

To scroll up one screen at a time, click directly on the scrollbar above the scroll box; to scroll down one screen at a time, click the scrollbar below the scroll box.

Using the Browse Buttons

Browsing is a fast way to move sequentially through your document. You can use several types of objects as the focus point for browsing—including pages headings, graphics, and footnotes—and you can change the browse object at any time. To browse, you use the three Browse buttons in the lower-left corner of the Word window (see Figure 3.10).

FIGURE 3.10

The Browse buttons let you move sequentially through your document.

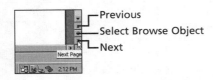

The default option is to browse by page, so the ScreenTips for the Next and Previous buttons are *Next Page* and *Previous Page*. Click the Next Page button to travel directly to the top of the next page; click the Previous Page button to go to the top of the previous page.

If you want to browse by a different type of object, click the Select Browse Object button. Word displays a grid containing various browse objects (see Figure 3.11). Point to each square to see its description in the gray area at the bottom of the grid. Some objects, such as Field and Comment, are useful only if you have used certain features in your document. The two squares on the left end of the lower row, Go To and Find, display the Find and Replace dialog box. (Go To is described in "Jumping to a Specific Page" later in this hour, and Find is described in Hour 14, "Editing Shortcuts.") Select the object that you want to use, and click OK.

FIGURE 3.11

Click the Select Browse Object and choose an object to browse by in the grid.

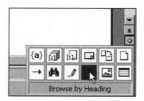

As soon as you choose a browse object other than Page, the Next and Previous buttons turn blue, and their ScreenTips change to reflect the currently selected object (*Next Heading* and *Previous Heading*, for example). Clicking these buttons now takes you to the next or previous instance of the browse object you selected.

Navigating with the Keyboard

You can, if you like, move the insertion point through an entire document by using only the four arrow keys (see the first four items in Table 3.1), but you won't get anywhere fast. To navigate more efficiently, use the keyboard shortcuts listed after the arrow keys in Table 3.1. Learning these shortcuts will save you huge amounts of time later on as you're editing your documents.

TABLE 3.1. KEYBOARD TECHNIQUES FOR MOVING THE INSERTION POINT

Keyboard Technique	Moves the Insertion Point
↓	Down one line
↑	Up one line
→	One character to the right
←	One character to the left

Keyboard Technique	Moves the Insertion Point
Ctrl+→	One word to the right
Ctrl+←	One word to the left
Ctrl+↓	Down one paragraph
Ctrl+↑	Up one paragraph
End	To the end of the line
Home	To the beginning of the line
Page Down	Down one screen
Page Up	Up one screen
Ctrl+Page Down	To the top of the next page
Ctrl+Page Up	To the top of the previous page
Ctrl+End	End of document
Ctrl+Home	Beginning of document

With the keyboard techniques that involve pressing two keys, you can continue to travel in the same direction by holding down the first key as you press the second key repeatedly. For example, to move the insertion point word by word to the right, hold down the Ctrl key as you press the right-arrow key repeatedly.

Take a moment to practice the keyboard techniques now. You might want to jot them on a Post-it and stick the "cheat sheet" on your monitor. That way, you can refer to the shortcuts easily until you have them memorized.

Jumping to a Specific Page

When you're typing a long document, you often need to get to a particular page to make a change. You can, of course, navigate to that page by using the standard mouse and keyboard techniques described in this hour. However, it's often faster to use Word's Go To feature, which enables you to jump directly to any page in your document.

To Do: Jump to a Specific Page

To use the Go To command to jump to a specific page, follow these steps:

1. Choose Edit, Go To to display the Go To tab of the Find and Replace dialog box.
2. Type the number of the page in the Enter Page Number text box (see Figure 3.12).

You can also double-click anywhere along the left two-thirds of the status bar, press Ctrl+G, or click the Go To object in the Select Browse Object grid (see "Using the Browse Buttons" earlier in this hour).

FIGURE 3.12

Type the desired page number in the Enter Page Number text box.

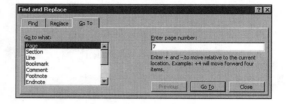

3. Click the Go To button (or press Enter). Word jumps to the page you specified. (You can check the page number in the status bar to confirm this.)

4. Repeat steps 2 and 3 if you want to go to other pages. Otherwise, click the Close button.

One unusual aspect of the Find and Replace dialog box (and a few other dialog boxes as well), is that you can click outside of the dialog box and edit your text while the dialog box is open. Most dialog boxes close as soon as you click the OK button, and you can't edit your document while the dialog box is displayed.

Word leaves the Find and Replace dialog box open after you click the Go To button so that you can continue using the dialog box to jump to other pages in the document. If you need to edit text on the current page, click outside of the dialog box to deactivate it and activate the document. The dialog box's title bar turns gray to let you know that it no longer has the focus. Revise your text, and then click the title bar of the dialog box to activate it again. You can then use the Go To command to travel to another page. When you're finished using Go To, click the Close button in the dialog box.

As you can see in Figure 3.12, the Go to What list in the Go To tab of the Find and Replace dialog box lets you go to other items besides pages. When you click a different item in this list—Line or Footnote, for example—the options on the right side of the dialog box change to enable you to tell Word which specific instance of the item you want to go to.

Summary

Typing in a word processing program is easy and straightforward. You now know how to type simple documents and navigate within them. Don't worry about editing your text and correcting mistakes yet. You will learn many ways to revise your documents in Hour 6. The most pressing task at the moment is learning how to save your documents so that you can come back to them later. You'll learn this and other document-management techniques in the next hour.

Q&A

Q How much of the page can I see onscreen?

A Assuming that you're using Word's default settings, you can probably see about one third of a page onscreen at a time.

Q I accidentally pressed the wrong key. How do I correct it?

A Click just past the character, press the Backspace key, and then type the correct character. (You'll learn many other alternative methods of correcting text in Hour 6.)

Q How can I tell how many pages long my document is?

A The left third of the status bar shows you the current page and the total number of pages, separated by a slash. If you see 5/14, for example, you are currently on page 5 out of 14 pages.

3

HOUR 4

Managing Documents

In this hour, you learn how to manage your Word documents. The topics in this hour read like a file clerk's job description: You learn how to store (save) files for later use, open existing files so that you can revise them, quickly access your favorite folders and files, and so on. You may already know how to use Windows Explorer or My Computer to create new folders, and rename, delete, move, and copy files. Here you learn how to perform these same tasks in Word so that you can handle them without leaving the Word window.

The highlights of this hour include

- Saving and opening files
- Accessing favorite folders and files
- Creating folders
- Switching among open documents
- Starting new documents
- Renaming and deleting files
- Moving and copying files

Saving Documents

As you are typing a new document, it exists only in your computer's memory. Memory (or RAM) is a temporary storage area. In other words, it is dependent on electricity. As soon as you turn off your computer, memory is wiped clean and everything in it is lost. For this reason, you need to save your documents to a permanent storage medium, such as your hard disk, a removable disk such as a floppy disk or a Zip disk, or a network drive (if you're on a network). These storage devices are not dependent on electricity, so the files stored on them remain there whether your computer is turned on or off.

You can think of your disk drives as filing cabinets. Just as a physical filing cabinet holds hanging folders that can contain other folders or files, so can your electronic storage devices contain folders, which can in turn contain other folders or files.

> A *disk drive* is basically a disk player. It's the device that plays the disk, just like a tape player plays a cassette tape. Because you can't remove a hard disk from the drive, the terms *hard disk* and *hard drive* are often used interchangeably. (In contrast, you can remove a floppy disk or Zip disk from its disk drive.) If your computer is on a network, your own hard drive is often called your *local drive* to distinguish it from *network drives*, which are storage locations on other computers on the network.

Saving a Document for the First Time

Before you save a document for the first time, it has a temporary name such as *Document1*, *Document2*, or *Document3*. When you save the file, you replace this name with one of your choosing. Here are the rules for filenames:

- They can contain up to 256 characters.
- They can include spaces.
- They cannot include these characters: / \ > < * . ? " | : ;
- They are not case sensitive; as far as your computer is concerned, the filenames *Letter to mom* and *letter to Mom* are the same.
- You can have only one file of any given name in a folder.

The number following *Document* in the temporary filename doesn't mean that you have that number of documents open. For example, if your document is named *Document8*, it doesn't mean that you have eight documents open. It means only that you've started eight documents in this session of using Word. (You may have closed some of them.) When you close all of your Word windows and start Word again, the temporary filenames start over at *Document1*.

To Do: Save a Document for the First Time

As soon as you decide that the document you're typing is worth saving, follow these steps:

1. Click the Save button on the Standard toolbar (or choose File, Save). Because this is the first time you are saving the document, Word displays the Save As dialog box to ask what you want to name the file and where you want to store it (see Figure 4.1).

Places Bar   Save In box   Up One Level

FIGURE 4.1

Use the Save As dialog box to choose a name and location for your file.

2. Look at the location in the Save In box. If you want to save the file in this location, skip to step 5. Otherwise, continue with the next step.

3. Click the down arrow to the right of the Save In list, and click the drive on which you want to save the file. For example, click 3 1/2 Floppy (A:) to save the file on your floppy disk. (If you want to save the file in a location on your network, choose Network Neighborhood. The main area of the dialog box then lists the drives and folders to which you have access on your network.)

4

FIGURE 4.2

*Choose a location in
the Save In list.*

The Places Bar on the left side of the Save As dialog box contains buttons for
some locations in which you might want to save your files. The History and
Web folders are useful if you're saving Web pages. My Documents is the
default folder for Word documents. Any file you save in the Desktop folder
appears on your Windows desktop. You'll learn how to use the Favorites
folder in "Getting to Your Favorite Folders and Documents" later in this hour.

4. Double-click folders in the main area of the dialog box until the desired folder
   appears in the Save In box. If you want to move back to a parent folder (the folder
   that contains the folder in the Save In box), click the Up One Level button.

5. Type the filename that you want to use in the File Name text box (see Figure 4.3).
   Word automatically adds the extension .doc to the name. (Depending on your
   Windows settings, your file extensions may not be visible.)

6. Click the Save button.

FIGURE 4.3

*Type the name for your
file in the File Name
text box.*

Word saves your document. If it finds an existing document in the same folder with the same name, it displays the message box shown in Figure 4.4. If you click the Yes button, Word replaces the existing file with the one you're saving. After you replace the existing file, you can't get it back. If you click the No button, it redisplays the Save As dialog box to let you choose a different name and/or location for the file so that it won't overwrite the existing file.

FIGURE 4.4

Word checks with you before overwriting a file with the same name.

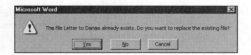

Saving As You Work

After you've saved your document for the first time, you need to continue to save it every few minutes as you work on it. Each time you save, Word updates the copy of the file on your hard disk with the copy on your screen (in memory). If you save religiously, then in the event of a crash or power outage, you lose, at most, a few minutes' worth of work.

To save your document periodically, click the Save button on the Standard toolbar (or choose File, Save or press Ctrl+S). It looks like nothing is happening when you issue the Save command because Word assumes that you want to keep the same filename and location, so it automatically overwrites the original file on disk without asking you any questions.

If you live in an area with frequent power outages, consider buying an uninterruptible power supply (UPS). This gizmo sits between your computer and the wall socket, and kicks in when there is an outage, at which time it powers your computer by battery for approximately 10 to 20 minutes—enough time to save and close your documents and shut down Windows. Some UPS devices also come with software that saves and closes your documents and shuts down for you if an outage occurs when you aren't at home.

Saving a Document with a New Name or Location

If you want to create a document that's very similar to one you have already saved, you don't need to type the new document from scratch. Rather, you can open the first document, make changes to it, and then save the new document under a different name. Because you're giving the document a new name, it won't overwrite the original file. For example, you can create monthly invoices for a particular company by opening the previous month's invoice, changing the invoice number and other details, and then saving the revised invoice under a new name.

> If you frequently use one document as the "jump-off point" for creating others, consider creating a template for this type of document, as described in Hour 12, "Working with Templates."

A variation of this idea is to open a document and then save it with the same name but in a different location. This is one way to copy a file from one place to another (you'll learn the standard method in "Moving and Copying Documents" later in this hour). For example, if you have a document on your hard drive that you want to put on a floppy disk, you can open the document from your hard drive, and then save it to your floppy drive.

To Do: Save a File with a Different Name and/or Location

To save a file with a different name and/or location, follow these steps:

1. Open the file (see "Opening Documents" later in this hour).

2. Choose File, Save As to display the Save As dialog box.

3. If you want to save the file to a new location, navigate to it so that it appears in the Save In box. (See the steps in "Saving a Document for the First Time" earlier in this hour if you need help.)

4. Optionally, type a different name in the File Name text box. (You have to choose a different name if you're keeping the same location, otherwise, you overwrite the original file.)

5. Click the Save button.

Recovering Documents After Crashes or Power Outages

As you're typing a document, you may have noticed that at periodic intervals, the Save icon (the icon that appears on the Save toolbar button) flashes briefly at the right end of the status bar. When this happens, Word's AutoRecover features is taking a "snapshot" of your document (saving a copy of the file in its current state). By default, the AutoRecover feature updates this snapshot every ten minutes when the document is open. If you close the document normally, it deletes the AutoRecover information.

However, if a computer crash or power outage prevents you from saving your document before Word closes, Word keeps the most recent snapshot for you. If you did not save for a long period of time before the crash or outage, the snapshot can contain a much more current version of your document than the one you most recently saved.

The next time you turn the computer on and start Word, Word displays the AutoRecover snapshot with the word *Recovered* in the title bar. If you want Word to replace the copy you most recently saved with this AutoRecover version, choose File, Save As, click the filename in the Save As dialog box, and click Save. When Word asks whether you want to replace the original file, click the Yes button.

> If you want AutoRecover to take a snapshot of your document more frequently (perhaps you're working on a critical document during a storm, you don't have a UPS, and you're less than diligent about saving), choose Tools, Options to display the Options dialog box. Then click the Save tab, make sure the Save AutoRecover Info Every X Minutes check box is marked, change the number of minutes, and click OK.

Opening Documents

When you want to work on a file that you previously saved to disk, you have to tell Word to open it.

To Do: Open a Document

Follow these steps to open a document:

1. Click the Open button on the Standard toolbar (or choose File, Open) to display the Open dialog box (see Figure 4.5).

2. Check the location in the Look In box. If the file you want to open is in this location, skip to step 5. Otherwise, continue with the next step.

3. Click the down arrow to the right of the Look In list, and click the drive that contains the file (see Figure 4.6). For example, click 3 1/2 Floppy (A:) if the file is on your floppy disk. (If you want to open a file from a location on your network, choose Network Neighborhood. The main area of the dialog box will then list the drives and folders to which you have access on your network.)

Places Bar   Look In box   Up One Level

FIGURE 4.5

Use the Open dialog box to open a file that you want to revise.

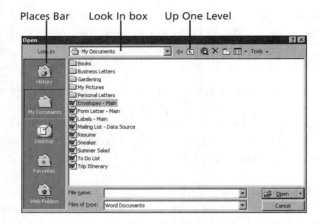

FIGURE 4.6

Choose a location in the Look In list.

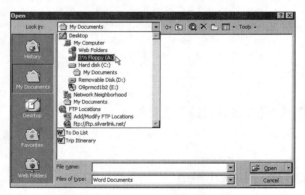

> The Open dialog box has a Places Bar just like the one in the Save As dialog box. If the file that you want to open is in one of the folders in the Places Bar, click the folder icon in the bar.

4. Double-click folders until the desired folder appears in the Look In box. If you want to move back to a parent folder, click the Up One Level button.

5. Double-click the filename, or click it and then click the Open button (see Figure 4.7).

FIGURE 4.7

Double-click the file that you want to open.

If you accidentally click twice instead of double-clicking the file in step 5, Word thinks you're trying to rename the file. (See "Renaming Documents" later in the hour.) If a thin box appears around the filename, indicating that you're in rename mode, press Escape or click on a blank area in the dialog box, and then double-click the file.

When you open a file, a copy of the file is placed in your computer's memory. The original file is still on disk. If you close the file without making any changes, you don't need to save because the onscreen copy is no different from the one on disk. You need to save only if you revise the file.

If you want to open several files in the same folder at once, you can select all of them in the Open dialog box before clicking the Open button. To select several files, use these techniques:

- If the files are adjacent to one another, click the first file, and then Shift+click (hold down your Shift key as you click) the last file.

- If the files are not adjacent, click the first file, and then Ctrl+click (hold down the Ctrl key as you click) the additional files.

You can also delete, move, or copy multiple files by selecting them as described here before issuing the appropriate command. See the sections "Deleting Documents" and "Moving and Copying Documents" later in this hour.

The four documents that you most recently opened are listed at the bottom of the File menu. If you want to open one of these files, you can dispense with the Open dialog box altogether. Just display the File menu and click the document that you want to open.

Viewing Files in the Save As and Open Dialog Boxes

Word lets you choose among four views to display folders and files in the Save As and Open dialog box:

- List view (the default option) lists the names of the folders and files.
- Details view displays the size, type, and date modified for each file or folder, in addition to its name.
- Properties view displays the information from the Properties dialog box (File, Properties) in a pane on the right side of the dialog box.
- Preview shows a preview of the document in a pane on the right side of the dialog box (see Figure 4.8); this view lets you take a peek at the contents of your files without actually opening them.

FIGURE 4.8

Use the Preview view to see what's in a file before opening it.

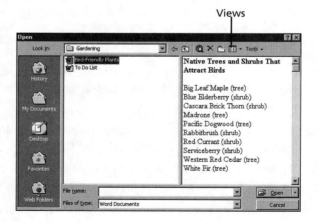

To change views, click the down arrow to the right of the Views button (see Figure 4.8), and then click the desired view in the list that appears. (Alternatively, you can click the View button itself one or more times to switch among all four views.)

By default, files and folders in the Save As and Open dialog boxes are ordered by name. To sort them by type, size, or date instead, click the down arrow to the right of the Views button, point to Arrange Icons, and choose the desired option in the submenu.

Getting to Your Favorite Folders and Documents

If a folder or document that you use frequently is buried deep in the folder structure on your hard disk or is off on another network computer, it can be time-consuming to navigate to it in the Open and Save As dialog boxes. Fortunately, you can avoid this hassle by creating a shortcut to the folder or document in your Favorites folder. The shortcut simply points to the folder or document; clicking it opens the folder or document just as if you clicked the item itself.

To Do: Create a Shortcut to a Folder or Document

Follow these steps to create a shortcut to a folder or document in your Favorites folder:

1. Display the Open or Save As dialog box. In the main area of the dialog box, select the file or folder that you want to create a shortcut for.

2. Choose Tools, Add to Favorites at the top of the dialog box.

3. Repeat steps 1 and 2 to add other shortcuts to your Favorites folder if you like, and then click the Cancel button to close the dialog box without opening or saving a file.

4. To open a folder or document that you've created a shortcut for, display the Open dialog box, and click the Favorites folder in the Places Bar (see Figure 4.9).

5. Double-click the desired shortcut in the Favorites folder. If the shortcut points to a file, the file opens. If it points to a folder, the folder appears in the Look In box.

6. To save a document to a folder for which you created a shortcut, display the Save As dialog box, and click the Favorites folder in the Places Bar.

7. Double-click the shortcut for the folder. It appears in the Save In box. Continue with the save process.

▼To Do

4

FIGURE 4.9

Click the Favorites folder in the Places Bar to access your favorite shortcuts.

If you want to delete a shortcut to a favorite folder or file, right-click the shortcut in the Favorites folder and click Delete. Deleting a shortcut does not remove the file or folder to which the shortcut pointed.

Creating Folders

Just as you might add a new hanging folder to a physical filing cabinet to hold a new group of related files, so you can create new folders on your hard drive (or a network drive) to store groups of related Word documents. For example, you might want to create a folder for your personal correspondence, or one for your child's homework assignments. Although you can create folders in either Save As or the Open dialog box, you're most likely to create them in the Save As dialog box when you're in the midst of saving a file.

To Do: Create a Folder

To create a folder, follow these steps:

1. Display either the Save As or the Open dialog box.

2. Navigate to the folder that you want to be the parent of the new folder so that it appears in the Save In or Look In box.

3. Click the Create New Folder button.

4. The New Folder dialog box appears (see Figure 4.10). Type the name you want to use, and click OK. (The rules for naming folders are the same as for naming files—see "Saving a Document for the First Time" earlier in this hour.)

Create New Folder

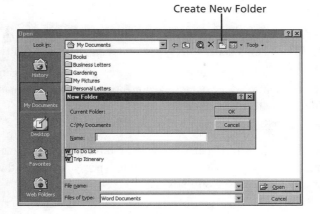

FIGURE 4.10

Word displays the New Folder dialog box to let you name your new folder.

If you are in the midst of saving a file, double-click the new folder so that it appears in the Save In box and continue the save process. Otherwise, click the Cancel button to close the dialog box.

Microsoft Office automatically creates the My Documents folder on your hard drive as a convenient place for you to store data files/including Word documents, Excel spreadsheets, PowerPoint presentations, and so on. You can create a set of subfolders within My Documents for the various types of documents you create. You aren't required to use the My Documents folder, but it's a good idea to designate one top-level folder for your data, and then store all of your files in subfolders of that folder. (If you want to use a different folder to store all of your data files, see the next section.) If you are on a network, ask your network administrator where you should save your Word documents.

Changing Your Default Documents Folder

By default, Word assumes that you want to store documents in the My Documents folder or one of its subfolders, so it automatically displays the contents of the My Documents folder when you first display the Open or Save As dialog box. If you use a different folder for your data files, you will probably want Word to automatically display its contents in the Open and Save As dialog boxes instead.

To Do: Change Your Default Documents Folder

To change your default documents folder, follow these steps:

To Do

4

▼ 1. Choose Tools, Options.

2. In the Options dialog box, click the File Locations tab.

3. Select Documents under File Types, and then click the Modify button.

4. In the Modify Location dialog box that appears, navigate to and select the folder that you want to be the default documents folder. When its name appears in the Folder Name text box, click OK.

▲ 5. Click the Close button in the Options dialog box.

Now when you display the Open dialog box, the folder you designated appears by default in the Look In box. By the same token, when you display the Save As dialog box, this folder appears in the Save In box.

Switching Among Open Documents

You can open as many Word documents at a time as you like. (Issue the File, Open command or click the Open toolbar button in any Word window to open additional documents.) In general, however, it's best to use a little restraint. The more documents you have open, the slower your computer runs. When you have more than one Word document open, you can switch among them by using the techniques described in the next three sections.

Taskbar Buttons

Each document that you open appears in its own Word window, with its own taskbar button. The simplest way to switch from one to another is to click their taskbar buttons. In Figure 4.11, six Word windows are open. The active Word window is maximized, so the other Word windows are hidden behind it.

If the active window isn't maximized and you can see a part of the window that you want to switch to behind it, just click a neutral part of the window, such as the title bar or the text area (so you don't accidentally issue a command) to bring it to the front.

FIGURE 4.11

Click the taskbar button of an open document to switch to it.

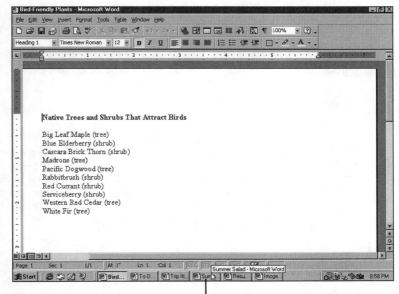

When you point to a taskbar button, the entire
document name appears in a ScreenTip.

If you have several Word documents open at once, you may have difficulty telling which
document is which because the taskbar buttons are so small that the document names
have to be truncated. You can always point to a button to display the entire filename in a
ScreenTip, as shown in Figure 4.11. Another option is to enlarge your taskbar so that the
taskbar buttons can increase in size enough to display more of the document names. If
you have Windows 98, one or more toolbars may be sharing the same edge of the desktop as the taskbar. You can enlarge the taskbar by hiding or moving these toolbars.
Alternatively, you can increase the height of the taskbar to allow two or more rows of
buttons. In Figure 4.12, the QuickLaunch toolbar—which appears to the right of the Start
button in Windows 98—has been hidden, and the taskbar has been resized to take up two
rows. Note that the taskbar buttons are considerably bigger than they are in Figure 4.11.
(Refer to the Windows help system if you need help hiding or moving Windows toolbars,
or resizing your taskbar.)

FIGURE 4.12

*Hiding the
QuickLaunch toolbar
and increasing the
height of the taskbar
creates more room for
the taskbar buttons.*

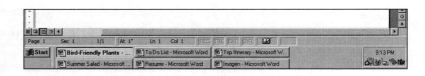

If you don't see your taskbar, it is set to hide when a window is active. To
bring it into view, rest your mouse pointer on the edge of the desktop
where it normally appears. If you want the taskbar to be visible all of the
time, click the Start button, point to Settings, and click Taskbar & Start
menu. In the Taskbar Options tab of the Taskbar Properties dialog box, clear
the Auto Hide check box and click OK.

Window Menu

You can also switch among open documents by using the Window menu in any Word
window. All of your open documents are listed at the bottom of the Window menu (see
Figure 4.13), and a check mark appears next to the one that's currently active. Click the
desired document to switch to it.

FIGURE 4.13

*Click the document
that you want to switch
to at the bottom of the
Window menu.*

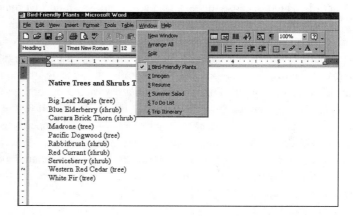

Alt+Tab

You can switch among all of your open windows, including the Word windows, by using the Alt+Tab keyboard combination. Press and hold down the Alt key as you press the Tab key to display a small window containing icons for each open window. An outline appears around the icon for the active window (see Figure 4.14). Keeping the Alt key held down, continue to press Tab until the icon for the document that you want to switch to is outlined, and then release the Alt key.

FIGURE 4.14

Release the Alt key when the desired document icon is outlined.

Summer Salad - Microsoft Word

Starting New Documents

Word presents a new blank document when you start the program. If, after you've started typing in this document, you decide to begin another new document, click the New Blank Document button at the far-left end of the Standard toolbar (or press Ctrl+N). A second Word window opens with a new blank document.

When you use the New Blank Document toolbar button to start a document, Word assumes that you want to base the document on the *Normal template*. All Word documents are based on a template, which is like a blueprint for a document that includes formatting and possibly text. The Normal template produces a plain-vanilla blank document with all of Word's default formatting. Word also comes with many other templates (including special templates called *wizards*) that can help you create a wide variety of documents, including letters, memos, fax cover sheets, reports, and so on. If you want to base your new document on one of these templates, you have to use the File, New command instead of the New Blank Document toolbar button. You learn how to use other templates in the next hour, and in Hour 12 you'll learn how to create your own templates.

Renaming Documents and Folders

You can rename your files in the Save As or Open dialog box. Make sure that the file you want to rename is not open. Then display either of these dialog boxes, and use one of these methods to switch to rename mode:

4

- Right-click the file and click Rename in the context menu.
- Select the file and then click it again.
- Select the file and press F2.
- Select the file, click the Tools button at the top of the dialog box, and choose Rename.

A thin box appears around the filename to inform you that you're in rename mode, and the current name is highlighted to let you easily replace it (see Figure 4.15). Type the new name and press Enter.

FIGURE 4.15

The Imogen file is ready to be renamed.

 You can rename folders in the exact, same way that you rename files.

Deleting Documents

You can delete files in either the Save As or Open dialog box. Make sure that the file you want to delete is not open. Display either dialog box, and delete the file by using one of these methods:

- Right-click the file and click Delete in the context menu.
- Select the file and click the Delete toolbar button at the top of the dialog box.
- Select the file and press the Delete key.
- Select the file, click the Tools button at the top of the dialog box, and choose Delete.

The Confirm File Delete message box appears to ask whether you want to send the document to the Recycle Bin. Click the Yes button. If you later want to get the document back, you can double-click the Recycle Bin icon on your Windows desktop, right-click the file, and choose Restore in the context menu. The file reappears in the folder in which it was originally stored.

> If you delete a file from a network drive or a removable drive (a floppy or Zip drive, for example), it does not go to the Recycle Bin—once it's gone, it's gone.

Moving and Copying Documents

As with creating folders, renaming files, and deleting files, you can move or copy files in either the Save As or Open dialog box. When you move a file, you remove it from its current location and place it in a new location. When you copy a file, you leave it in its current location and place a duplicate copy in the new location.

To Do: Move or Copy a Document

To move or copy a document, follow these steps:

1. Make sure that the file you want to move or copy is not open, and display either the Save As or the Open dialog box.

2. Navigate to the folder containing the file you want to move or copy, so that the folder appears in the Save In or Look In box.

3. Right-click the file and choose Cut or Copy in the context menu. (You can also press Ctrl+X to cut or Ctrl+C to copy.)

4. Navigate to the folder in which you want to paste the file so that the folder appears in the Save In or Look In box.

5. Right-click a blank part of the main area in the dialog box and choose Paste in the context menu (or press Ctrl+V).

Summary

In this hour, you learned everything that you need to know to manage your Word documents. You can save them to disk, open them when you want to revise or print them, and perform other standard file-management tasks. In the next hour, you learn how to enlist the help of Word's templates and wizards to produce nicely formatted documents.

Q&A

Q **I have Excel spreadsheets and Word documents in my My Documents folder. Why do I see the Word documents in the Open dialog box only when the My Documents folder is in the Look In box?**

A By default, Word displays Word documents (files with an extension of .doc) only in the Open dialog box. If you want to see all of the files in a folder, including non-Word documents, choose All Files in the Files of Type drop-down list at the bottom of the dialog box.

Q **How can I record tracking information about my documents when I save them?**

A Choose File, Properties, enter information about the document (its title, subject, and so on) in the Summary tab of the Properties dialog box, and click OK. If you want Word to prompt you to fill in this information each time you save, choose Tools, Options, click the Save tab, mark the Prompt for Document Properties check box, and click OK.

Hour 5

Creating Documents with Templates and Wizards

You can type and format all of your documents from scratch, but you don't have to. Word's templates can help you create a variety of documents, from memos and letters to fax cover sheets, résumés, and reports. A *template* is a rough blueprint for a document that includes some combination of text and formatting. The default template, Normal, produces a blank document with "plain-vanilla" formatting. In this hour, you learn to use other templates that have more complex formatting and text. You also try out a couple of wizards. A *wizard* is a special kind of template that asks you a series of questions, and then creates a "made-to-order" document based on your answers.

The highlights of this hour include

- Finding out how templates and wizards can help you
- Selecting a template or wizard for a new document

- Creating a document with a template
- Creating a document with a wizard

The Advantages of Using a Template or Wizard

The most obvious advantage of using a template (or wizard) is that it's fast. If you use a template that includes the standard text that doesn't change from one document to the next, you can avoid the tedium of typing this text yourself.

Another benefit of using templates is that the formatting is handled for you. Professionals who know how to use Word's formatting features to their best advantage designed the templates that come with Word. With the help of templates, you can produce documents with sophisticated formatting that you haven't yet learned how to apply yourself (although by the end of this book, you will know how to apply most of the formatting included in Word's templates).

Templates also enable you to create a consistent look for all of your documents. This is especially helpful in an office, where you can use templates to standardize the letters, memos, reports, and so on that you and your coworkers generate.

Finally, templates can be used repeatedly without ever being overwritten. If you have to type the same basic document over and over, each time making only minor changes to it, you may be inclined to use one Word document as the "boilerplate" for all of the others. If you wanted to employ this technique to create letters, for example, you would open the boilerplate letter, fill in the recipient's name and address, type the body of the letter, and then use the Save As command to save the file under a new name. By using Save As, you wouldn't overwrite your boilerplate file with the revised version. The problem with this technique is that sooner or later you would probably have a brain lapse and use the Save command instead of Save As. When you did, the boilerplate letter would get replaced with the revised version, and you would have to create the boilerplate all over again.

You can avoid this potential problem by using a template instead of a document for your boilerplate. When you save a document based on a template, the document is automatically saved as a separate file from the template, regardless of whether you use Save or Save As. You thus never run the risk of overwriting your boilerplate text.

Selecting a Template or Wizard

In the last hour, you learned that when you click the New Blank Document button in the Standard toolbar to start a new document, Word assumes that you want to base the document on the Normal template. If you want to use a different template or wizard, you have to use the File, New command.

To Do: Select a Template or Wizard

Follow these steps to start a document based on a template or wizard other than the Normal template:

1. Choose File, New to display the New dialog box (see Figure 5.1).

FIGURE 5.1

Use the New dialog box to choose a template other than the Normal template.

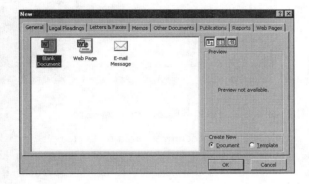

The Blank Document icon in the General tab is selected by default. If you leave this icon selected and click OK, Word creates a document based on the Normal template, just as if you had clicked the New Blank Document toolbar button. (Microsoft also refers to the Normal template as the Blank Document template, just to confuse you.)

5

2. Click the tab that contains the template or wizard that you want to use.

You may see a different set of tabs than the ones shown here. As you'll learn in Hour 12, you can create your own tabs in the New dialog box to store custom templates. If you are missing some tabs, some templates may not have been included in your Word installation.

3. Click the icon for the template or wizard, and check the Preview area on the right side of the dialog box. If you see the message "Template not installed yet. Click OK to install it now." dig out your Office or Word CD and insert it into your CD-ROM drive. (As soon as you click OK, Word will copy the necessary files from the CD to your hard drive.)

▼   4. If the template is already installed, you'll see a picture of it in the Preview area of the New dialog box (see Figure 5.2).

FIGURE 5.2

The Preview area of the New dialog box shows you what the currently selected template looks like.

▲   5. Click OK (or double-click the template or wizard).

In a moment, you'll see a new document based on the template or wizard. You need to complete the document by adding all of your personalized text. In the next two sections, you practice using templates and wizards to create a fax cover sheet, a résumé, a memo, and a letter.

Creating a Document with a Template

Each template is unique, but there are a few characteristics that crop up in most of them. The Contemporary Fax and Professional Résumé templates are typical examples. After you've used both of them, you should feel comfortable trying the others.

The Contemporary Fax Template

It takes only a few moments to put together a nicely formatted fax cover sheet if you use a template or wizard.

To Do: Use the Contemporary Fax Template to Create a Fax Cover Sheet

To create a fax cover sheet by using the Contemporary Fax template, follow these steps:

1. Choose File, New to display the New dialog box.

2. Click the Letters & Faxes tab, and double-click Contemporary Fax.

3. If the template isn't already installed, Word installs it now (make sure to have your Office CD handy). A document based on the Contemporary Fax template then appears onscreen (see Figure 5.3).

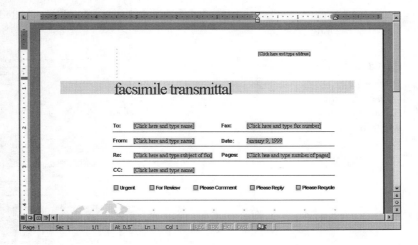

FIGURE 5.3

A document based on the Contemporary Fax template, before it's been filled in.

4. In the upper-right corner, click the gray [Click Here and Type Address] text. (The prompts are gray to indicate that you need to replace them with your own text. The gray color won't print.) Type your address, pressing Enter after each line. The text you type replaces the dummy text.

> Documents that you start from wizards or templates (other than Normal) display onscreen at a reduced magnification so that you can see the full width of the page. As a result, some of the text may too small to read clearly. If you need to increase the magnification of the document to see what you're typing, see "Zooming a Document" in Hour 7 ("Viewing and Printing Your Documents").

5

5. Continue to replace the other [Click Here and Type] prompts with the text that you want to include in the fax coversheet. If you want to leave an area blank (for example, you don't want to type a name after CC:), click the prompt text and press Delete.

6. Double-click any of the check boxes (Urgent, For Review, Please Comment, and so on) in which you want to mark to place a check mark. (You can double-click when your I-beam mouse pointer is over the check box.)

7. In the body of the memo, drag over the text following the word Notes: to select it. (To drag, press and hold down your mouse button as you move the mouse pointer across the text. The text becomes selected as you drag. You'll learn much more

about selecting text in the next hour.) Type over it with the text that you want in the body of the memo. The memo should now be completely filled in, as shown in Figure 5.4.

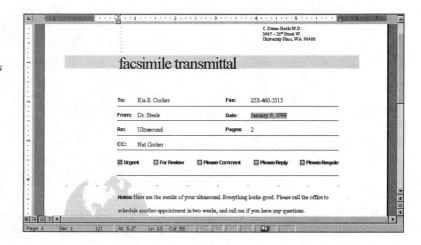

 The "dummy" text after Notes: includes instructions for modifying the template to include your personal information so that you don't have to type it each time you use the template. You'll learn how to do this in Hour 12, "Working with Templates."

8. Click the Save button in the Standard toolbar. In the Save As dialog box, notice that Word Document is selected in the Save As Type drop-down list (see Figure 5.5). This tells you that Word saved the file as a Word document, and not as a template, so it won't overwrite the template itself. Choose a name and location for the file, and click the Save button.

FIGURE 5.5

Save your document after you've filled it in.

Word saves the file as a Word document.

9. Click the Close button in upper-right corner of the Word window to close the document.

The Professional Résumé Template

Designing a résumé can be quite time-consuming to create if you have to handle all of the formatting on top of drafting the text. If you use one of Word's résumé templates, you can use the built-in formatting in the template, which lets you focus on the writing.

To Do: Use the Professional Résumé Template to Create a Résumé

To create a résumé using the Professional Résumé template, follow these steps:

1. Choose File, New to display the New dialog box.

2. Click the Other Documents tab, and double-click Professional Résumé.

3. If the template isn't already installed, Word installs it now (have your Office CD handy). A document based on the Professional Résumé template then appears onscreen (see Figure 5.6).

5

FIGURE 5.6

A document based on the Professional Résumé template, before it's been filled in.

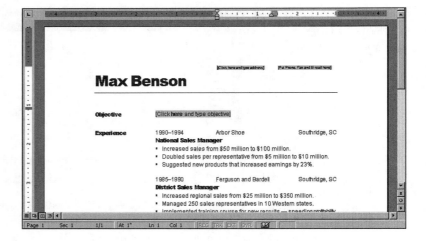

4. One by one, click the [Click Here and Type Address], [Put Phone, Fax, and E-mail Here], and [Click Here and Type Objective] prompts to select them, and type over them with your own personal information.

5. Notice that this template includes fictitious data about a person named Max Benson to show you where your text should go. Drag over all of this text to select it, and type over it with your own information. Figure 5.7 shows the document after the "dummy text" has been replaced.

6. Save and close the document.

FIGURE 5.7

A document based on the Professional Résumé template, after it's been filled in.

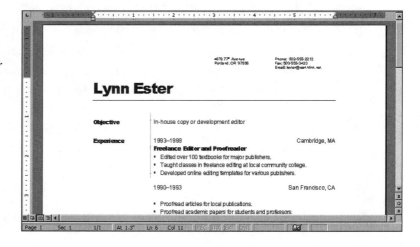

Creating a Document with a Wizard

Wizards give you as much hand-holding as possible, short of sending you the final document in the mail. Here, you practice using two kinds of wizards. The first one, the Memo Wizard, is an example of the standard type that you find in the New dialog box. You progress through a series of dialog boxes, answering a different set of questions in each one. Clicking Finish at the end generates the document. The second one, the Letter Wizard, is a bit atypical. You access it through the Tools menu, not the New dialog box, and instead of presenting a series of dialog boxes, it gives you only one dialog box, with all of the questions arranged in different tabs. After you've made your selections in each tab, you click OK to generate the document.

The Memo Wizard

When you need to dash off a quick memo, the Memo Wizard can be a great help. It fills in most of the details so you need to do little more than type the memo text.

To Do: Use the Memo Wizard to Create a Memo

To create a memo by using the Memo Wizard, follow these steps:

1. Choose File, New to display the New dialog box.

2. Click the Memos tab, and double-click Memo Wizard.

3. If the wizard isn't already installed, Word installs it now (insert your Office CD if necessary).

4. The first of the Wizard dialog boxes appears onscreen (see Figure 5.8). Along the left side of the dialog box is a "progress line" that shows you all of the steps you'll go through to get from start to finish. This progress line appears in all of the wizard dialog boxes. As you move through the wizard, the box next to the current step turns green so that you know where you are.

▼ To Do

5

FIGURE 5.8

The first dialog box of the Memo Wizard.

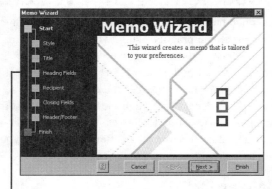

└─The progress line lets you keep track of where you are in the wizard.

5. Click Next to move to the next dialog box, and choose the style for your memo. Continue clicking Next to move from one dialog box to the next, answering the wizard's questions about the memo title, heading fields, recipient, and so on. If you change your mind about the options you chose in a previous dialog box, click the Back button to move back to it and change your settings, and then click Next to get back to where you were.

6. When you get to the last step, click the Finish button. A memo that incorporates all of your instructions appears onscreen. Replace the [Click Here and Type Your Memo Text] prompt with the text you want in the memo (see Figure 5.9).

▲   7. Save and close the document.

FIGURE 5.9

Type the body of the memo; the wizard has done everything else for you.

interoffice memo

Date: 10/26/99
To: Product Development Department
From: Peter Jarvin
RE: Brown Bag Lunches
Priority: [Urgent]

Today is the last day to submit ideas for speakers at the Brown Bag Lunch series. Please send email or stop by my office to get your suggestions in before 5:00pm. Thanks.

PJ

The Letter Wizard

The Letter Wizard, although different in its appearance, performs the same role as the Memo Wizard. If you don't have much time to compose a letter, you should find it helpful.

To Do: Use the Letter Wizard to Create a Letter

To create a letter by using the Letter Wizard, follow these steps:

1. Choose Tools, Letter Wizard to display the Letter Wizard dialog box, as shown in Figure 5.10.

FIGURE 5.10

Design your letter in the Letter Wizard dialog box.

2. In the Letter Format tab, mark the Date Line check box if you want a date at the top of the letter, and choose the format for the date in the drop-down list to the right of the check box. Choose a page design and a letter style in the two drop-down lists in the middle of the dialog box. If you have preprinted letterhead, mark the Pre-Printed Letterhead check box, and specify where the letterhead is on the page and how much space it needs.

3. Click the Recipient Info tab and fill in the recipient's name and address and the salutation.

4. Click the Other Elements tab. If you want to include a reference line, mailing instructions, an attention line, or a subject line, mark the appropriate check boxes. For each check box you mark, choose the exact text from the associated drop-down list, or type your own text in the box at the top of the list. At the bottom of the dialog box, type the names of any people who you want to receive courtesy copies.

5

5. Click the Sender Info tab, and fill in the sender's name and address. Mark the Omit check box if you are using letterhead that includes the return address. Under Closing at the bottom of the dialog box, choose standard text from the drop-down lists for the complimentary closing, your job title, and so on, or type your own text in the text boxes at the top of each list. The Preview area shows what your closing will look like.

6. After you've made your selections, click OK.

7. The letter appears onscreen. Type the body of the letter (see Figure 5.11) and then save and close it.

FIGURE 5.11

A letter written with the help of the Letter Wizard.

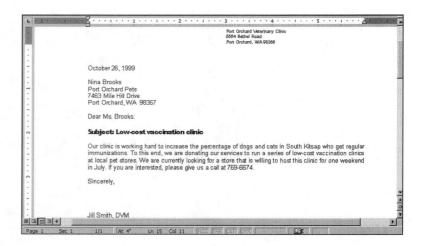

Summary

If you need to dash off a letter, memo, or fax and don't have the time or inclination to fiddle with formatting, use a template or wizard. They can help you produce professional documents with a minimum of hassle. In the next hour, you learn everything you need to know about revising text, including many shortcuts enabling you to edit documents quickly and efficiently.

Q&A

Q **I don't have the templates that you describe in my New dialog box. What is going on?**

A When you install Office (or Word as a standalone program), you can choose which templates to include. Your company may not have installed all of the Word templates, or it may only have installed custom templates that someone designed specifically for your company. Check with your network administrator if you want to use a template that you don't see in your New dialog box. If you are using Word on a standalone computer, follow the instructions in Appendix A to add more templates to your installation.

Q **When I use the Memo Wizard, I don't want to change any of the default choices. Do I still have to click Next repeatedly to go all the way to the last wizard dialog box before clicking Finish?**

A No. If you want to keep all of the default options, just click Finish in the first wizard dialog box that appears. The Memo Wizard remembers the options that you chose the last time you ran the wizard. If you don't want to change them the next time you use the wizard, just click Finish in the first dialog box.

5

PART III

Revising and Printing Your Documents

Hour

Hour 6

Revising Your Text

For all the bells and whistles that come with a word processing program, you spend the bulk of your time with a much more prosaic activity: editing your text. In Hour 3, "Entering Text and Moving Around," you learned how to get text onto your page and move the insertion point within it. In this hour, you learn all of the skills required to polish your text, including inserting new text, deleting text, and moving or copying text from one spot to another.

The highlights of this hour include

- Inserting new text into existing text
- Selecting text in preparation for doing something to it
- Deleting text
- Undoing mistakes, including restoring deleted text
- Moving and copying text

Inserting Text

When you want to insert text in the middle of text that you've already typed, Word assumes that you want the existing text to move out of the way to make room for the new text. Word calls this default behavior *insert mode*. To insert text, then, you simply move the insertion point to the place where you want the text to go and start typing. Any text to the right of the insertion point shifts over as you type. Note that when you insert text, you usually need to add a space either at the beginning or the end of the insertion.

> If you are revising text throughout your document and want to return to the previous editing location, press Shift+F5.

Typing over Existing Text

Once in a while, you might want the text that you insert to replace existing text. To do this, press the Insert key to switch to *Overtype mode*. When you're using Overtype mode, every character you press replaces the character immediately to the right of the insertion point. The Insert key is a toggle, so you press it again when you want to return to Insert mode.

Watch your screen carefully when you're using Overtype mode. If you forget that you're in Overtype mode and merrily type away, you'll likely replace not only the text you wanted to delete but a sizable chunk of text that you wanted to keep as well.

> The Insert key is right next to the Home, Delete, and End keys on the keyboard, so it's easy to press it accidentally when you mean to press another key. If you notice that your existing text is getting "gobbled up" as you type, it's a sure sign that you inadvertently switched to Overtype mode. Press the Insert key again to switch out of it, and then click the Undo button in the Standard toolbar one or more times to restore the deleted text.

> You can also switch to Overtype mode by double-clicking the letters OVR in the right half of the status bar. The letters turn dark to indicate that you're in Overtype mode (see Figure 6.1). To return to Insert mode, double-click OVR again.

FIGURE 6.1

When you're in Overtype mode, the letters OVR in the status bar are dark.

Double-click to get in and out of Overtype mode.

Double-Clicking to Move the Insertion Point Anywhere on the Page

Word 2000 introduces *click-and-type,* a feature that enables you to start typing in a blank area of your document by simply double-clicking at the desired location. For example, you can double-click in the middle of the page to center your text, double-click on the right margin to make the text flush right, or double-click several lines below your last line of text to create a large block of white space above the text. You don't have to first change your alignment, insert custom tabs, or press Enter repeatedly to create white space at the end of the document. (You learn about alignment and custom tabs in Hour 9, "Formatting Paragraphs.") Word makes these changes for you when you double-click.

Click-and-type works only in Print Layout view and Web Layout view. To make sure you're using Print Layout view (Web Layout view is useful only if you're using Word to design Web pages), choose View, Print Layout. You learn more about views in the next hour.

To practice using click-and-type, start a new document, and move your I-beam to the right margin of the page. After a moment, an icon appears next to the I-beam indicating your text is right-aligned (see Figure 6.2). Double-click to move the insertion point to this spot. If you start typing, your text is flush against the right margin.

FIGURE 6.2

This click-and-type I-beam indicates right alignment.

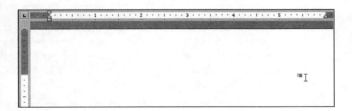

6

If double-clicking doesn't move the insertion point, choose View, Print Layout if you haven't already. Choose Tools, Options, click the Edit tab, make sure the Enable Click and Type check box is marked, and click OK.

Now position the I-beam about halfway across the page. The I-beam icon changes to indicate center alignment (see Figure 6.3). Double-click to move the insertion point. Any text you type now is centered horizontally on the page.

FIGURE 6.3

This click-and-type I-beam indicates center alignment.

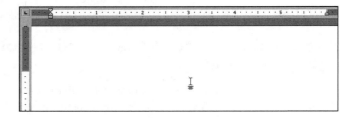

Next, point to a location approximately midway between the horizontal center of the page and the left margin. The I-beam icon indicates left alignment (see Figure 6.4). Double-click to move the insertion point. If you start typing now, your text is left-aligned at the location you double-clicked.

FIGURE 6.4

This click-and-type I-beam indicates left alignment.

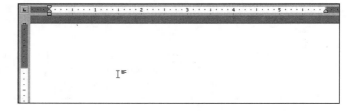

Finally, move the I-beam several inches down from the top margin of the page, and double-click. Word moves the insertion point down to the line you double-clicked on. If you start typing now, you have several blank lines above your text.

You don't have to use click-and-type if you don't want to. You can still move the insertion point into blank areas of the page by using the traditional formatting methods, which you'll learn about in Hour 9. If you'd like to disable click-and-type, choose Tools, Options, click the Edit tab, clear the Enable Click-and-Type check box, and click OK.

Combining and Splitting Paragraphs

As you're typing, you may at times want to combine two paragraphs into one, or split a longer paragraph into two or more shorter ones. While there is nothing mysterious about doing this, it can be a little puzzling to beginners.

To join two paragraphs, click at the very end of the first paragraph, just past the period, and press the Delete key one or more times until the second paragraph moves up to join the first. (Alternatively, you can click at the very beginning of the second paragraph and press the Backspace key one or more times.) You may need to add a space where the two paragraphs came together.

When you press the Delete or Backspace key to join paragraphs, you're actually removing the hidden paragraph marks separating the paragraphs. (See "Deleting Text" later in this hour for more about deleting hidden characters.) Remember that you can click the Show/Hide button in the Standard toolbar to make paragraph marks and other hidden characters visible.

To split a paragraph into two separate ones, click just before the first letter of the sentence that begins the second paragraph, and press Enter. If you want a blank line between the two paragraphs, press Enter again.

Selecting Text

Selecting (highlighting) text is an essential word processing skill. In many situations, you have to select text before issuing a command so that Word knows what text you want the command to affect. For example, you have to select text before cutting and pasting it or applying many kinds of formatting.

The most basic way of selecting text is to drag across it with the mouse. To do this, you position the I-beam at the beginning of the text you want to select, press and hold down the mouse button, drag across the text, and then release the mouse button. When text is selected, it becomes white against a black background, as shown in Figure 6.5. If you want to deselect text (remove the highlighting) without doing anything to it, click anywhere in the text area of the Word window, or press a navigation key such as one of the arrow keys, Home, or End.

If you accidentally drag over too much text, you can remove the extra text from the selection by keeping the mouse button held down as you drag back up and/or to the left.

6

FIGURE 6.5

Selected text is white against a black background.

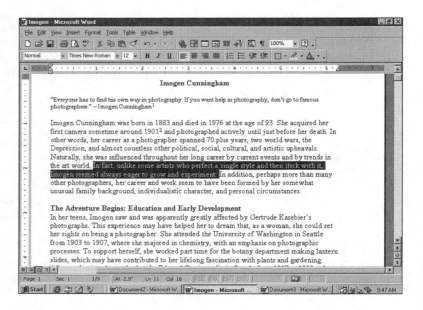

If you select some text, release the mouse button, and then realize that you selected too much or too little, you can't point to the end of the selection and start dragging to extend or shorten it. If you do this, you end up *moving* the selected text. (Dragging selected text performs a type of cutting and pasting called *drag-and-drop*.) Instead, you need to either click to deselect the text and then start dragging again, or extend or shorten the selection with the keyboard (described in just a moment).

Although dragging always works to select text, it is often not the most efficient method. Table 6.1 lists some shortcuts for selecting different amounts of text.

Three of the shortcuts involve clicking in the *selection bar,* the white area in the left margin of the page (see Figure 6.6). When the mouse pointer is in this area, it becomes a white arrow angled toward your text. Some of the shortcuts also require you to Ctrl+click or Shift+click—in other words, hold down the Ctrl key or Shift key as you click.

FIGURE 6.6

The selection bar is the white area to the left of your text.

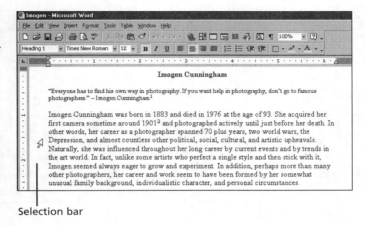

Selection bar

TABLE 6.1. SELECTION SHORTCUTS

Amount of Text Selected	Shortcut
One word	Double-click the word.
One sentence	Ctrl+click the sentence.
One line	Click in the selection bar to the left of the line.
One paragraph	Double-click in the selection bar to the left of the paragraph. (You can also triple-click directly on the paragraph.)
Entire document	Triple-click or Ctrl+click anywhere in the selection bar.
Any amount of text	Click at the beginning of the text you want to select, and then Shift+click at the end of the text.

If you like using the keyboard, you may prefer to select text by using only the keyboard. All of the keyboard selection techniques involve adding the Shift key to a navigation keyboard shortcut (whichever one travels the distance that you want to select). Table 6.2 lists some of the most common keyboard selection techniques.

TABLE 6.2. KEYBOARD SELECTION TECHNIQUES

Keyboard Technique	Amount Selected
Shift+→	One character to the right
Shift+←	One character to the left
Shift+↓	One line down
Shift+↑	One line up
Shift+Ctrl+→	One word to the right

continues

6

TABLE 6.2. CONTINUED

Keyboard Technique	Amount Selected
Shift+Ctrl+←	One word to the left
Shift+Ctrl+↓	One paragraph down
Shift+Ctrl+↑	One paragraph up
Shift+End	From the insertion point to the end of the line
Shift+Home	From the insertion point to the beginning of the line
Shift+Ctrl+End	From the insertion point to the end of the document
Shift+Ctrl+Home	From the insertion point to the beginning of the document
Ctrl+A	The entire document (same as choosing Edit, Select All)

With the keyboard techniques involving pressing an arrow key, you can add to the selection by keeping the other keys in the combination held down as you repeatedly press the arrow key. For example, to select six words to the right, you would hold down the Shift and Ctrl keys as you pressed the right-arrow key six times.

One of the handiest uses of keyboard selection techniques is to adjust the size of a selection after you've already released the mouse button. For example, if you dragged over a couple of sentences, but accidentally didn't include the period at the end of the last sentence, you can press Shift+→ to extend the selection to include the period.

> You can also press the Shift key and then click with the mouse to extend or shrink the selection.

Deleting Text

Knowing how to delete text is almost as important as knowing how to type it in the first place. Although you can delete any amount of text if you bang on the Delete or Backspace key enough times, it's much more efficient to use other methods when you want to select more than a few characters. Table 6.3 lists techniques for deleting different amounts of text.

TABLE 6.3. TECHNIQUES FOR DELETING TEXT

Technique	Result
Delete key	Deletes character to the right of the insertion point
Backspace key	Deletes character to the left of the insertion point

Technique	Result
Ctrl+Delete	Deletes word to the right of the insertion point
Ctrl+Backspace	Deletes word to the left of the insertion point
Select text and press the Delete key	Deletes selected text (can be any amount)
Select text and start typing	Deletes selected text (can be any amount) and replaces it with the text you type

To delete several words, hold down the Ctrl key as you press Delete or Backspace several times. If you want to delete only the end of a word—for example, you want to change the word *functionality* to *function*—click in front of the part you want to delete (before the letter *a* in this example) and press Ctrl+Delete. If you want to delete the beginning of a word—to change the word *ultraconservative* to *conservative,* for instance—click just after the part you want to delete (just past the letter *a* in this example) and press Ctrl+Backspace.

Word treats paragraph marks, tabs, and spaces just like other characters, so you can delete them with the Delete and Backspace keys, just as you delete other characters. In most cases, it's obvious where they are even though they are hidden. At times, however, you may find it helpful to display these hidden characters onscreen so that you can see exactly where they are. To do this, click the Show/Hide button in the Standard toolbar. (You learned about the Show/Hide feature in the section "Seeing Your Paragraph, Tab, and Space Marks" in Hour 3.)

Undoing Mistakes

If you know how to delete text, you surely want to know how to restore it when you delete it accidentally. Word's Undo feature enables you to bring back deleted text as well as undo many other actions. You are not limited to undoing the most recent action you performed; Undo enables you to undo multiple actions. For example, if you delete a paragraph by mistake and then go on to issue a few more commands before realizing that the paragraph was gone, you can undo all of your actions back to, and including, the deletion.

6

> Word can undo most actions related to editing and formatting your document. Two actions that Word can't undo are saving and printing.

To undo the most recent action, click the Undo button on the Standard toolbar (see Figure 6.7) or press Ctrl+Z. To continue undoing previous actions one by one, keep clicking the Undo button or pressing Ctrl+Z.

FIGURE 6.7

Click the Undo toolbar button to undo your most recent action.

If you know that you want to undo something you did a few minutes ago and don't want to click the Undo button several times, click the down arrow to the right of the Undo button (refer back to Figure 6.7). This displays a list of all of your actions, with the most recent action at the top (see Figure 6.8). Scroll down the list and click the action that you want to undo. Word undoes all of your actions back to and including the one you click.

FIGURE 6.8

Click an action in the Undo drop-down list to undo everything back to that point.

If you undo an action and then decide that you want to perform it after all, click the Redo button on the Standard toolbar (refer to Figure 6.7) or press Ctrl+Y or F4. As with Undo, you can redo multiple actions by clicking the button repeatedly, or by choosing an action in the Redo drop-down list.

Cutting and Pasting

The capability to move and copy text from one place to another is one of the most appreciated features of word processing programs. The term *cutting and pasting* actually refers to both moving and copying text. When you *move* text, you remove (*cut*) it from one location in your document and paste it in another. When you *copy* text, you leave the text in its original location and paste a duplicate of it somewhere else.

The location that contains the text you want to move or copy is called the *source*, and the place you want to paste it is called the *destination*. The destination can be in the same document, another Word document, another Office document (such as an Excel spreadsheet or a PowerPoint presentation), or a document created in another Windows application.

When you cut or copy text, it is placed on the Windows Clipboard, a temporary storage area available to all Windows applications. Issuing the Paste command copies the text from the Windows Clipboard into your document. (It actually stays on the Windows Clipboard until you perform the next cut or copy, so you can paste the same text multiple times if you like.)

> A major limitation of the Windows Clipboard is that it can hold only one selection at a time. Each time you cut or copy another block of text, it replaces the text that was previously on the Windows Clipboard. As you'll see in "Moving and Copying Multiple Items" later in this hour, Office 2000 offers a way around this restriction with the Office Clipboard.

Moving Text

As you're typing a document, you'll probably want to restructure it a bit. You may need to move a word or phrase within a sentence, reorganize the flow of sentences within a paragraph, or change the order of some paragraphs.

To Do: Move Text

Follow these steps to move text:

1. Select the text that you want to move. (Use any method described in "Selecting Text" earlier in this hour.)
2. Click the Cut button on the Standard toolbar (see Figure 6.9) or press Ctrl+X. The text disappears from its current location.

Cut

FIGURE 6.9

Click the Cut button to remove the selected text from its current location.

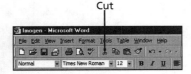

6

▼ 3. Navigate to the destination, and place the insertion point exactly where you want the text to appear.

> If the destination is in a different document that is currently open, click the document's taskbar button to switch to it, and then navigate to the place where you want to insert the text. If the destination document isn't open, open it now (see "Opening a Document" in Hour 4, "Managing Documents").

4. Click the Paste button in the Standard toolbar (see Figure 6.10) or press Ctrl+V. The text is pasted into the destination, and existing text to the right of the insertion point moves over to make room for the inserted text.

▲

FIGURE 6.10

Click the Paste toolbar button to paste the text into the destination.

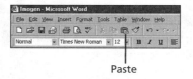

Paste

> If you're trying to move text and the Cut toolbar button is dim, you forgot to select the text you want to move. The Cut and Copy toolbar buttons become active only when you have selected text.

Copying Text

If you want to insert a block of text that you've already typed somewhere else, it's much faster to copy it than to type it from scratch.

To Do: Copy Text

Follow these steps to copy text:

1. Select the text that you want to copy.

2. Click the Copy button on the Standard toolbar (see Figure 6.11) or press Ctrl+C. The original text remains in its current location.

FIGURE 6.11

Click the Copy button to make a copy of the selected text.

Copy

3. Navigate to the destination, and make sure that the insertion point is exactly where you want the text to appear. (See the note in the steps for moving text in the preceding section if the destination is not in the current document.)

4. Click the Paste button in the Standard toolbar or press Ctrl+V. The text is pasted into the destination, and existing text to the right of the insertion point moves over to make room for the inserted text.

> If you want to copy an entire file into the current document, click at the location where you want to insert the file, choose Insert, File, select the file in the Insert File dialog box, and click the Insert button.

Moving and Copying with Drag-and-Drop

If you are handy with the mouse, you may find it easiest to move and copy text with *drag-and-drop*. This feature enables you to select text and then drag it to its destination. Drag-and-drop is best suited for moving or copying small amounts of text a short distance.

To Do: Move Text with Drag-and-Drop

To move text with drag-and-drop, follow these steps:

1. Select the text that you want to move or copy and release the mouse button.

2. Point to the selected text. The mouse pointer becomes a white arrow.

3. To move the text, drag it to the destination. As you drag, the mouse pointer changes to indicate that you're performing a drag-and-drop (see Figure 6.12). Drag until the dashed insertion point attached to the mouse pointer is in the right place, and then release the mouse button.

6

FIGURE 6.12

A special drag-and-drop mouse pointer shows where the text will be inserted.

> Naturally, she was influenced throughout her long career by current events and by trends in the art world. In fact, unlike some artists who perfect a single style and then stick with it, Imogen seemed always eager to grow and experiment. In addition, perhaps more than many other photographers, her career and work seem to have been formed by her somewhat unusual family background, individualistic character, and personal circumstances.

Drag-and-drop mouse pointer

To copy the text, Ctrl+drag it to the destination (hold down the Ctrl key as you drag). The drag-and-drop mouse pointer gains a plus sign to indicate that you're performing a copy, not a move (see Figure 6.13). When the dashed insertion point is in the right place, release the mouse button and then the Ctrl key. (If you release the Ctrl key before the mouse button, Word performs a cut instead of a copy.)

FIGURE 6.13

The drag-and-drop mouse pointer includes a plus sign when you're copying text.

> Imogen could also have been influenced by the two photographers Albert Renger-Patzsch and Karl Blossfeldt, both of whom photographed plants extensively. Remember, she both spoke and read German, so their work would have been accessible to her. But her photos seem less "scientific" and "clinical" than theirs, and are also in many cases less straightforward and immediately recognizable, with shadows often playing as important a role as the plants themselves.[6] (See Figure 9, "Sempervivum Percarneum," by
>
> On the West Coast, Margrethe Mather did plant photographs that Imogen admired greatly. In

Drag-and-drop mouse pointer

4. Click anywhere to deselect the text.

If you accidentally drop the selected text in the wrong place, click the Undo button on the Standard toolbar.

Moving and Copying Multiple Items

With the traditional cut-and-paste procedure, you can cut or copy only one selection at a time. The Office Clipboard, new to Office 2000, enables you to "collect" up to 12 selections of cut or copied data and then paste them in any order into any Office 2000 document. The Office Clipboard can handle all of the standard data types, including text, numbers, graphic images, and so on.

To Do: Move or Copy Multiple Items with the Office Clipboard

To practice using the Office Clipboard, follow these steps:

1. Choose View, Toolbars, Clipboard to display the Clipboard toolbar and the Office Clipboard.
2. Select a block of text in a Word document, and click the Cut or Copy button on the Standard toolbar, and then cut or copy another block of text in the document. Two Word icons appear on the Office Clipboard to represent the two items that you've cut or copied (see Figure 6.14).

FIGURE 6.14

Each item you cut or copy appears as an icon on the Office Clipboard.

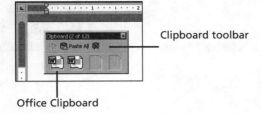

Clipboard toolbar

Office Clipboard

3. Cut or copy a couple more items to the Office Clipboard, and then point to one of them. A ScreenTip appears with the beginning of the text in that item so that you can identify it (see Figure 6.15).

FIGURE 6.15

Use ScreenTips to identify each item on the Office Clipboard.

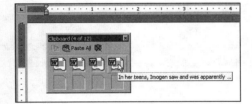

4. Click in a location where you want to insert one of the items on the Office Clipboard, and then click the item to paste it into that spot.

5. Paste some of the other items in the Office Clipboard if you like, and then click the Close button in the Clipboard toolbar to close it and the Office Clipboard.

> If the Clipboard toolbar is visible, you can click its Copy button instead of the Copy button in the Standard toolbar to copy text. If you want to paste all of the items in the Office Clipboard at once, click the Paste All button in the Clipboard toolbar. To remove all of the items from the Office Clipboard, click the Clear Clipboard button (the button to the right of the Paste All button).

6

When the Clipboard toolbar is visible, you can cut or copy items from any Windows application to the Office Clipboard. (When it isn't visible, you can still use it to cut or copy items in an Office 2000 application.) Items that you've cut or copied from applications other than Word have different icons. In Figure 6.16, the Office Clipboard holds nine items: four from Word documents, two from a Web page, one from an Excel spreadsheet, one from a PowerPoint presentation, and one from Paint Shop Pro (a graphics program).

FIGURE **6.16**

*You can cut or copy
items from any
Windows application.*

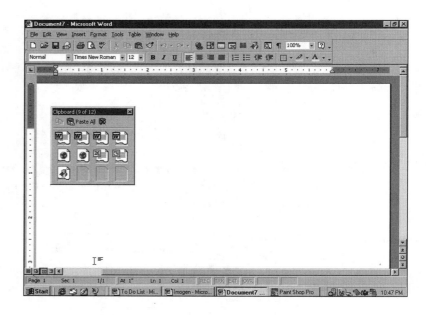

Summary

Revising text is at the heart of word processing. As soon as the techniques described in
this hour become second nature, you'll be able to place your attention squarely on the
content of your document, where it belongs, rather than the commands required to edit
text. Word's editing features are so easy to master that you should feel comfortable tinkering with the text of your document in no time. In the next hour, you learn different
ways of viewing and printing your documents.

Q&A

Q When I tried to move text with drag-and-drop, it didn't work. What is wrong?

A Some people disable drag-and-drop if they find that they are moving text accidentally. If someone turned this feature off on your computer, you can turn it back on
by choosing Tools, Options, clicking the Edit tab, marking the Drag-and-Drop Text
Editing check box, and clicking OK.

**Q If I use the Office Clipboard in a Word document and then close Word, does
the Office Clipboard remain available?**

A The Office Clipboard is available as long as you have at least one Office 2000
application open. If you want to use the Office Clipboard to cut or copy data in a

non-Office 2000 application, display the Clipboard toolbar first, and then switch to the application in which you want to cut or copy data. Select the item that you want to cut or copy and issue the Cut or Copy command. When you switch back to the Office 2000 application, you see an icon for the item you just cut or copied on the Office Clipboard. When you close all Office 2000 applications, the Office Clipboard is cleared.

Q How exactly does the Office Clipboard relate to the Windows Clipboard?

A The Office Clipboard and Windows Clipboard are separate, but their functions overlap. When you cut or copy items to the Office Clipboard, the last item is placed on the Windows Clipboard. When you click the Paste button in the Standard toolbar (or choose Edit, Paste or press Ctrl+V), the item in the Windows Clipboard (the last item in the Office Clipboard) is pasted into your document. If you keep issuing the Paste command, this same item is pasted each time, until you cut or copy another item. Clicking the Clear Clipboard button in the Clipboard toolbar also clears the Windows Clipboard.

6

Hour 7

Viewing and Printing Your Documents

Word offers a wide assortment of options for changing the appearance of your document onscreen. If you type only simple letters and memos, you may never need to change these settings. However, if you create documents with sophisticated formatting, have trouble reading small print, or want to view different parts of a document or more than one document at the same time, you can tailor the view options to suit your preferences. And when you've finished typing your documents and like their appearance onscreen, you'll most likely want to print them out. In this hour, you explore a whole host of viewing and printing options.

The highlights of this hour include

- Switching views
- Zooming your document
- Viewing separate parts of your document at the same time
- Arranging multiple Word documents on the desktop

- Previewing your document before you print
- Printing your document
- Printing envelopes and labels

Viewing Your Document

Word's view options are so plentiful that you can surely find one or two that work well for you. You can use any of these six views to work with your documents:

- Print Layout (View menu)
- Normal (View menu)
- Full Screen (View menu)
- Print Preview (File menu)
- Web Layout (View menu)
- Outline (View menu)

You'll learn about Print Layout, Normal, and Full Screen view in the next three sections. Print Preview is discussed in "Previewing a Document Before Printing" later in this hour. Web Layout view is covered in Hour 24, "Word and the Web," and Outline view is explained in Hour 15, "Working with Long Documents."

You can switch to Normal, Web Layout, Print Layout, and Outline views by using the four View buttons in the lower-left corner of the Word window (see Figure 7.1).

FIGURE 7.1

Using the View buttons to switch among four of the views.

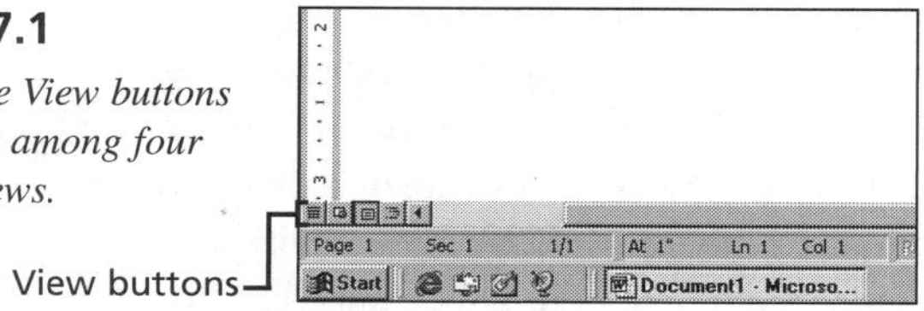

View buttons ⅂

> Word remembers the view you choose for a document and uses it the next time you open the document.

Using Print Layout View

Print Layout view is the default view option, and it probably works for you most of the time. If you aren't sure whether you're using it, choose View, Print Layout or click the Print Layout View button in the lower-left corner of the Word window.

Print Layout view gives you the sense that you're typing directly onto a piece of paper (see Figure 7.2). It includes horizontal and vertical rulers so that you always know where your text appears on the page, and it shows you the top, bottom, left, and right margin areas. If you have typed text in the headers and footers (you learn how to do this in Hour 10), it will be visible in the top and bottom margins. All page breaks (regardless of type) appear as a gap between the bottom edge of one page and the top edge of the next.

FIGURE 7.2

Print Layout view enables you to see the margin areas of your document.

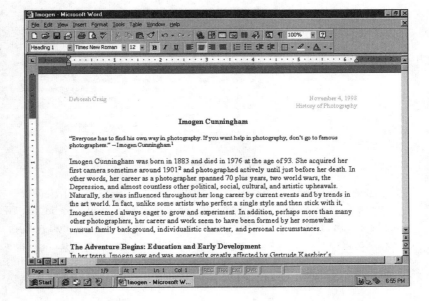

You don't have to use Print Layout view if you're typing documents with simple formatting. However, you do need to use it if you're working with more complex formatting such as columns, tables, and graphics. (These features do not display correctly in Normal view, described in the next section.)

Using Normal View

In earlier versions of Word, Normal view was the default view option. Although Print Layout view is now the default, Normal view is still useful in some situations. To switch to it, choose View, Normal or click the Normal View button in the lower-left corner of the Word window.

Normal view displays only the horizontal ruler, not the vertical ruler. And it doesn't display the margin areas of the page, so you can't see headers and footers (see Figure 7.3).

7

FIGURE 7.3

Normal view doesn't display the margin areas of your document.

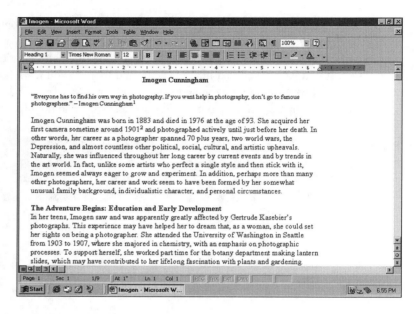

One advantage of Normal view is that unlike Print Layout view, it shows you what type of page breaks are in your document. A soft page break—one that Word adds for you when the text flows on to the next page—appears as a dotted horizontal line running across the page. A hard page break—one that you insert to end a page before it's full— appears as a dotted horizontal line with the words *Page Break* on it. Figure 7.4 shows a soft and hard page break in Normal view.

Normal view also displays *section breaks*, which you have to use to apply certain kinds of formatting to only a portion of your document. You learn more about page and section breaks in Hour 10, "Formatting Pages."

Using Full Screen View

If you like working in a completely uncluttered environment, you'll appreciate Full Screen view. To switch to this view, choose View, Full Screen. Your document window enlarges to cover the entire desktop (see Figure 7.5). The title bar, menu bar, and toolbars in the Word window are temporarily hidden to give you as much room as possible to see your text. If you want to issue a menu command, point to the thin gray line running across the top of your screen to slide the menu bar into view.

FIGURE 7.4

Switch to Normal view if you need to see what kind of page breaks are in your document.

Soft page break ———

Hard page break ———

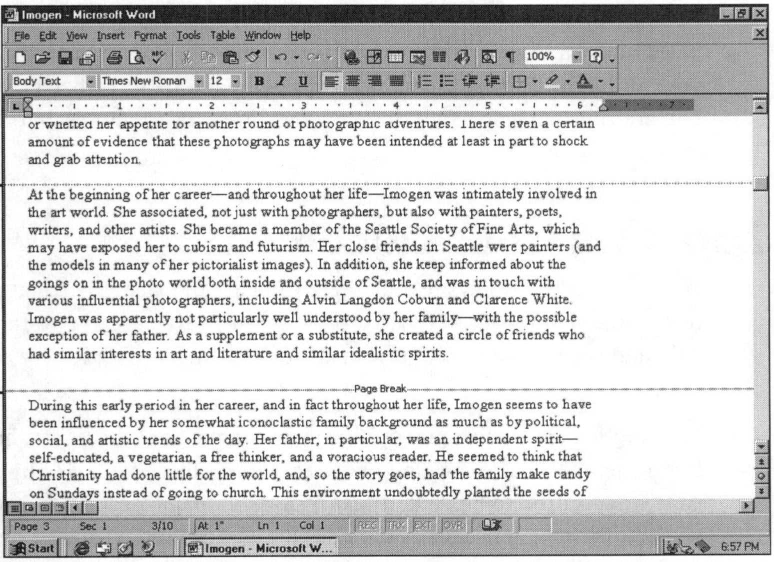

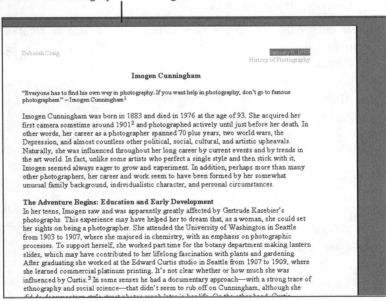

Point to the thin gray line to bring the menu bar into view.

FIGURE 7.5

Full Screen view gives you an uncluttered view of your document.

7

Full Screen view works in conjunction with whatever other view you are using, not in place of it. In Figure 7.5, the document is in Print Layout and Full Screen view. While you are in Full Screen view, you can switch among the other views as you like. When you are finished using Full Screen view, bring the menu bar into view and choose View, Full Screen again.

Zooming Your Document

Word normally displays text at approximately the size it is when printed. In some situations, you might want to enlarge or shrink the text onscreen to make it easier to read, edit, and format. You change your document's magnification by adjusting the Zoom setting.

You might want to change your Zoom setting if your document has especially large or small fonts, if you're printing on a paper size other than 8 1/2 by 11, or if your eyesight isn't what it used to be. When you shrink the magnification to anything less than 100 percent, the text appears smaller and you can see more of your document. When you enlarge the magnification to anything over 100 percent, the text appears bigger and you can see less of your document. Changing the magnification of your document onscreen does not affect the way it prints.

To change the Zoom setting, click the down-arrow to the right of the Zoom box at the right end of the Standard toolbar to display the Zoom list (see Figure 7.6), and then click the desired setting.

FIGURE 7.6

Choose the desired magnification setting in the Zoom list.

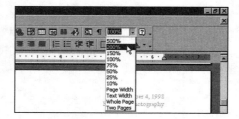

In Figure 7.7, the document has been zoomed to 200 percent. Word remembers the setting and uses it the next time you open the document.

FIGURE 7.7

The Zoom setting was changed to 200 percent.

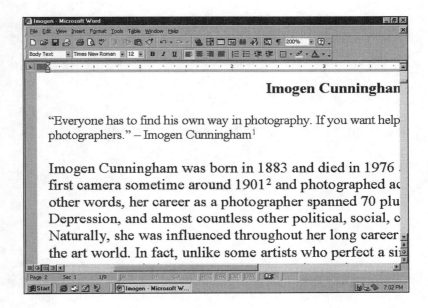

If you enlarge the magnification of your document, as shown in Figure 7.7, you may need to use the horizontal scrollbar at the bottom of the Word window to bring the right side of the document into view.

The four options at the bottom of the Zoom list also come in handy. They automatically adjust your document's magnification just the right amount to display the full width of the page (Page Width), the width of the text only (Text Width), the entire page (Whole Page), and two entire pages (Two Pages). In Normal view, the Text Width, Whole Page, and Two Pages options are not available.

You aren't limited to the magnification percentages shown in the Zoom list. If you want to magnify your document at a setting not in the list, 85 percent, for example, click in the Zoom box to select the current setting, type over it with the percentage you'd like, and press Enter.

Viewing Separate Parts of Your Document at the Same Time

With a longer document, you may find it convenient to view separate parts of it at the same time. For example, if you're typing a report that begins with a table of contents, you may want to keep it in view as you're typing later portions of the report to make sure that you're sticking to your outline.

To practice using this feature, open any document that is too long to fit onscreen. Then point to the *split bar*, the short horizontal bar directly above the up-arrow at the top of the vertical scrollbar (see Figure 7.8).

FIGURE 7.8

Drag the split bar to divide your screen into two panes.

Split bar

When you point to the split bar, your mouse pointer changes to two horizontal lines with a vertical double arrow. Drag about halfway down the Word window. As you drag, a gray horizontal line shows where the window will be split (see Figure 7.9). When the line is in the right place, release the mouse button.

FIGURE 7.9

Release the mouse button when the horizontal gray line is in the right spot.

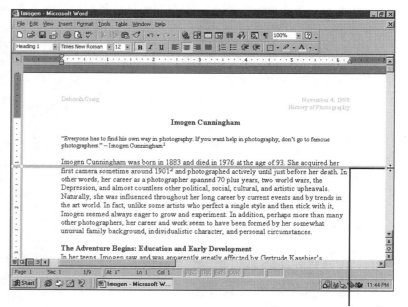

Drag to create the split.

Word divides the window into two *panes*. Each pane has its own rulers and scrollbars. Click in the lower pane to activate it, and then use its vertical scrollbar to scroll down in the document. As you scroll, the portion of the document displayed in the upper pane doesn't change. If you want to scroll the upper pane, click in it and then use its vertical scrollbar. The status bar at the bottom of the Word window shows you the page number of the active pane. In Figure 7.10, the first page of a 9-page document is displayed in the upper pane, and the last page is displayed in the lower pane.

FIGURE 7.10

The first and last pages of a nine-page document are visible at the same time.

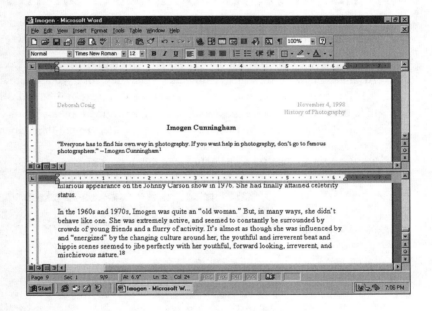

When the Word window is split, you can use the Go To feature in the active pane to scroll only that pane to the page you specify. (See the section "Jumping to a Specific Page" in Hour 3, "Entering Text and Moving Around.")

If you want to adjust the relative size of the two panes, point to the gray dividing line and drag it up or down. To remove the split, double-click the gray line or drag it all the way up to the top of the Word window.

When the Word window is split, you can drag and drop text from one pane into the other. This makes it easy to use drag-and-drop to move or copy text over long distances in a multiple-page document.

7

> Another way to create a split is to choose Window, Split. Word displays a gray horizontal line and moves the mouse pointer over it. Move the mouse to get the line in the right spot, and then click to create the split. When you want to remove the split, choose Window, Remove Split.

Arranging Word Documents on Your Screen

If you have more than one Word document open, you may want to display them next to one another to compare their content, or to drag and drop text between them.

To arrange your open Word documents so that all of them are visible, choose Window, Arrange All. Word tiles the documents so that they cover your entire desktop (see Figure 7.11). If you want to create more room to see your text in tiled Word windows, you can hide the rulers and place the Standard and Formatting toolbars on one row, as shown in Figure 7.11. (To hide the rulers, choose View, Ruler. To put the Standard and Formatting toolbars on the same row, choose Tools, Customize, mark the Standard and Formatting Toolbars Share One Row check box, and click the Close button.)

FIGURE 7.11

The two open Word windows are visible at the same time.

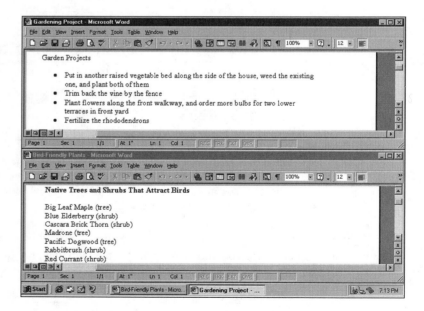

To return to viewing only one Word window, click the Maximize button in the upper-right corner of the window that you want to use.

Previewing a Document Before Printing

Word's Print Preview feature enables you to see what a document looks like before you send it to the printer. Using Print Preview is a great way of saving paper because you can catch things that you'd like to change before you print. To use Print Preview, click the Print Preview button on the Standard toolbar (see Figure 7.12) or choose File, Print Preview.

FIGURE 7.12

Click the Print Preview button in the Standard toolbar to switch to Print Preview.

Print Preview

Word switches to Print Preview. When you're using this view, the title bar contains the word [Preview], and a Print Preview toolbar appears (see Figure 7.13).

Print   Zoom   Shrink to Fit

FIGURE 7.13

Print Preview gives you a good idea of what your document will look like after it's printed.

Magnifier

One Page

Multiple Pages

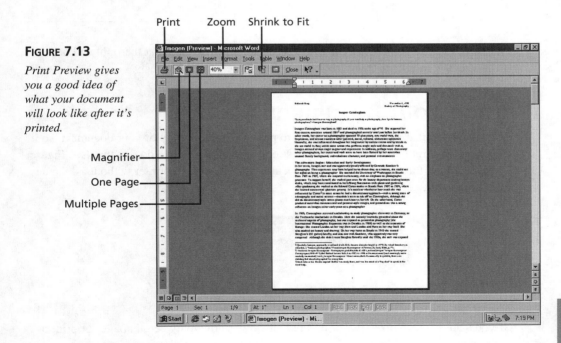

7

To scroll through the document page by page, press the Page Down and Page Up keys. If you want to view several pages at once, click the Multiple Pages toolbar button and drag through the desired number of squares in the grid that drops down (each square represents a page). To go back to viewing one page, click the One Page toolbar button. If you want to print your document directly from Print Preview, click the Print toolbar button.

Another handy feature in Print Preview is Shrink to Fit. If you'd like your document to fit onto one page and it's spilling onto two (or you want it to fit onto two pages and it's spilling onto three, and so on), you can click the Shrink to Fit toolbar button to make it fit on one less page than it currently does. Word accomplishes this by making small adjustments to your document's formatting (reducing the font size, decreasing the amount of white space, and so on).

> You can edit your document while you're viewing it in Print Preview if you like. Click the Magnifier toolbar button to turn it off. An insertion point appears in the document. You can now type and revise your text as usual. (You may want to use the Zoom box in the Print Preview toolbar to increase the magnification so that you can see your text more clearly.) Click the Magnifier button again when you are finished.

When you're finished using Print Preview, click the Close button at the right end of the Print Preview toolbar to return to the view you were using previously.

Printing Your Document

Word assumes that you frequently want to print a complete copy of your document, so it provides the Print button on the Standard toolbar enabling you to do just that (see Figure 7.14). Clicking this button sends your document to the default printer without asking any questions at all.

FIGURE 7.14

Click the Print button on the Standard tool-bar to print one copy of the entire document.

Print

If you want to customize your printing at all—by printing only certain pages or printing more than one copy, for example—you need to use the Print dialog box.

To Do: Print Your Document from the Print Dialog Box

Follow these steps to print from the Print dialog box:

1. Choose File, Print or press Ctrl+P (see Figure 7.15).

FIGURE 7.15

Use the Print dialog box to customize your printing.

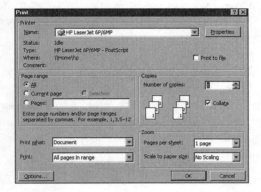

2. Check the printer listed in the Name drop-down list. If you have only one printer, you won't need to change this setting. If your computer is hooked up to multiple printers, you can select a different printer in this list.

3. Under Page Range, the All option button is marked by default. This option prints your entire document. To print only the page containing the insertion point, mark the Current Page option button. To print more than one page but not the entire document, type the page numbers you want to print in the Pages text box. Use commas to separate nonsequential pages and dashes indicate a range of pages. For example, you would type *1,3-6, 8* to print pages 1, 3, 4, 5, 6, and 8. If you want to print only one block of text in your document, select the text before displaying the Print dialog box, and then mark the Selection option button.

4. If you want to print more than one copy of your document, enter the number in the Copies text box by typing it or clicking the spinner arrows.

5. Under Zoom, click the desired number of pages in the Pages per Sheet drop-down list if you want to print more than one document page on a sheet of paper. (You might do this to conserve paper.) Select a paper size in the Scale to Paper Size drop-down list to print on a different paper size than the one that's set for the document. (You learn how to set a document's paper size in Hour 10.)

6. Click the OK button to send the document to the printer. (If you decide not to print, click the Cancel button.)

7

Word enables you to print a document without opening it. To do so, display the Open dialog box, navigate to the document that you want to print, right-click it, and choose Print in the context menu. To print more than one document in a folder, Ctrl+click each document in the Open dialog box (or, if the documents are adjacent to one another, click the first document and Shift+click the last one). Right-click any one of the selected documents and choose Print.

Printing Envelopes

Printing envelopes in Word is simple. You check the recipient's address and the return address, load your envelope in the printer, issue the command to print. Word assumes that you want to print on a standard business-size envelope, but you can choose a different envelope size if necessary.

Instead of printing one envelope or label at a time, you can also print a bunch of them at once as part of a mass mailing. You learn how to do this in Hour 20, "More on Mass Mailings."

To Do: Print an Envelope

Follow these steps to print an envelope:

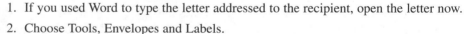

1. If you used Word to type the letter addressed to the recipient, open the letter now.
2. Choose Tools, Envelopes and Labels.
3. Click the Envelopes tab in the Envelopes and Labels dialog box (see Figure 7.16).

FIGURE 7.16

Use the Envelopes tab of the Envelopes and Labels dialog box to specify the addresses to print on your envelope.

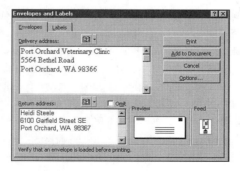

4. Word finds the address in the document you have open onscreen. Edit it in the Delivery Address box if needed.

5. Word automatically includes your return address on the envelope. If you have envelopes with a preprinted return address, mark the Omit check box.

6. If you want to print a return address, check the address in the Return Address box, and edit it if necessary.

7. If your envelope is not the standard business size, or if you want to change the font or position of the addresses, click the Options button to display the Envelope Options dialog box (see Figure 7.17). Use the Envelope Size list to choose a different envelope size. To change fonts, click the Font button under Delivery Address or Return Address. To adjust the position of the return or recipient address, click the spinner arrows to the right of the appropriate From Left and From Right text boxes. When you're finished, click OK to return to the Envelopes and Labels dialog box.

FIGURE 7.17

The Envelope Options dialog box enables you to customize your envelope.

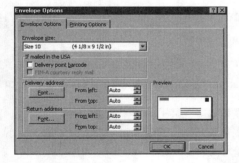

8. Put the envelope in your printer and click the Print button to print it. Alternatively, you can click the Add to Document to add the envelope to the top of the current document so that it prints every time you print the document. (If you do this, remember to always have an envelope loaded when you print the document because it prints as the first page.)

If you aren't sure how to feed your envelope into the printer, check the Feed area in the Envelopes tab of the Envelopes and Labels dialog box (see Figure 7.16). This diagram is usually correct. If it's not, check your printer's documentation for the right way to load the envelope.

7

9. If you changed your return address in step 6, Word asks whether you want to save the new address as the default return address. Click the Yes button if you want to use this return address in the future, or click No to use it just this once.

Word finds your return address in the User Information tab of the Options dialog box. If you change it while printing an envelope, Word updates your address here. You can edit your return address and other user information at any time. To do so, choose Tools, Options, click the User Information tab, revise the information, and click OK.

Printing Labels

The steps for printing labels are very similar to those for printing envelopes. The one difference is that you'll likely need to choose another label type because labels come in such a wide variety of sizes.

To Do: Print a Label

Follow these steps to print a label:

1. Choose Tools, Envelopes and Labels.

2. Click the Labels tab in the Envelopes and Labels dialog box (see Figure 17.18).

FIGURE 17.18

Use the Labels tab of the Envelopes and Labels dialog box to specify the address to print on your label.

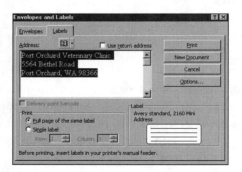

3. Type or edit the address in the Address box. If you want to print your return address instead, mark the Use Return Address check box.

4. Click the Options button to display the Label Options dialog box (see Figure 17.19).

FIGURE 17.19

The Label Options dialog box enables you to specify the type of labels you're using.

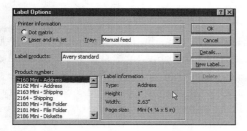

5. Select the product number for your labels in the Product Number list, and click OK. (If you don't have standard Avery labels, choose a different label from the Label Products drop-down list.)

> The product number for most labels is printed on the packaging. If you can't find your labels' product number or it isn't in the Product Number list, click the New Label button in the Label Options dialog box. In the New Custom Laser dialog box (or New Custom Dot Matrix if you marked the Dot Matrix option button in the Label Options dialog box), type a name for your labels, enter their dimensions, and click OK. Your new label type is added to the Product Number list so you can choose it in the future.

6. Mark the Full Page of the Same Label check box if you want a whole page of labels with the same address on each one.

7. If you want a single label, mark the Single Label option button, and then enter the label's row and column number.

8. Put the sheet of labels in your printer, and click the Print button to print the label or sheet of labels. (If you aren't sure which paper tray to use, check your printer's documentation.) If you are printing a sheet of labels and want to print them in the future, you can click the New Document button instead of the Print button. Word creates a separate one-page document of your labels. Save this document, print as many copies as you need, and then close it. You can open this document at any time in the future to print more of these labels.

> Even though Word enables you to print a single label at a time, it is not a good idea to run a sheet of labels through a laser printer more than once. Doing so can cause labels to come off inside the printer, something that is not cheap to repair.

7

Summary

Word gives you all the flexibility you need for viewing and printing your documents. In addition to switching views, you can adjust the magnification of your documents, display different parts of a document at the same time, and tile open Word documents on the desktop. Before printing, you can preview your document to make sure it looks the way you want it to, and then optionally adjust your print job in a variety of ways. In the next hour, you start learning how to format your documents, beginning with changing the appearance of characters.

Q&A

Q In Print Layout view, header and footer text appears dim. Will it print that way?

A No. Header and footer text appears dim because the header and footer areas are not active in Print Layout view by default. If you want to edit your header or footer, double-click it to activate it. The text turns dark. When you are finished, double-click the document text to reactivate it. You'll learn more about headers and footers in Hour 10.

Q I use a high-resolution setting on my monitor, and the text in Word documents is too small to read easily. Will the Zoom feature help in this situation?

A Yes. Many people who have large monitors (17-inch or more) like to use a high resolution (1024×768 or greater) so that they can see more on their screen. The downside of choosing a high resolution is that you'll experience a corresponding reduction in onscreen text size. To compensate, you can increase the Zoom setting for Word documents slightly (to 110 percent perhaps).

Q Can I print Word documents without even opening Word?

A Yes. If you have a shortcut to your printer on your desktop, you can drag the document icon from Windows Explorer or My Computer and drop it onto the printer shortcut. If you don't have a printer shortcut on your desktop, double-click the Printers folder in your My Computer window, right-drag the icon for your printer onto the desktop, release the mouse button, and choose Create Shortcut Here.

PART IV
Formatting Your Documents

Hour

Hour 8

Formatting Characters

Changing the appearance of characters is one of the parts of word processing that most people enjoy—even stodgy workaholics and high-octane business managers. The formatting that you can apply to individual characters—fonts, font sizes, bold, italic, underline, and so on—is referred to as *font formatting* or *character formatting*. You can apply font formatting to as little as one character, or as much as an entire document. In this hour, you learn how to apply a wide range of font formatting, and then you find out about a few more tricks for handling this type of formatting in your documents.

The highlights of this hour include

- Changing fonts and font size
- Applying boldface, italic, and underline
- Changing font color
- Adjusting character spacing
- Applying text effects
- Choosing a different default font
- Copying and removing font formatting

Applying Font Formatting

Word assumes that you want to use a Times New Roman, 12-point font. To make any changes to this default setting, you use one of the font-formatting features described in this hour. As you're exploring the different formatting options, keep these three points in mind:

- In general, you need to select the text you want to format before issuing the formatting command. This is your way of telling Word what exact text you want to affect.

> There are two exceptions to the "select first" rule. First, if you're applying the font formatting to a single word, you can just click in the word without selecting it, and then issue the commands. The formatting is applied to the entire word. Second, if you haven't yet typed the text that you want to format, you can place your insertion point at the location where you want to type, turn on the font formatting options, and then type your text. The text takes on the formatting you chose.

- The easiest way to tell what font, font size, font style (boldface, italic, underline), and font color has been applied to a block of text is to click in it. The options in the Formatting toolbar show you the formatting in effect wherever the insertion point is resting.
- If you want to apply the same font formatting to several blocks of text, a fast way to do it is to use the F4 key. F4, the *repeat* key, repeats whatever command you last issued. To increase the font size of several headings, for example, you could apply the new font size to the first heading, and then select the next heading, press F4, select the next heading, press F4, and so on. (You can use F4 to repeat many other commands as well—try using it throughout the rest of this book.)

Changing Fonts

In the world of personal computers, the term *font* is used to refer to the typeface of your text. Each computer has a different set of fonts, depending on what software is installed and what printer you're using. Office 2000 detects what fonts you have available and enables you to select them in Word. As a general rule, it's best to use only one or two fonts in a document. If you apply more, your document is likely to look overly busy.

The quickest way to change a font is to the use Font drop-down list in the Formatting toolbar, although you can also change fonts in the Font dialog box, as you'll see in a moment.

To Do: Apply a Font Using the Font List

To apply a font using the Font list, follow these steps:

1. Select the text you want to change.

2. Click the down-arrow to the right of the Font list in the Formatting toolbar. The list of fonts shows you what each font looks like (see Figure 8.1). Scroll down until you find the one you want to use, and click it.

FIGURE 8.1

The Font list shows you what the fonts look like. Click the one you want to use.

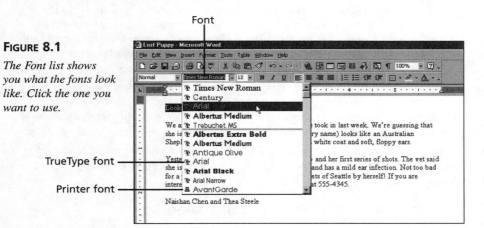

Word applies the font to the selected text. To see the change more clearly, click once to deselect the text. In Figure 8.2, the title was changed to Arial font.

FIGURE 8.2

Word applies the font you chose to selected text.

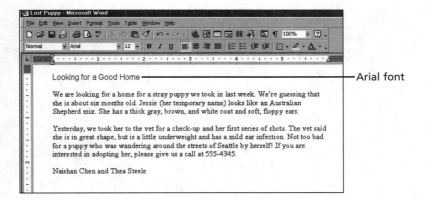

Word places the fonts you use frequently above the double line in the Font list (refer back to Figure 8.1) so that you can get at them easily. Below the double line is an alphabetical list of all your fonts.

The symbols to the left of the fonts in the Font list indicate the font type. The TT icon represents a *TrueType* font. These fonts come with Windows or other Windows applications, and they are the best ones to use because they look the same onscreen as they do when printed. TrueType fonts are also scalable, meaning that they can be flexibly resized. (You may have some fonts that are not scalable.) The printer icon represents a *printer* font. These fonts come with your printer. They print just fine, but their onscreen appearance may not match the way they print.

If you'd like to change other font formatting at the same time as you're changing the font, you may find it more convenient to use the Font dialog box. The dialog box gives you a "one-stop shopping" experience. All of the font formatting features described in this hour are accessible in this dialog box, although in many cases it's faster to use the Formatting toolbar or a keyboard shortcut.

To Do: Apply a Font Using the Font Dialog Box

▼ To Do

To apply a font using the Font dialog box, follow these steps:

1. Select the text you want to change.

2. Choose Format, Font or press Ctrl+D to display the Font dialog box (see Figure 8.3).

FIGURE 8.3

The Font dialog box provides access to all of the font-formatting commands.

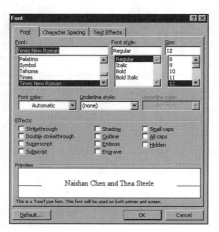

3. Click the Font tab if it isn't already in front.

4. Scroll through the Font list and click the fonts that you're interested in to see what they look like in the Preview area at the bottom of the dialog box. (This is the same list as the one in the Font list in the Formatting toolbar.)

5. When you find the font that you want to use, select it and click OK. (Again, you may want to deselect the text to see the font more clearly.)

Changing Font Size

Font size is measured in *points*. The larger the point size, the taller the font. There are approximately 72 points in an inch, so a 72-point font is about one inch tall. Typically, business documents are written in a 10- or 12-point font.

> If you use more than one font size in a document, it looks best if the sizes differ by at least 2 points.

As with changing fonts, you can change font size by using either the Formatting toolbar or the Font dialog box, but there is no advantage to using the dialog box unless you want to make other font-formatting changes at the same time.

To Do: Change the Font Size Using the Font Size List

To change the font size by using the Font Size list, follow these steps:

1. Select the text you want to change.

2. Click the down-arrow to the right of the Font Size list in the Formatting toolbar, scroll down the list, and click the size that you want to use (see Figure 8.4).

FIGURE 8.4

Word includes commonly used font sizes in the Font Size list. Click the one you want to use.

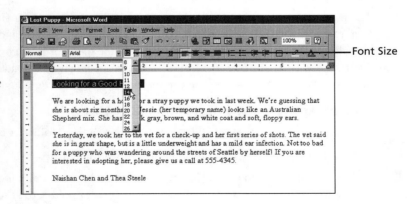

Word applies the font size to the selected text. To see the change more clearly, click to deselect. In Figure 8.5, the title was changed to a 14-point font.

FIGURE 8.5

Word applies the chosen font size to selected text.

14-point font ⌐

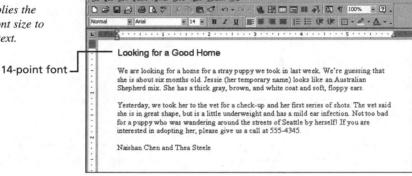

 If you like, you can adjust font size one point at a time by pressing Ctrl+] to increase the size and Ctrl+[to decrease it.

 You aren't limited to the point sizes in the Font Size list. If you want to use a size smaller than 8-point or larger than 72-point, click in the Font Size box to select the current size, type over it with the size that you want to use, and press Enter.

Applying Bold, Italic, and Underline

The most common type of font formatting other than font and font size is *font style*. This term refers collectively to boldface, italic, and underline. You can apply font styles individually, or you can apply two or more to the same block of text. For example, you could add boldface and italic to a word. Judicious use of font styles can add just the right emphasis to a document—overuse can make a document cluttered and difficult to read.

To Do: Apply Font Bold, Italic, and Underline

The easiest way to apply font styles is via the Formatting toolbar or a keyboard shortcut:

1. Select the text to which you want to apply a font style.

2. Click the Bold, Italic, or Underline button in the Formatting toolbar (see Figure 8.6). Alternatively, you can also press Ctrl+B for bold, Ctrl+I for italic, or Ctrl+U for underline.

Bold   Italic   Underline

8

FIGURE 8.6

Click the Bold, Italic, or Underline button in the Formatting toolbar to apply a font style to the selected text.

Bold text —

Underlined text —

Italic text —

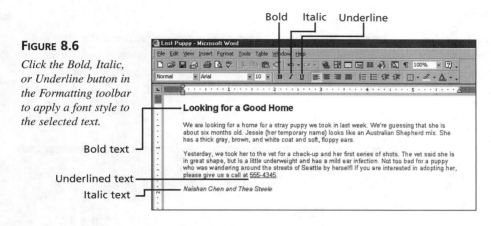

Word applies the font style. To see the change, click anywhere to deselect the text. Figure 8.6 shows a document that includes all three font styles.

To remove a font style from a block of text, select the text and then click the toolbar button (or press the keyboard shortcut) again.

> The Underline button on the Formatting toolbar applies a single underline. Word provides a wide variety of other underlining options in the Font tab of the Font dialog box (words only, double, thick, dashed, and so on). Choose the style you want in the Underline Style list, and optionally select a color for the underline in the Underline Color list. (To remove special underlining, select the text, choose Format, Font, and choose None in the Underline Style list or Automatic in the Underline Color list.) Another quick way to apply double underlining is to select the text and press Ctrl+Shift+D.

Changing Font Color

Changing the color of your text can brighten up a document and make key parts of it stand out. Remember that changing font color won't do much if you're printing on a black-and-white printer. (The colors print in shades of gray.) If, on the other hand, you have a color printer or your readers view the document onscreen, font colors can greatly enhance your document's appearance.

To Do: Apply a Font Color

As usual, the easiest way to apply font color is to use the Formatting toolbar, as described in these steps:

1. Select the text to which you want to apply font color.

2. Click the down-arrow to the right of the Font Color toolbar button at the right end of the Formatting toolbar. A palette appears with a large selection of colors (see Figure 8.7). Pointing to a color displays a ScreenTip with the color's name. Click the one you want to use.

Font Color

FIGURE 8.7

Word gives you many colors to choose from. Click the one you want to use.

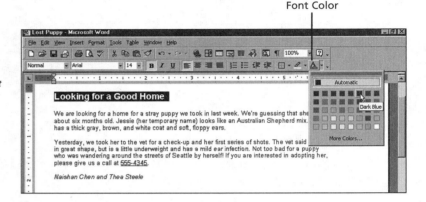

Word applies the color to the selected text. To see what it looks like, deselect the text. If you don't see a color that you want to use in the Font Color palette, click the More Colors button at the bottom of the palette to display the Colors dialog box. Click a color you like, and click OK.

> Font colors change the color of the text itself. You can also use the Highlighting feature to draw a transparent color over the selected text, just as you'd mark text with a highlighter pen. You learn how to apply highlighting in Hour 21, "Collaborating on Documents."

Adjusting Character Spacing

Word gives you several ways to adjust the amount of space between characters. In most documents, you won't need to adjust spacing, but once in a while you may want to change the spacing in a heading.

To Do: Change Character Spacing

To adjust character spacing, follow these steps:

1. Select the text in which you want to change character spacing.

▼   2. Choose Format, Font or press Ctrl+D to display the Font dialog box.

3. Click the Character Spacing tab (see Figure 8.8).

FIGURE 8.8

The Character Spacing tab contains four options for adjusting spacing.

▲   4. Select the desired options, and click OK.

Here is an explanation of how to use the options in the Character Spacing tab:

- Scale—Use this list to expand or condense your text horizontally by a particular percentage. Any percentage over 100 percent expands the text; any percentage under 100 percent condenses it. If you like, you can click in the Scale box, type a percentage that doesn't appear in the list (120 percent, for example), and press Enter. In Figure 8.9, the top version of *Fernwood* is scaled at 100 percent. The lower one is scaled at 120 percent.

- Spacing—Use this list if you want to expand or condense your text by a number of points, and then type the number of points in the By text box. Figure 8.9 shows two versions of the heading *Lighthouse Times*. The first has normal character spacing; the second is expanded by 2 points.

- Position—Use this list to raise the text above the baseline or lower it beneath the baseline without decreasing its size (as you would if you applied superscript or subscript formatting, as described in the next section). Type the number of points by which you'd like to raise or lower the text in the By text box. In Figure 8.9, the word *fork* is lowered 6 points below *spoon* and *knife*.

- Kerning—Mark this check box if you want to adjust the amount of space between certain combinations of letters. When kerning is not turned on and you're using a large point size, large gaps appear between some letters. Kerning closes these gaps.

In the Points and Above text box, type the smallest point size for which you want to adjust kerning. Figure 8.9 shows two versions of the heading *AVIARY NEWS*. Kerning is not turned on for the first one and there is a noticeable gap between the *A* and the *V*. In the second version, kerning is turned on and the gap between the *A* and the *V* is gone. Kerning works only with TrueType and Adobe Type Manager fonts.

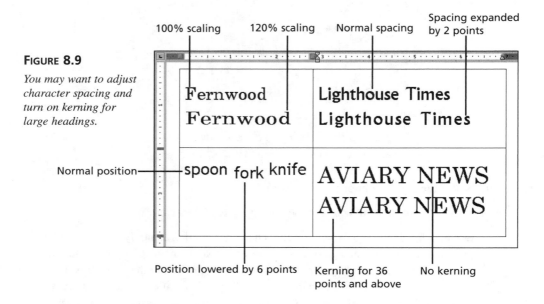

FIGURE 8.9

You may want to adjust character spacing and turn on kerning for large headings.

To return character spacing for a block of text to its default settings, select the text, choose Format, Font, click the Character Spacing tab, choose 100% in the Scale list, Normal in the Spacing and Position lists, clear the Kerning check box, and click OK.

Adding Effects

If you're feeling adventurous, try some of the effects available in the Font dialog box. Depending on the kind of documents you create, you may need to use one or two of these—superscript and subscript, perhaps—all the time. Other more specialized ones, such as emboss and engrave, you may never need.

To Do: Add Text Effects

To apply text effects, follow these steps:

1. Select the text to which you want to apply an effect.

2. Choose Format, Font or press Ctrl+D to display the Font dialog box.

▼   3. Click the Font tab if it isn't already in front.

   4. Mark the desired check boxes under Effects (refer to Figure 8.3). You can see what
      an effect does by marking its check box and looking at the Preview area at the bot-
      tom of the dialog box.

▲   5. When you're done, click OK.

To remove any of these effects, select the text to which the effect is applied, choose
Format, Font, and clear the appropriate check box under Effects.

> Some of the effects have convenient keyboard shortcuts. For example, you
> can select the text and then press Ctrl+Shift+A for all caps, Ctrl+Shift+K for
> small caps, Ctrl+equal sign for subscript, Ctrl+Shift+plus sign for superscript.

> The Hidden option hides the selected text both onscreen and in the printed
> document. Word closes up the text around the hidden text so that you can't
> even tell it's there unless you click the Show/Hide button in the Standard
> toolbar. When you turn on Show/Hide, hidden text appears with a dotted
> line underneath it. This feature comes in handy in some documents. You
> could use it to hide confidential parts of a report before printing it, for
> example.

One other effect you can apply to your text is animation. When you animate your text, it
"comes alive" with neon lights, shimmers, or sparkles. This feature was probably
designed with the junior high school set in mind, but even sober-minded adults may find
it a good distraction during tax time. Note that animation can't be appreciated unless
your readers view the document onscreen. To try it out, select some text, choose Format,
Font, and click the Text Effects tab. Click a few options in the Animations list to see
what they look like. When you find one that you like, click OK. (To later remove animation, select the text, display the Text Effects tab of the Font dialog box, choose None, and
click OK.)

Changing the Case of Letters

If you realize after you type some text that you want to change its case, you don't have
to retype it. Instead, just select the text, choose Format, Change Case to display the
Change Case dialog box (see Figure 8.10), choose the option you want, and click OK.

FIGURE 8.10

Use the Change Case dialog box to change the case of text without retyping it.

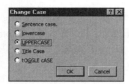

The Title Case option capitalizes articles and prepositions. So "a day at the beach" would become "A Day At The Beach." If you'd rather leave articles and prepositions lowercase (as in "A Day at the Beach"), you need to change their case manually.

The keyboard shortcut for changing case is Shift+F3. Select the text and then press Shift+F3 one or more times until you see the case you want.

Changing the Default Font Settings

If you use a different font than Times New Roman 12-point for most of your documents, you might want to change the default font. If you do, Word assumes the new font in all new documents based on the Normal template. (You can always change the font in specific documents if you choose.)

To Do: Change the Default Font

To change the default font, follow these steps:

1. Choose Format, Font to display the Font dialog box.
2. Choose all of the font options that you want for the default font.
3. Click the Default button.
4. Word displays a message box asking whether you want to change the default font, and reminding you that this change affects all new documents based on the Normal template (see Figure 8.11). Click the Yes button.

FIGURE 8.11

Word confirms that you want to change the default font.

If you want to change the default font to something else in the future, repeat these steps.

Copying Font Formatting

If you have carefully applied several font formats to one block of text and then decide that you'd like to use the same combination of formats somewhere else in the document, you don't have to apply the formatting from scratch. Instead, you can use Word's Format Painter feature to copy the formatting of the original block of text and then "paint" it across the other text.

To Do: Copy Font Formatting

Follow these steps to copy font formatting:

1. Click anywhere in the text that has the formatting you want to copy.
2. Click the Format Painter button on the Formatting toolbar (see Figure 8.12).

Format Painter

FIGURE 8.12

Use the Format Painter button on the Standard toolbar to copy font formatting.

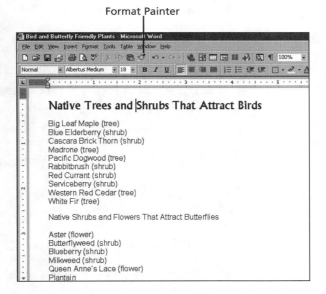

3. The mouse pointer becomes an I-beam with a paintbrush attached to it. Drag over the text to which you want to apply the formatting (see Figure 8.13).

FIGURE 8.13

The Format Painter is a great way to copy font formatting quickly.

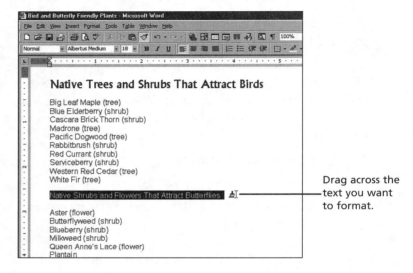

Drag across the text you want to format.

4. Release the mouse button. Word applies the formatting to the selected text (see Figure 8.14).

FIGURE 8.14

The formatting is copied as soon as you release the mouse button.

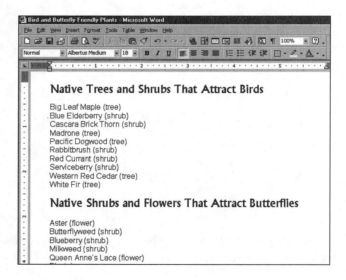

If you want to apply the same set of font formats to several blocks of text, double-click the Format Painter toolbar button in step 2. The Format Painter stays turned on while you drag over multiple blocks of text. When you're finished, click the button again to turn it off.

8

Removing Font Formatting

If you have applied several different font formats to a block of text and then decide you want to turn all of them off, you can, of course, select the text and then turn each one off individually. This method can be quite tedious, however, because you may have to use several dialog boxes, toolbar buttons, or keyboard shortcuts. A much faster method is to select the text and press the keyboard shortcut Ctrl+Spacebar, which strips off all font formatting.

This shortcut also comes in handy if you have to edit a document in which the font formatting is badly botched. To strip the font formatting from an entire document and start over, press Ctrl+A to select the document, and then press Ctrl+Spacebar.

Ctrl+Spacebar does not remove font formatting that is part of a *style* (a collection of formatting commands). It will, however, remove any font formatting that was added after the style was applied. (You'll learn about styles in Hour 11, "Working with Styles.")

Summary

Judicious use of font formatting can greatly enhance the appearance of your document. Experiment with different combinations of the font-formatting options you learned in this hour to see what is most effective for your documents. In the next hour, you learn how to apply paragraph formatting.

Q&A

Q What is the difference between a *serif* and a *sans serif* font, and which type should I use where?

A A serif font has "tails" at the ends of the letters. A good example of serif font is Times New Roman. Serif fonts are ideal for body text. A sans serif font is one that doesn't have the tails. Arial and Helvetica are examples of sans serif fonts. These fonts work well for headings and short blocks of text.

Q **In Word 97, the default font size was 10-point. Why has it changed to 12-point in Word 2000?**

A Microsoft finally caught on to the fact that almost everyone uses 12-point fonts for business documents. For most people, 10-point fonts are just a little too small for regular body text.

Q **I tried to change a font format for some text in my document and nothing happened. What did I do wrong?**

A You probably forgot to select the text first.

HOUR 9

Formatting Paragraphs

Now that you know how to apply font formatting, you're ready to delve into *paragraph formatting*, the second of the three formatting categories. Paragraph formatting includes all of the formatting that can affect, at a minimum, a single paragraph. As you wend your way through this jam-packed hour, you'll learn about such paragraph formatting features as alignment, line spacing, custom tabs, and indentation. Some of these you will almost certainly need at some point. Others you may not need at all. Feel free to quickly skim over any features that aren't relevant to the documents you create. After you've learned how to apply paragraph formatting, you end this hour by learning how to copy this type of formatting and remove it from your text.

The highlights of this hour include

- Changing alignment and line spacing
- Setting custom tabs and indents
- Adding space above and below paragraphs
- Controlling how paragraphs break across pages
- Creating bulleted and numbered lists

- Adding borders and shading
- Copying and removing paragraph formatting

Applying Paragraph Formatting

Just as Word makes some assumptions about font formatting (it assumes you want a Times New Roman, 12-point font unless you tell it otherwise), it also sets default paragraph formatting for you. The most obvious of these default settings are left alignment and single spacing. To change any of the default paragraph formatting in your document, use one of the features described in this hour. As you're exploring the different formatting options, keep these four points in mind:

- Paragraph formatting affects individual paragraphs. If you want to apply paragraph formatting to only one paragraph, you simple place the insertion point in that paragraph before applying the change. Word alters just that paragraph and no others. You can select the paragraph instead of placing the insertion point in it if you like, but it isn't necessary.

- If you want to apply a paragraph formatting feature to more than one adjacent paragraph, you have to select them first. (Actually, you just have to make sure that at least a portion of all the paragraphs is included in the selection.) As you know, Word considers any text followed by a paragraph mark to be a paragraph. So, for example, a three-line title contains three paragraphs. If you want to center the title, you have to select all three lines first. By the same token, if you want to make an entire document double-spaced, you have to select the whole document first.

- Each new paragraph you begin takes on the paragraph formatting of the previous paragraph. So if you want to apply the same paragraph formatting to several paragraphs that you haven't yet typed, you can just type and format the first one, and then continue typing the remaining paragraphs. The formatting you applied to the first paragraph carries down to the others.

- As with font formatting, the options in the Formatting toolbar show you the paragraph formatting that's in effect for the paragraph containing the insertion point. The same is true with the settings on the horizontal ruler. To quickly see what paragraph formatting has been applied to a paragraph, you can simply click in it, and then look at the options that are turned on in the Formatting toolbar and the ruler.

Many paragraph features are accessible via the Formatting toolbar or keyboard shortcuts. If you use one of these methods for issuing a formatting command, you can save yourself a more time-consuming trip to a dialog box. In this hour, you learn the fastest way to issue each command, but also find out about alternatives where they are available.

9

If you find yourself applying a certain combination of font and paragraph formatting over and over, consider using a *style* to "collect" this set of formatting features into a group and apply them all at once to your paragraphs. (You'll learn about styles in Hour 11, "Working with Styles.")

Aligning Paragraphs

Alignment refers to the way the right and left edges of a paragraph line up along the right and left margins of your document. Word gives you four alignment choices—left, centered, right, and justified—as shown in Figure 9.1.

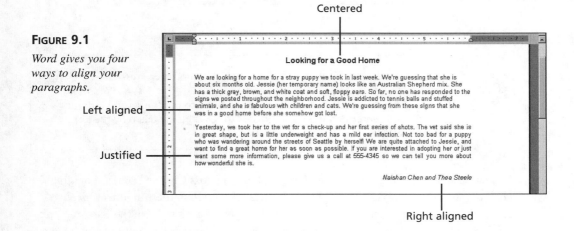

FIGURE 9.1

Word gives you four ways to align your paragraphs.

By default, Word uses *left alignment*, which produces a straight left edge and a ragged right edge. Left alignment is usually the best choice for body text in standard business documents such as letters, memos, reports, and so on. *Center alignment* centers your text horizontally between the right and left margins. You use centering for headings and other short lines of text. *Right alignment* lines up your text at the right margin and gives it a ragged left edge. This type of alignment works well for short lines of text that you want to appear on the far-right edge of the page. Finally, you may occasionally want to use *justification.* This type of alignment makes both the right and left edges of a paragraph straight. Word makes slight adjustments to the spacing between characters to produce the straight right edge. Justified text can be a little hard on the eyes because the spacing is uneven, but it is appropriate in some situations. For example, text that is indented from both sides or arranged in columns often looks better if it's justified.

To Do: Change Alignment

To change alignment using the Formatting toolbar, follow these steps:

1. Click in the paragraph in which you want to change alignment (or select multiple adjacent paragraphs to change the alignment of all of them).

2. Click the Align Left, Center, Align Right, or Justify button on the Formatting toolbar (see Figure 9.2).

▲

FIGURE 9.2

Click one of the alignment buttons to change alignment.

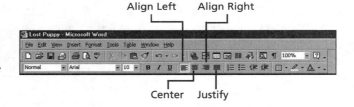

Align Left   Align Right

Center   Justify

You can also change alignment with keyboard shortcuts: Press Ctrl+L to left align, Ctrl+E to center, Ctrl+R to right align, or Ctrl+J to justify. (Yes, using Ctrl+E for centering is a bit odd. Microsoft had to use the second letter in the word *center* because the shortcut Ctrl+C is already taken by the Copy command.)

You can also change alignment in the Paragraph dialog box. Choose Format, Paragraph, click the Indents and Spacing tab, choose the desired option in the Alignment list, and click OK. The only reason to use this method is if you happen to be in the Paragraph dialog box already to change some other setting. Otherwise, it's faster to use the alignment toolbar buttons or the keyboard shortcuts.

Changing Line Spacing

Line spacing is the amount of space between lines in a paragraph. By default, paragraphs are single-spaced. You might want to double-space a school paper or a rough draft of a report (so that you have room to scribble edits between the lines). Some people like 1.5 line spacing better than single spacing because it can make the text a little easier to read. In Figure 9.3, the document has been double-spaced.

FIGURE 9.3

This document is double-spaced.

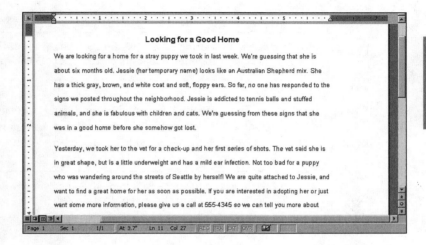

To Do: Changing the Line Spacing

To change line spacing using the Paragraph dialog box, follow these steps:

1. Click in the paragraph in which you want to change line spacing (or select multiple adjacent paragraphs to change the line spacing for all of them).

2. Choose Format, Paragraph to display the Paragraph dialog box (see Figure 9.4).

FIGURE 9.4

The Paragraph dialog box gives you access to most of the paragraph-formatting commands, including line spacing.

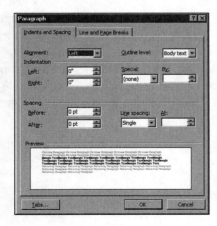

3. Click the down-arrow to the right of the Line Spacing list, and click the line spacing you want. If you choose one of the last three options, At Least, Exactly, or Multiple, you need to type an amount (in points) in the At text box.

4. Click OK.

> To change line spacing with keyboard shortcuts, press Ctrl+1 for single spacing, Ctrl+2 for double spacing, or Ctrl+5 for 1.5 line spacing.

If you change line spacing frequently, you might want to add buttons for single, double, and 1.5 line spacing to the Formatting toolbar (see "Adding or Removing Toolbar Buttons" in Hour 2, "Getting Acquainted with Word").

> You can quickly display the Paragraph dialog box at any time by double-clicking one of the indent markers on the ruler.

Working with Custom Tabs

Word's default tabs are *left* tabs, meaning that they left-align text at the tab stops. The default tab stops are positioned every half-inch across the horizontal ruler. You can see them on the bottom edge of the ruler—they look like faint gray tick marks. Each time you press the Tab key, your insertion point moves to the next default tab stop, pushing over any text to the right of the insertion point.

In regular body text, the default tabs work just fine. In some situations, however, you may want to create a custom tab at the exact location on the horizontal ruler where you want to align your text. For example, if you wanted to line up several lines of text at the 3-inch mark by using the default tabs, you would have to press the Tab key six times at the beginning of each line. A much more efficient solution is to create a custom tab at the 3-inch mark. When you insert the custom tab, all of the default tabs to its left disappear. You can then press the Tab key once to bring the insertion point directly to the spot where you want to type your text.

Another advantage of custom tabs is that in addition to creating custom left tabs, you can also create right, center, decimal, and bar tabs to align text in different ways. Figure 9.5 shows a document including all five types of custom tabs.

Left tab   Center tab   Right tab

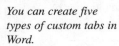

FIGURE 9.5

You can create five types of custom tabs in Word.

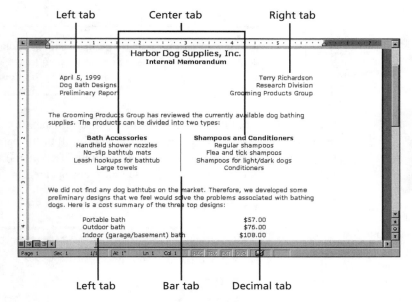

Left tab   Bar tab   Decimal tab

Left tabs left-align text at the tab stop. *Right tabs* right-align text at the tab stop. *Center tabs* center text over the tab stop, and *decimal tabs* align numbers along the decimal point. *Bar tabs* create a vertical line at the tab stop. You can use a bar tab to add a vertical line between columns of text that you've aligned with the other types of custom tabs.

> Custom tabs are great for creating simple lists in two or more columns. If your lists or charts require more complex formatting, however, the powerful table feature is a much better option (see Hour 16, "Columns and Tables").

To Do: Create and Use Custom Tabs

To create a custom tab using the ruler, follow these steps:

1. Click in the paragraph to which you want to add the tab (or select multiple adjacent paragraphs to add the tab to all of them). If you haven't yet typed the text in the paragraph, just click on the blank line where you want the custom tabs to begin.

2. Click the Tab Stop Indicator button at the left end of the ruler (see Figure 9.6) until you see the symbol for the tab that you want to insert. Each symbol is labeled with a ScreenTip, so you can easily tell which is which.

> The Tab Stop Indicator button also displays symbols for first-line and hang-
> ing indents. It's probably easier to create these indents by dragging the
> indent markers on the ruler, as you'll see later in this hour.

3. Click at the desired location on the ruler to insert the tab. In Figure 9.6, a decimal
tab is added at the 2.5-inch mark on the ruler for all of the paragraphs in the list of
budget items (in preparation for typing a column of numbers). Note that all of the
default tabs to the left of the custom tab have disappeared.

Tab Stop Indicator

FIGURE 9.6

*When you insert a cus-
tom tab, the default
tabs to its left disap-
pear.*

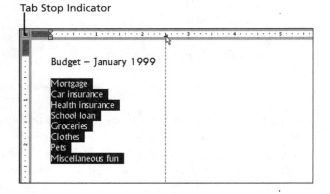

4. Repeat steps 2 and 3 to insert any additional custom tabs.

To use your custom tabs, press Tab to move to the first custom tab stop, and type your
text. Press Tab to get to next tab stop (if any) and type your text. If you accidentally
press the Tab key too many times, delete the extra tabs by pressing Backspace (if the
insertion point is just past the tabs) or Delete (if the insertion point is just before them).
Press Enter after typing the last block of text on the line, and type the remaining paragraphs that use the custom tabs. Figure 9.7 shows the budget with all of the dollar
amounts typed in and lined up on the decimal tab. The Show/Hide button in the
Formatting toolbar is turned on so that you can see where the Tab and Enter keys were
pressed.

FIGURE 9.7

Press the Tab key to move out to your custom tab stops, and type your text.

As a reminder, you can see what custom tabs are in effect for any paragraph by clicking anywhere in the paragraph, and then looking at the ruler.

Unlike the other custom tabs, the bar tab doesn't require you to press the Tab key. As soon as you add the bar tab to the ruler, a vertical line automatically appears at the location of the tab, running down the paragraph containing the insertion point (or the selected paragraphs).

To Do: Move Custom Tabs

When you work with custom tabs, you frequently need to adjust their positions on the horizontal ruler. To move a custom tab, follow these steps:

1. Click in the paragraph containing the tab (or select multiple adjacent paragraphs if they all contain the tab and you want to move it in all paragraphs).

2. Point to the tab on the ruler, drag it to the new position, and release the mouse button (see Figure 9.8). The text at that tab stop adjusts to the new position of the tab.

FIGURE 9.8

To move a custom tab, simply drag it along the ruler.

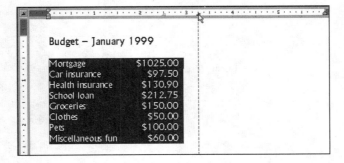

> If you need to move the tab to a precise location on the ruler, hold down the Alt key as you drag. The ruler displays the exact location of the tab in inches as you drag it along the ruler.

If you select several adjacent paragraphs and notice that a custom tab on the ruler is gray instead of black, it means that that the tab is set in some of the selected paragraphs, but not all. If you drag the tab, it creates the same tab in all of the selected paragraphs.

To Do: Delete Custom Tabs

If you insert a custom tab by accident (easy enough to do), you need to know how to get rid of it. As soon as you delete a custom tab, all of the default tabs to its left automatically reappear. To delete custom tabs, follow these steps:

1. Click in the paragraph that contains the tab that you want to remove (or select several adjacent paragraphs if they contain the same tab and you want to delete it in all paragraphs). If you haven't yet typed the text in the paragraph, just click on the blank line.

2. Point to the tab on the ruler, drag straight down into the text area of the Word window, and then release the mouse button.

3. Optionally repeat step 2 to delete any other custom tabs in the paragraph (or selected paragraphs).

If you want to restore all of the default tabs below a paragraph that contains custom tabs, click in the paragraph where you'd like the default tabs to begin, and simply drag all of the custom tabs off the ruler.

Adding a Dot Leader to a Tab

You can add a *dot leader*—a dotted line extending out to the tab stop—to any type of custom tab. Figure 9.9 shows a phone list created with a custom left tab that has a dot leader.

FIGURE 9.9

Dot leaders are great for phone lists.

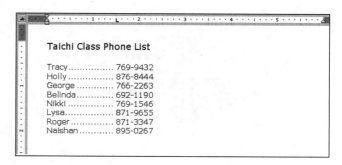

To Do: Add a Dot Leader to a Tab

To add a dot leader to a tab, follow these steps:

1. Click in the paragraph that has the tab to which you want to add the dot leader (or select multiple adjacent paragraphs if they all contain the same tab).

2. Choose Format, Tabs to display the Tabs dialog box.

3. In the Tab Stop Position list, click the tab to which you want to add the leader (all of the custom tabs in the paragraph containing the insertion point or the selected paragraphs are listed). Mark the option button for the type of leader you want under Leader, and click the Set button. In Figure 9.10, a dot leader is added to the right tab at the 5-inch mark.

9

FIGURE 9.10

You can use the Tabs dialog box to add a dot leader to a tab.

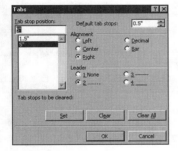

4. Click OK.

You can also create custom tabs from scratch in the Tabs dialog box. In the Tab Stop Position text box, type the position of the tab you want to add in inches, mark the desired option buttons under Alignment and Leader, and click the Set button. Add any other custom tabs you like, and click OK. The tabs appear on the ruler just as if you had added them directly to the ruler.

Indenting Paragraphs

Word's indentation feature enables you to indent paragraphs from the left and right margins. You can also create a *first-line indent*, which indents only the first line of a paragraph, or a *hanging indent*, which indents all of the lines in a paragraph except the first. Figure 9.11 illustrates all four types of indentation.

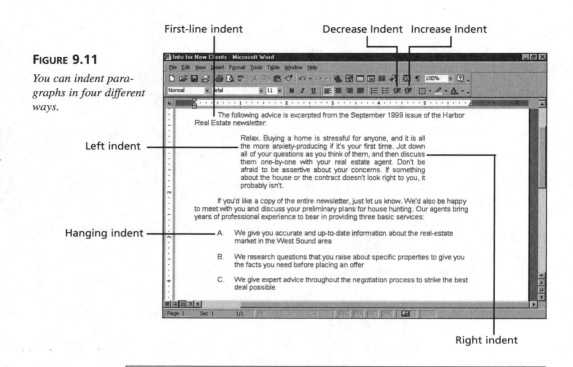

FIGURE 9.11

You can indent paragraphs in four different ways.

First-line indent   Decrease Indent   Increase Indent

Left indent

Hanging indent

Right indent

By default, Word sets a first-line indent of one-half inch when you press Tab at the beginning of a paragraph that you've already typed. This indent carries down to additional paragraphs you type, so you won't have to press Tab at the beginning of each paragraph. If you don't like this behavior, choose Tools, Options, click the Edit tab, clear the Tabs and Backspace Set Left Indent check box, and click OK.

To Do: Set Indents with Increase Indent and Decrease Indent Buttons

Word provides several ways to set indents. If you want to set a left indent at a half-inch increment on the ruler, you can use the Decrease Indent and Increase Indent buttons on the Formatting toolbar (see Figure 9.11), as described in these steps:

1. Click in the paragraph you want to indent (or select multiple adjacent paragraphs to indent them all).

2. Click the Increase Indent button to indent the text one-half inch. If you want to indent the text further, continue clicking this button. To decrease the indentation, click the Decrease Indent button.

The keyboard equivalent of clicking the Increase Indent toolbar button is Ctrl+M. The equivalent of the Decrease Indent button is Shift+Ctrl+M.

The most efficient way of setting indents is to drag the indent markers on the ruler. When no indentation is set for a paragraph, the First-Line Indent, Hanging Indent, and Left Indent markers are positioned at the left margin, and the Right Indent marker is positioned at the right margin, as shown in Figure 9.12.

First-line Indent

FIGURE 9.12

When no indents are set, the indent markers appear at the margins.

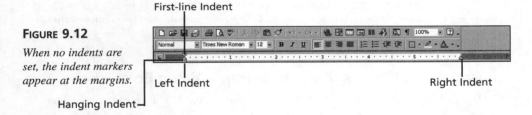

Left Indent

Right Indent

Hanging Indent

To Do: Set an Indent with Indent Markers

Follow these steps to set an indent by dragging the indent markers:

1. Click in the paragraph you want to indent (or select multiple adjacent paragraphs to indent them all).

2. Point to the indent marker that you want to use. ScreenTips label each marker to make it clear which one is which.

3. Drag the desired indent marker to the right spot on the ruler, and release the mouse button.

If you like, you can drag more than one marker for the same paragraph. For example, you can drag both the Left Indent and Right Indent markers to indent a paragraph from both sides, or drag the First Line and Hanging Indent markers to create a hanging indent in which the first line in the paragraph is indented a little, and the remaining lines are indented further. In Figure 9.13, the insertion point is in a paragraph with this type of hanging indent. Note the position of the indent markers on the ruler.

FIGURE 9.13

Hanging indents are useful for creating simple lists.

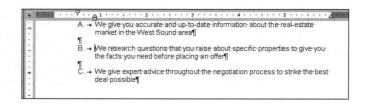

The Show/Hide button is turned on in Figure 9.13 so that you can see where the Tab key and Enter keys were pressed. To create a list like the one shown in the figure, set the hanging indent, and type the letter or number that begins the first item (*A.* in this example). Press the Tab key to move out to the hanging indent position, type the text in the item, press Enter once (or twice to create a blank line), and then continue with the remainder of the list.

To Do: Create Indents in the Paragraph Dialog Box

Finally, you can create indents in the Paragraph dialog box. If you and your mouse don't get along, this is probably the best method for you:

1. Click in the paragraph you want to indent (or select multiple adjacent paragraphs to indent all of them).

2. Choose Format, Paragraph to display the Paragraph dialog box (refer to Figure 9.3 earlier in this hour).

3. Click the Indents and Spacing tab if it isn't already in front.

4. Under Indentation, type the amount (in inches) that you want to indent the paragraph in the Left and/or Right text boxes. To create a first-line or hanging indent, choose that option from the Special list, and type the desired amount for the special indentation (in inches) in the By text box.

5. Click the OK button.

To move an indent that you've set via any method, simply select the indented paragraphs and drag the appropriate marker on the ruler.

If you select several paragraphs and notice that an indent marker on the ruler is gray, not black, it means that the indentation is set for some of the selected paragraphs, but not all. If you drag the indent marker, it creates the same indentation in all of the selected paragraphs.

To remove an indent, select the indented paragraphs, and drag the appropriate marker back to the left or right margin on the ruler.

Another quick way to remove all indents from the selected paragraphs is to choose Format, Paragraph, click the Indents and Spacing tab if necessary, set the Left and Right text boxes to zero inch, choose None in the Special list, and click OK.

Adding Paragraph Spacing

One way to add a blank line between paragraphs is to press Enter twice at the end of each paragraph. You can avoid having to press Enter a second time to create the blank line by adding *paragraph spacing* before and/or after your paragraphs. For example, if you are using a 12-point font, you can add 12 points of spacing below each paragraph to automatically get one blank line's worth of white space between each paragraph.

Paragraph spacing also enables you to fine-tune the amount of space above or below a paragraph to improve your document's appearance. In Figure 9.14, the paragraphs are separated by 6 points (one half line) of space. The Show/Hide button is turned on so that you can see that no paragraph marks appear in the white spaces between paragraphs. These spaces were created with the paragraph spacing feature, not by pressing Enter.

FIGURE 9.14

Paragraph spacing enables you to control the amount of white space above and below paragraphs.

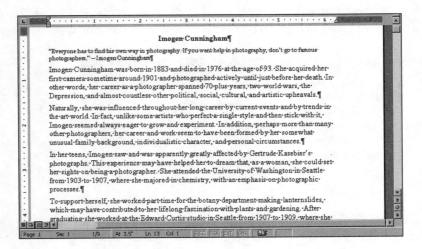

To Do: Add Spacing Before or After a Paragraph

To add spacing before or after a paragraph, follow these steps:

1. Click in the paragraph to which you want to add spacing (or select multiple adjacent paragraphs to add the spacing to all of them).

▼ 2. Choose Format, Paragraph to display the Paragraph dialog box.

3. Click the Indents and Spacing tab if it isn't already in front.

4. Under Spacing, type a number in points in the Before and/or After text box (or use the spinner arrows to increment the spacing 6 points at a time).

▲ 5. Click OK.

> If you select several adjacent paragraphs and add space before and after, you may end up with double the amount of white space between paragraphs that you expected. It's usually simpler to add spacing before or spacing after, but not both.

Adjusting Line and Page Breaks

Word enables you to control how paragraphs break across pages. You can, for example, prevent a paragraph from being split across pages, or instruct Word to insert a page break immediately before a paragraph so that it always appears at the top of a page.

To make these kinds of changes, click in the paragraph you want to affect (or select multiple adjacent paragraphs to affect all of them), choose Format, Paragraph, click the Line and Page Breaks tab (see Figure 9.15), mark the desired check boxes, and click OK.

FIGURE 9.15

The Line and Page Breaks tab of the Paragraph dialog box enables you to control how your paragraphs break across pages.

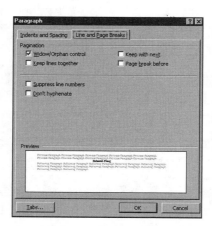

Here is a description of the options in the Line and Page Breaks tab:

- Widow/Orphan Control—This option, marked by default, prevents widows and orphans (single lines of text at the top and bottom of a page). When Word has to split a paragraph across a page break, it adjusts the position of the break to keep a minimum of two lines above or below the break.

- Keep Lines Together—If you mark this check box, the paragraph does not split across a page break. If the paragraph won't fit in its entirety at the bottom of a page, Word moves it to the top of the next page.

- Keep with Next—This option keeps the paragraph on the same page as the paragraph that follows it.

- Page Break Before—This option forces a page break immediately above the selected paragraph. You can mark this check box for a heading that you want to appear at the top of a page.

Creating Bulleted and Numbered Lists

Setting off items in a list with numbers or bullets is a great way to present information clearly. Word's bulleted and numbered list features add the bullets or numbers for you, and they create hanging indents so that when text in an item wraps to the next line, it doesn't wrap underneath the number or bullet. Also, when you use the numbered list feature to create a list and then add, delete, or move items in the list, Word keeps the numbering sequential.

Word enables you to create single-level lists, or lists with two or more levels. Figure 9.16 shows single-level bulleted and numbered lists, and one multilevel list.

FIGURE 9.16

You can create single-level and multilevel lists.

Bulleted list

Numbered list

Multilevel list

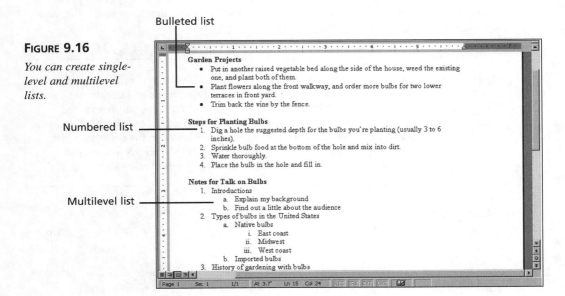

To Do: Creating Single-Level Lists

Follow these steps to create a single-level bulleted or numbered list:

1. Click where you want the list to start.
2. Click the Bullets or Numbering button on the Formatting toolbar (see Figure 9.17). Word inserts a bullet or number.

Numbering

FIGURE 9.17

The Bullets and Numbering buttons on the Formatting toolbar let you create lists quickly.

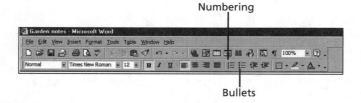

Bullets

3. Type the first item in the list, and press Enter. Word inserts a bullet or number on the next line for you. Continue typing items in your list.
4. After the last item, press Enter twice to turn off the bullets or numbers. (You can also turn off the bullets or numbering by clicking in the paragraph where you don't want the bullets or numbers, and clicking the Bullets or Numbering toolbar button again.)

To switch from numbers to bullets (or vice versa), select all of the items in the list, and then click the Bullets or Numbering button.

> If you want a blank line between items in a bulleted or numbered list, press Shift+Enter and then Enter at the end of each item (instead of just pressing Enter). Pressing Shift+Enter inserts a *line-break character,* which ends the line without ending the paragraph, so you don't get a bullet or number on the blank line. (Word inserts a bullet or number only at the beginning of a paragraph.) If you click the Show/Hide button on the Formatting toolbar, you'll see that the symbol for the line-break character looks like this: ↵.

Instead of turning on the bulleted or numbered list feature and then typing the list, you can also type the list first, select it, and then click the Bullets or Numbering toolbar button.

You may notice that Word automatically turns on the bulleted or numbered list feature as soon as you type a line of text that begins with an asterisk (*) or a number and press

Enter. If you like this behavior, great. If you don't, you can turn it off: Choose Tools, AutoCorrect, click the AutoFormat As You Type tab, clear the check boxes for Automatic Bulleted Lists and Automatic Numbered Lists, and click OK.

> If you want to insert a bullet or two but don't want to turn on the bulleted list feature, see "Inserting Symbols and Special Characters" in Hour 14, "Editing Shortcuts."

If you have more than one numbered list in a document, Word starts each new list at number 1. If you want the numbering to continue from the previous list, click on the first paragraph of the new list, choose Format, Bullets and Numbering, click the Numbering tab, mark the Continue Previous List option button, and click OK. (By the same token, if Word assumes you want to continue the previous numbering and you want to restart it, mark the Restart Numbering option button.)

Changing the Appearance of Your Bullets and Numbers

In many documents, the default bullets and numbers that Word uses suit you just fine. If you have a hankering for a different look, though, you can choose from a wide range of options.

To Do: Change the Bullets in Your Bulleted List

Follow these steps to change the bullet used in your bulleted list:

1. Click where you want the bulleted list to start (or, if you've already typed your list, select the entire list).

2. Choose Format, Bullets and Numbering to display the Bullets and Numbering dialog box.

3. Click the Bulleted tab if it isn't already in front. This tab contains a *gallery* of different bullets (see Figure 9.18). The one you are currently using has a box around it. If you see a bullet that you want to use here, click it, and then click OK.

FIGURE 9.18

You may see the bullet you want to use in the Bulleted tab.

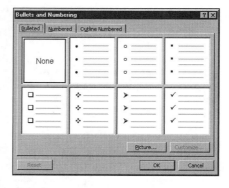

4. If you don't see a bullet you want to use, click any of the seven gallery positions (other than None), and click the Customize button to display the Customize Bulleted List dialog box (see Figure 9.19).

FIGURE 9.19

The Customize Bulleted List dialog box enables you to modify your bullet.

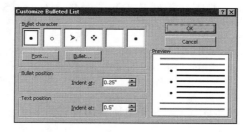

> Some bullets look much better when they are larger. You can increase the size of your bullet by clicking the Font button in the Customize Bulleted List button and then increasing the point size in the Font dialog box that appears.

5. Click the Bullets button to display the Symbol dialog box (see Figure 9.20). Look for the symbol you want to use for your bullet. (When you click a symbol, it enlarges so that you can see it more clearly.) If you don't see the one you want, choose a different character set in the Font list. (The Webdings and Wingdings sets contain a lot of fun symbols.)

FIGURE 9.20

Hunt down the symbol you want to use in the Symbol dialog box.

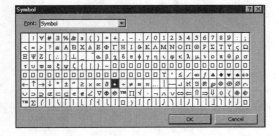

6. When you find the symbol you want, click it and click OK twice to return to your document and insert the new bullet.

The new bullet is now the default, so clicking the Bullets toolbar button inserts this bullet until you repeat these steps to choose something else.

> If you choose a new bullet, it takes over a position in the Bulleted tab of the Bulleted and Numbered dialog box. If you want to return that position to the bullet that appears there by default, click the position, and click the Reset button.

To Do: Change the Numbering in Your Numbered List

Follow these steps to change the numbering used in your numbered list:

1. Click where you want the numbered list to start (or, if you've already typed your list, select the entire list).

2. Choose Format, Bullets and Numbering to display the Bullets and Numbering dialog box.

3. Click the Numbering tab. If you see the numbering that you want to use here, click it, and then click OK (see Figure 9.21).

4. If you don't see the numbering you want to use, click any of the gallery positions other than None, and click the Customize button to display the Customize Numbered List dialog box (see Figure 9.22).

5. If you want to revise the format of the numbers, type the change in the Number Format text box. (Leave the number in the box, but type any text you like before or after it.) Use the Number Style list to change to another style, such as Roman numerals, ordinals, or letters. Change the number in the Start At text box to begin the list at a number other than 1. The Preview area on the right side of the dialog box shows you the effect of your changes. When you're finished, click OK twice to close this dialog box and the Bullets and Numbering dialog box.

FIGURE **9.21**

You may see the numbering you want to use in the Numbered tab.

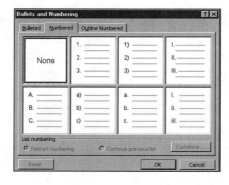

FIGURE **9.22**

The Customize Numbered List dialog box lets you modify your numbering.

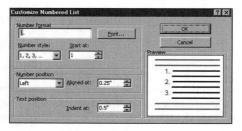

The new numbering is now the default, so clicking the Numbering toolbar button inserts this numbering until you repeat these steps to change it to something else.

> If you modify your numbering, the new numbering takes over a position in the Numbered tab of the Bullets and Numbering dialog box. If you want to return that position to the numbering that appears there by default, click the position, and click the Reset button.

Creating Multilevel Lists

Word enables you to turn any bulleted or numbered list into a multilevel list. When you want to create a sublist within your main list, click the Increase Indent button on the Formatting toolbar or press Alt+Shift+Right arrow. Then type the first item in the sublist and press Enter. Word assumes you want to type another item in the sublist. If you do, continue typing sublist items. When you are ready to type another item one level up, click the Decrease Indent toolbar button or press Alt+Shift+Left arrow.

You can customize the numbering in a multilevel list by using the same method you use to customize bullets or numbers in a single-level list. Click where you want the list to begin (or select the list if you've already typed it), choose Format, Bullets and Numbering, and click the Outline Numbered tab (see Figure 9.23).

FIGURE 9.23

You may see the numbering you want to use in the Outline Numbered tab.

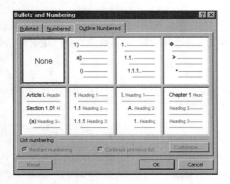

9

If you see the numbering scheme you want to use in the top row of gallery positions, click it and click OK. (The lower row is used for creating outlines, which you'll learn about in Hour 15, "Working with Long Documents.") If you don't, click the scheme in the top row that most resembles the one you want to use, and click the Customize button to display the Customize Outline Numbered List dialog box. Under Level in the upper-left corner of the dialog box, click the list level that you want to change, and then select the desired options for that level. Repeat this process to adjust the appearance of any other levels, and then click OK.

As with the single-level lists, the new multilevel list takes a position in the Outline Numbered tab of the Bullets and Numbering dialog box. To reset the position to the default, click it and click the Reset button.

Adding Borders and Shading

You don't have to know anything about graphics to set off paragraphs with attractive borders. You can also use the shading feature to add a background color to the paragraph. Figure 9.24 shows a little chart formatted with borders and shading.

FIGURE 9.24

This chart is enhanced by borders and shading.

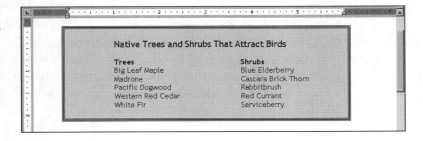

You can apply borders and shading by using the Borders and Shading dialog box (Format, Borders and Shading) or the Tables and Borders toolbar. Here, you learn how to use the toolbar. You will work with this same toolbar extensively in Hour 16 when you learn how to create tables.

To Do: Add Borders and Shading to Your Text

Follow these steps to add borders and shading to your text:

1. Click in the paragraph to which you want to add the borders and shading (or select multiple adjacent paragraphs to format all of them).

2. Click the Tables and Borders button on the Standard toolbar to display the Tables and Borders toolbar (see Figure 9.25).

FIGURE 9.25

Clicking the Tables and Borders toolbar button displays the Tables and Borders toolbar.

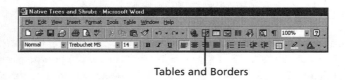

Tables and Borders

3. If the Draw Table button looks like it's pushed in, as it is in Figure 9.26, click it once to turn it off.

Draw Table   Line Weight

FIGURE 9.26

The Tables and Borders toolbar makes it fast to apply borders and shading.

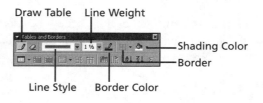

Shading Color

Border

Line Style   Border Color

4. Click the down-arrow to the right of the Line Weight button, and select a thickness for your border in the list that appears.

5. If you want to create a color border, click the Border Color button and select a color in the palette that appears.

6. Click the down-arrow to the right of the Border button, and click the desired border in the palette that appears. (For example, to create a bottom border under the paragraph containing the insertion point, click the Bottom Border option. To create a border around several selected paragraphs, click the Outside Border option.)

▲ 7. Finally, if you want to apply shading, click the down-arrow to the right of the Shading Color button, and click a color in the palette that appears.

To remove borders from your text, select the paragraph, display the Tables and Borders toolbar, and choose the No Border option in the Border list. To remove shading, choose the No Fill option at the top of the Shading Color palette.

You can adjust the position of top and bottom borders by dragging them up or down with the mouse. You can also drag left and right borders out toward the margins. However, if you want to bring the left and right borders in toward the center of the page, you need to set left and right indents (the borders automatically move to the position of the indents).

9

> If you like, you can add a border around your entire page. To learn how, see "Adding a Border Around Your Page" in the next hour.

> If you want to add a single horizontal border running from the left to the right margin, you don't need to use the Tables and Borders toolbar. Instead, click on the blank line where you want the border to go, type --- (three hyphens), and press Enter. To create a double line, type === (three equal signs) and press Enter. To get fancier borders, try using the ~ (tilde), # (pound), and * (asterisk) symbols. To disable these automatic borders, choose Tools, AutoCorrect, click the AutoFormat As You Type tab, clear the Borders check box, and click OK.

Copying Paragraph Formatting

In the last hour, you learned how to copy font formatting from one part of your document to another by using the Format Painter toolbar button. You can also use the Format Painter button to copy paragraph formatting—including all of the formatting you've learned about in this hour—from one paragraph to another.

To Do: Copy Paragraph Formatting

▼ To Do

The steps you use to copy paragraph formatting are the same general ones you used to copy font formatting in Hour 8, "Formatting Characters":

1. Select the paragraph containing the formatting you want to copy. Word stores the paragraph-formatting information for a paragraph in the paragraph mark at the end of the paragraph, so you have to make sure to include it in the selection. (If you aren't sure whether it's selected, turn on the Show/Hide button in the Standard toolbar.)

▼   2. Click the Format Painter button on the Formatting toolbar.

    3. A paintbrush is now attached to the I-beam mouse pointer. Click in the paragraph
▲   to which you want to apply the formatting.

The paragraph formatting is copied to the second paragraph. If you want to copy the formatting to several paragraphs, double-click the Format Painter button in step 2. It stays on while you click in multiple paragraphs. When you are finished using it, click it again to turn it off.

Removing Paragraph Formatting

You learned in the last hour that you can strip font formatting off of a block of text by pressing Ctrl+Spacebar. The equivalent keyboard shortcut that removes paragraph formatting is Ctrl+Q. If you have applied several different paragraph formats to a paragraph and now want to turn all of them off, it's much faster to select the paragraph and press Ctrl+Q than to turn each one off individually.

This shortcut also comes in handy if you have to patch up a document with sloppy paragraph formatting. To strip the paragraph formatting from an entire document and start over, press Ctrl+A to select the document, and then press Ctrl+Q.

> Ctrl+Q does not remove paragraph formatting that is part of a *style* (a collection of formatting commands). It does, however, remove any paragraph formatting that was added after the style was applied. (You'll learn about styles in Hour 11.)

Summary

Of the three categories of formatting—font, paragraph, and page—paragraph formatting undoubtedly takes center stage. It includes a large number of features, some of which can require a little practice to master. You covered a lot of territory in this hour, so don't expect to retain everything! You can always return to specific sections when you need to apply particular paragraph-formatting features. In the next hour, you learn how to apply page formatting, the third and final category of formatting in Word.

Q&A

Q **I want two blocks of text on the same line—one against the left margin and one against the right. How do I do that?**

A Type the phrase on the left margin, and then add a custom right tab at the right margin (you can place it directly on top of the right indent marker). Press the Tab key to move out to the right tab, and type the text that you want flush against the right margin.

Q **I notice there is a Border button in the Formatting toolbar as well as the Tables and Borders toolbar. Are they different?**

A No. They work in exactly the same way, so you can use either one.

Q **When I cut and pasted a paragraph, it lost all of its paragraph formatting. Why did that happen?**

A You didn't include the paragraph mark when you selected the paragraph before cutting it. Remember that all of the paragraph formatting is stored in the paragraph mark, so if you leave it behind when you cut and paste the paragraph, you'll leave behind the paragraph formatting as well.

9

HOUR 10

Formatting Pages

In this last hour on formatting techniques, you learn about *page formatting*. This category includes all of the formatting that affects the entire page, including margins, paper size, page numbers, and so on. After you learn how to apply page formatting, you find out how to control where your pages break, and how to vary the page formatting in different sections of your document. (You will learn about one other page formatting feature, columns, in Hour 16, "Columns and Tables.")

The highlights of this hour include

- Changing margins
- Page orientation and size
- Centering text vertically on the page
- Adding page numbers
- Working with headers and footers
- Adding page borders
- Inserting page breaks
- Inserting section breaks

Applying Page Formatting

Once again, Word decides what's best for you (in a well-intentioned sort of way). It makes two main assumptions about page formatting: You want 1-inch top and bottom margins, and 1 1/4-inch left and right margins, and you are printing on 8 1/2-×11-inch paper. To change these and other default page-formatting options, use the techniques described in this hour. You need to know three things up front to understand how page formatting works:

- Page formatting is automatically applied to every page in your document. Therefore, it doesn't matter where your insertion point is when you apply the formatting.

- You shouldn't select any text before you apply page formatting. If you do, Word assumes that you want to apply the formatting to only the selected text, and it inserts section breaks above and below the text to make this possible (see the next point).

- If you want to apply different page formatting to different portions of a document— for example, set different margins on one page of a multipage document—you need to insert *section breaks* to divide your document into two or more sections. You'll learn how to do this in "Varying the Page Formatting in Your Document" at the end of this hour.

Unlike font and paragraph formatting, you can't issue page-formatting commands via the Formatting toolbar. Word assumes that you won't need to apply page formatting as frequently, so it reserves the space on the Formatting toolbar for font and paragraph-formatting commands. To apply page formatting, you'll use a combination of dialog boxes (primarily the Page Setup dialog box), the rulers, and keyboard shortcuts.

As you practice applying the page formatting available in the Page Setup dialog box, you may discover that you make a particular change in almost every document you create. For example, if you're using preprinted letterhead, you may need to change the margins on all of your documents. In these situations, you can modify the Normal template to assume the page formatting you use. To do so, display the Page Setup dialog box (File, Page Setup), set the option that you want to use, click the Default button in the lower-left corner of the dialog box, and click the Yes button in the message box that appears.

Changing Margins

The default margins are a perfectly good starting point, but you frequently encounter situations in which you need to change them. For example, you might want to narrow the margins to fit more text on the page, increase the top or left margin to make room for a preprinted letterhead, or widen the inner margins for a document that will be bound.

To Do: Change the Margins Using the Page Setup Dialog Box

To change the margins using the Page Setup dialog box, follow these steps:

1. Choose File, Page Setup to display the Page Setup dialog box.

> As a shortcut, you can display the Page Setup dialog box by double-clicking in the gray margin areas at the ends of the horizontal and vertical rulers.

10

2. Click the Margins tab if it isn't already in front (see Figure 10.1).

FIGURE **10.1**

Use the Margins tab of the Page Setup dialog box to change your margins.

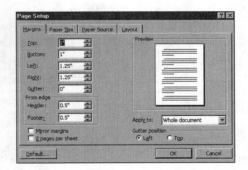

3. The value in the Top text box is highlighted. If you want to change the top margin, type a new value in inches to replace the selected value (you don't have to type the inch mark). Press the Tab key to move to the Bottom, Left, or Right text box, and type new values for any of these margins. (You can also use the spinner arrows to the right of any of these text boxes to increment the margins 1/10 inch at a time.)

 4. Click the OK button.

You can see your new margins in Print Layout view (change the Zoom setting to Page Width or Whole Page) or in Print Preview.

If you are going to bind your document, you probably want to increase the margins that are to be bound. If the document will be bound on the top edge of the pages, mark the

Top option button under Gutter Position. Otherwise, leave the Left option button marked. Type the amount that you want to increase the bound margins in the Gutter text box. (For example, type .5 to increase the margins by one-half inch.) If you are binding the document on the left side of the pages and printing single-sided pages, leave the Mirror Margins check box cleared. Word adds the amount of space you specify in the Gutter text box to the left margin of all of the pages. If you are printing double-sided pages, mark the Mirror Margins check box to have Word add the space to the inside margin of all of the pages.

To Do: Change the Margins with the Rulers

You can also change margins by using the horizontal and vertical rulers. To set margins this way, follow these steps:

1. Make sure you're using Print Layout view (View, Print Layout).

2. Point to the dividing line between the gray margin area and the white part of the ruler. The mouse pointer becomes a double-headed arrow, and the ScreenTip says `Left Margin`, `Right Margin`, `Top Margin`, or `Bottom Margin`, depending on which margin you're changing (see Figure 10.2).

FIGURE 10.2

Drag the inside edge of the margin on the ruler.

>
>
> When you're adjusting the left margin, it can be a little tricky to get the double-headed arrow to appear because Word may think you're pointing to one of the left indent markers. If you have trouble getting the `Left Margin` ScreenTip to appear, use the Page Setup dialog box to change the margin instead.

3. Drag in the desired direction. As you drag, a vertical dashed line shows you the width of the margin. When it's the right size, release the mouse button.

If you start dragging and then press and hold down the Alt key, Word changes the display on the ruler to show you the precise width of the margin in inches.

Changing Paper Orientation

Word assumes that you want to use *portrait* orientation, which means that the top of the document prints across the short edge of the paper. Occasionally, you may need to change to *landscape* orientation, so that the top of the document prints across the long edge of the paper.

 ### To Do: Change to Landscape Orientation

To change to landscape orientation, follow these steps:

1. Choose File, Page Setup to display the Page Setup dialog box.
2. Click the Paper Size tab (see Figure 10.3).

10

FIGURE 10.3

Use the Paper Size tab of the Page Setup dialog box to change orientation.

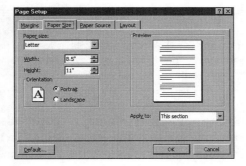

3. Mark the Landscape option button.

▲ 4. Click OK.

To see the change in paper orientation, use either Print Layout view or Print Preview. Figure 10.4 shows a document in Print Layout view whose orientation was changed to landscape. (The Zoom setting is set to Whole Page.)

FIGURE 10.4

Landscape orientation enables you to fit more text across the width of your page.

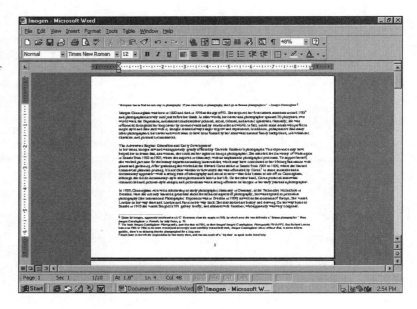

When you're using landscape orientation and the Zoom setting is 100 percent, you have to use the horizontal scrollbar to bring the entire width of the page into view. To avoid having to scroll horizontally, change the Zoom setting to Page Width.

Your rulers also reflect changes in paper orientation. If you switch to landscape mode and don't change the default margins, your horizontal ruler is 9 inches long with 1-inch margins, and your vertical ruler is 6 inches long with 1 1/4-inch margins.

Changing Paper Size

Word assumes that you want to print on 8 1/2-×11-inch paper, but it can adjust to most other standard sizes, and you can even set a custom size if you like.

To Do: Change the Paper Size

To print on a different paper size, follow these steps:

1. Choose File, Page Setup to display the Page Setup dialog box.
2. Click the Paper Size tab if it isn't already in front.

3. Display the Paper Size drop-down list and choose the desired size. (If you are printing on a nonstandard paper size, choose the last option, Custom Size, and then type the width and height of your paper in the Width and Height text boxes.)

4. Click OK.

Just as when you change margins or paper orientation, the rulers change to reflect the new paper size. Depending on the size, you may need to change the Zoom setting to avoid having to scroll horizontally.

Centering a Page Vertically

Many people try to center text vertically on the page by moving the insertion point to the top of the page and then pressing Enter several times to force the text down. More often than not, you end up pressing Enter too many (or too few) times and then have to add or delete blank lines to position the text where you want it. A more straightforward method is to let Word center the page vertically for you.

To Do: Center a Page Vertically

To vertically center the text on a page, follow these steps:

1. Remove any blank lines from above and below the text you want to center vertically.

2. Choose File, Page Setup to display the Page Setup dialog box.

3. Click the Layout tab if it isn't already in front (see Figure 10.5).

FIGURE 10.5

Use the Layout tab of the Page Setup dialog box to center your text vertically.

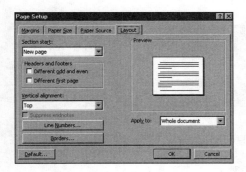

4. Click the down arrow to the right of the Vertical Alignment drop-down list, and click Center.

5. Click the OK button.

To see what the vertical centering looks like, use Print Preview or Print Layout view. If you decide not to use vertical centering, change the setting in the Vertical Alignment drop-down list back to Top.

Adding Page Numbers

Word offers two methods for adding page numbers to your document. First, you can use the Insert, Page Numbers command, as described here, to tell Word what type of page number you want and where it should appear. Word then adds the page number field to the header or footer for you. Second, you can enter the page number field by inserting it directly in the header or footer (see the next section). This second method gives you more control over the appearance of your page numbers, and you can add other text to the header or footer at the same time if you like. (A *field* is a "holding place" for information that can be updated. In this case, the page number field updates automatically to display the correct page number on each page. Later in this hour, you'll learn how to insert other fields in the header or footer, and in Hour 14, "Editing Shortcuts," you learn about fields in more depth.)

To Do: Add Page Numbering Using the Page Numbers Dialog Box

To add the page number to your document using the Page Numbers dialog box, follow these steps:

1. Choose Insert, Page Numbers to display the Page Numbers dialog box (see Figure 10.6).

FIGURE 10.6

Use the Page Numbers dialog box to quickly add page numbering to the header or footer.

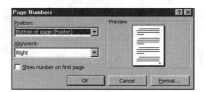

2. If you want the number at the bottom of the page, skip to the next step. To place the number at the top of the page, display the Position drop-down list, and choose Top of Page (Header).

3. Display the Alignment drop-down list and choose the alignment you prefer for your page numbers.

4. Mark the Show Number on First Page check box if you want the page number to print on the first page of your document.

▲   5. Click the OK button.

If you clear the Show Number on First Page check box, Word creates a *first page header* or *first page footer* and leaves it blank. (You'll learn more about this in "Creating a Different Header or Footer on First or Odd and Even Pages" later in this hour.)

If you need the page numbering to start on a number other than 1, click the Format button in the Page Numbers dialog box to display the Page Number Format dialog box. Type the desired number in the Start At text box, and click OK.

You can view your page numbers—and any other text in the header or footer—in Print Layout view and Print Preview, among others. Page numbers are not visible in Normal view.

Removing a page number field that you inserted via the Page Numbers dialog box is easier said than done. First, display the header or footer and activate the footer area if necessary (see the next section). Depending on how Word is set to display fields on your computer, the page number may appear with a light gray background. (If it isn't gray now, it may turn gray when you click it.) Click the page number. A crosshatched box appears around it. Point to this box (your mouse pointer changes to a four-headed arrow) and click it to select it—small black squares appears on all four sides of the box. At this point, you can press the Delete key to remove the field. Thankfully, when you insert the page number field using the Header and Footer toolbar, as described in "Inserting the Page Number or Date in the Header or Footer" later in this hour, the field is not enclosed in a crosshatched box, and you can simply drag over it and press Delete to get rid of it.

Creating Headers and Footers

A *header* appears at the top of every page, and a *footer* appears at the bottom of every page. You might want to use headers and footers to display the document title, your name, the name of your organization, and so on. Figure 10.7 shows a document in Print Preview. The author's name and the date are entered in the header, so they print on every page.

FIGURE 10.7

By default, the text in headers and footers prints on every page of your document.

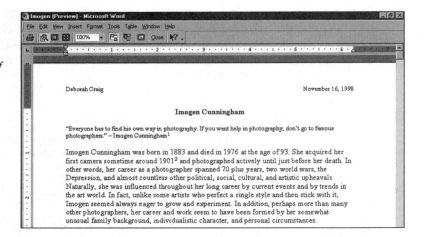

As you'll see, Word makes it easy to center and right-align header and footer text by providing a center tab in the middle of the header and footer and a right tab at the right edge of the header and footer.

To Do: Create a Header and/or Footer

To create a header and/or footer, follow these steps:

1. Choose View, Header and Footer.

> After you have text in your header, you can double-click it when you're in Print Layout view to activate it instead of choosing View, Header and Footer. You can always double-click the footer to activate it, regardless of whether it contains text.

2. Word activates the header area and displays the Header and Footer toolbar (see Figure 10.8). Note the custom tabs in the center and on the right. If you want to create a footer, click the Switch Between Header and Footer toolbar button to activate the footer area. (Click the same button again when you want to switch back to the header area.)

▼

Center tab   Right tab

FIGURE 10.8

The View, Header and Footer command activates the header area of your document and displays the Header and Footer toolbar.

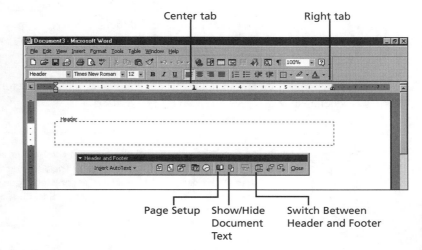

Page Setup   Show/Hide   Switch Between
              Document   Header and Footer
              Text

10

3. Type any text that you want to appear at the left margin.

4. If you want any text centered, press the Tab key to jump to the center tab, and type the text.

5. If you want some text to be right-aligned at the right margin, press the Tab key twice to move to the right tab, and type the text.

6. Apply any formatting that you like to text (and fields) in your header or footer by selecting it and using the standard formatting techniques, including the Formatting toolbar, the Font and Paragraph dialog boxes, keyboard shortcuts, and so on. To select all of the text in the header or footer, click when your mouse pointer is in the left margin, outside of the dashed-line that demarcates the header or footer area. Figure 10.9 shows a footer with text on the left and right margins, formatted in an Arial 10-point font.

FIGURE 10.9

You type whatever text you want in the header and footer.

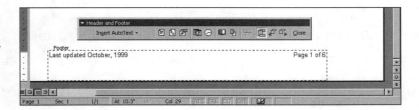

> It's common to make header and footer text a couple point sizes smaller than your document text to set it apart from the text stream.

▲ 7. Click the Close button in the Header and Footer toolbar to return to viewing your document text.

> The Insert AutoText button at the left end of the Header and Footer toolbar displays a list of typical header and footer entries, such as the filename of the document, the date on which it was last printed, and so on. Most of the entries are a combination of regular text and fields. Clicking an entry in this list is faster than creating it yourself.

By default, the document text is dim but visible when you're working with headers and footers. If you like, you can hide it completely by clicking the Show/Hide Document Text button in the Header and Footer toolbar. To bring the document text back into view, click the toolbar button again. If you want to display the Page Setup dialog box to modify the header or footer (see "Creating a Different Header or Footer on the First or Odd and Even Pages"), click the Page Setup toolbar button.

To delete text in your header or footer, activate the header or footer area and then delete the text by using any of the usual methods. To delete a field, double-click it or drag over it (it changes from black text on a light-gray background to white text on a dark-gray background), and then press the Delete key.

Inserting the Page Number or Date in the Header or Footer

The Header and Footer toolbar makes it easy to insert fields for the page number and the date or time. As with the page number field, fields for the date and time automatically update to display the current date and time.

To Do: Insert the Page Number in the Header or Footer

To insert the page number in the header or footer, follow these steps:

1. Choose View, Header and Footer.
2. Click the Switch Between Header and Footer button if you want to insert the page number in the footer.
3. Press Tab once or twice if you want to center or right-align the page number.
4. Click the Insert Page Number button on the Header and Footer toolbar (or press Alt+Shift+P).

▼

> If you want to use the format *Page 1 of 8, Page 2 of 8, Page 3 of 8,* and so
> on, click the Insert AutoText button, and then click Page X of Y in the list
> that appears. If you like doing things the hard way, you can do the same
> thing yourself: Type *Page* and press the Spacebar, click the Insert Page
> Number toolbar button and press the Spacebar, type *of* and press the
> Spacebar again, and then click the Insert Number of Pages button.

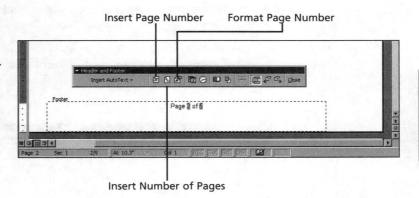

FIGURE 10.10

*The Header and Footer
toolbar has buttons
that make it simple to
add page numbering.*

10

5. Format the header or footer however you like, and then click the Close button on
   the Header and Footer toolbar.

▲

> If you want to begin page numbering with a number other than 1, click the
> Format Page Number button on the Header and Footer toolbar to display
> the Page Number Format dialog box, type the desired number in the Start
> At text box, and click OK. If you have divided your document into multiple
> sections (see "Varying the Page Formatting in Your Document" later in this
> hour), Word automatically continues the page numbering from one section
> to the next. To restart the page numbering in each section, activate the
> header and footer in each section, as described in "Creating Different
> Headers and Footers in Different Sections of Your Document" later in this
> hour, and enter 1 in the Start At text box.

To Do: Insert the Date or Time in the Header or Footer

To insert the date or time in the header or footer, follow these steps:

1. Choose View, Header and Footer.

    2. Click the Switch Between Header and Footer button if you want to insert the date or time in the footer.

    3. Press Tab once or twice if you want to center or right-align the date or time.

    4. Click the Insert Date toolbar button (or press Alt+Shift+D) to insert the date. Click the Insert Time toolbar button (or press Alt+Shift+T) to insert the time. Figure 10.11 shows the date field inserted at the right edge of the header.

FIGURE 10.11

Use buttons in the Header and Footer toolbar to add date and time fields to your header or footer.

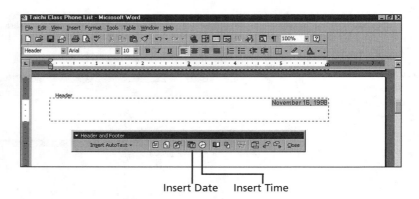

Insert Date   Insert Time

    5. Format the header or footer as you like, and then click the Close button.

Word inserts the date field in the default format. If you want to change the default to something else (from 11/18/99 to November 18, 1999, for example), choose Insert, Date and Time to display the Insert Date and Time dialog box, click the format you want in the Available Formats list, click the Default button, click Yes, and then click OK. You'll learn more about the Date and Time dialog box in Hour 14.

> If you have created AutoText entries, you can insert them in your header or footer by clicking the Insert AutoText button and then clicking the entry in the list that pops up. You'll learn how to create AutoText entries in Hour 14.

Creating a Different Header or Footer on the First or Odd and Even Pages

Word gives you a straightforward way to create a different header and footer for the first page of a multipage document. The most common reason to do this is to keep the header and footer from printing on the first page. And it is equally easy to create different headers and footers for your odd and even pages. You may want to do this if the document is to be double-sided and bound.

To Do: Suppress the Header and Footer on the First Page

In many documents, you want to print the header and footer on every page but the first. For example, you probably don't want the page number to appear on the first page of a letter. To suppress the header and footer on the first page of a document, you tell Word that you want a different header and footer on the first page, and then you simply leave the first page header and footer blank:

1. Choose File, Page Setup to display the Page Setup dialog box. If you are viewing your headers and footers already, you can also click the Page Setup button on the Header and Footer toolbar (refer to Figure 10.8).

2. Click the Layout tab (refer to Figure 10.5).

3. Mark the Different First Page check box.

4. Click OK.

5. Choose View, Header and Footer.

6. When you are viewing the header or footer for the first page, the left side of the header or footer indicates First Page Header or First Page Footer, as shown in Figure 10.12. If you don't want any header or footer text on the first page, leave the first page header and footer blank.

FIGURE 10.12

You can create a separate header and footer for the first page.

Leave the first page header or footer blank if you like.

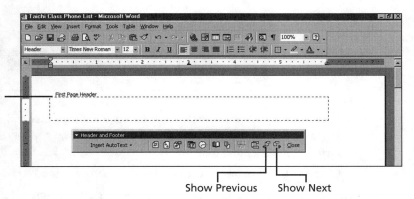

Show Previous   Show Next

7. Click the Show Next button in the Header and Footer toolbar to move to the header and footer for the remainder of the document, and insert and format the desired text and fields. (If you want to move back to the first page header and footer, click the Show Previous toolbar button.)

8. Click the Close button in the Header and Footer toolbar.

To Do: Create Different Odd and Even Headers and Footers

To create different headers or footers for odd and even pages in your document, follow these steps:

1. Choose File, Page Setup to display the Page Setup dialog box.

2. Click the Layout tab (refer to Figure 10.5).

3. Mark the Different Odd and Even check box.

4. Click OK.

5. Choose View, Header and Footer.

6. When you are viewing the header and footer for odd pages, the left side of the header or footer indicates Odd Page Header or Odd Page Footer, as shown in Figure 10.13. Type and format the text that you want to appear in the odd header and footer.

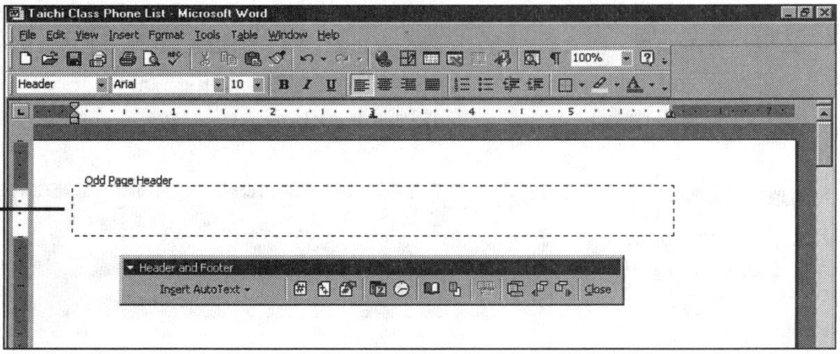

FIGURE 10.13

You can create different headers and footers for odd and even pages.

Click the Show Next button to move to the Even Page header.

7. Click the Show Next toolbar button to move to the header and footer for even pages (they are labeled Even Page Header and Even Page Footer) and type and format the header and footer text.

8. Click the Close button in the Header and Footer toolbar.

Creating Different Headers and Footers in Different Sections of Your Document

If you divide your document into sections, as described in "Varying the Page Formatting in Your Document" at the end of this hour, you can then create different headers and footers in each section. You might do this if you're printing a long document with multiple chapters and you want to include the chapter name and number in the header or footer, for example.

Word makes a less-than-intuitive assumption about headers and footers in documents that are divided into multiple sections. Unless you tell it otherwise, Word makes the header and footer text in each section the same as the previous section. You have to turn on this feature if you want to vary the header and footer text from section to section. Figure 10.14 shows the header in section 2 of a document. Note that the section number appears on the left side of the header, and `Same As Previous` appears on the right side. To "unlink" the header and footer in the current section from the previous section, click the Same As Previous button in the Header and Footer toolbar to turn it off (it's pushed in by default).

FIGURE 10.14

Click the Same As Previous button to unlink the header and footer from the previous section.

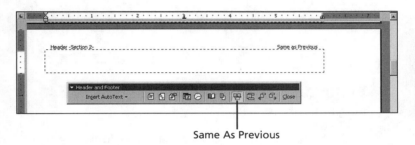

10

Same As Previous

You have to do this in each section individually. After the sections are unlinked, you can click the Show Previous and Show Next buttons in the Header and Footer toolbar to move from section to section, and type and format each one separately.

You can specify different first page and/or different odd and even page headers and footers within each section of a document, if you like.

Adding a Page Border

In the last hour, you learned how to add borders to individual paragraphs. Using a related feature, you can add borders to entire pages. Page borders can snaz up documents such as announcements, flyers, and title pages. Figure 10.15 shows a decorative border around a flyer for a singing group.

FIGURE 10.15

Page borders can focus the reader's attention on your text.

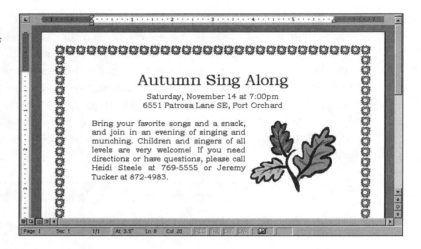

To Do: Add a Page Border

To add a border around the page, follow these steps:

1. Choose Format, Borders and Shading to display the Borders and Shading dialog box.
2. Click the Page Border tab (see Figure 10.16).

FIGURE 10.16

Use the Page Border tab of the Borders and Shading dialog box to create your page border.

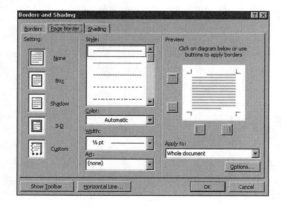

3. Click the option under Setting that most closely matches the border you want to create.
4. Using the Style, Color, Width, and Art lists in the middle of the dialog box, specify the type of border you want to use. The border shown in Figure 10.15 is one of the options in the Art list. As you choose options, the Preview area on the right side of the dialog box shows what the border looks like.

5. When you've made all of your selections, click OK.

If you have divided your document into multiple sections, Word automatically adds the page border to every page in the document. If you like, you can restrict the page border to the first page of the current section, to all pages except the first page in the current section, or to all pages in the current section. To choose one of these options, click the desired setting in the Apply To list in the Page Border tab.

Choosing What Printer Paper Trays to Use

By default, Word pulls paper from the default paper tray in your printer. If your office uses preprinted letterhead, you probably want to use the letterhead for the first page of your documents and plain paper for the remaining pages. To do this, you need to instruct your printer to pull the paper for the first page from one paper tray, and the paper for the remaining pages from another. (This assumes that your printer has more than one paper tray.)

10

To Do: Select Your Paper Trays

Follow these steps to tell Word which paper trays to use for the first page and remaining pages of your document:

1. Choose File, Page Setup to display the Page Setup dialog box.
2. Click the Paper Source tab if it isn't already in front (see Figure 10.17).

FIGURE 10.17

Use the Paper Source tab of the Page Setup dialog box to specify which paper trays your printer should draw paper from.

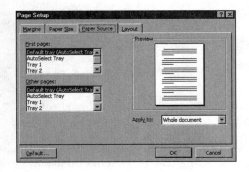

3. Choose the paper tray to use for the first page in the First Page list, and choose the tray for the remaining paper in the Other Pages list. (The names of the trays vary depending on your printer. If you aren't sure which trays to choose, check your printer manual.)

4. Click OK.

Controlling Page Breaks

As you know, Word inserts automatic page breaks when your pages are full of text. If you want to break a page that isn't full, you have to insert a *manual* (or *hard*) *page break*. You might want to insert a manual page break to end a section of a report, or to separate a title page from the rest of the document.

To Do: Insert a Manual Page Break

The steps to insert a manual page break are extremely simple:

1. Move the insertion point to the location where you want to insert the break.
2. Press Ctrl+Enter (or choose Insert, Break, mark the Page Break option button, and click OK).

A manual page break looks just like an automatic page break in Print Layout view. In Normal view, however, it is labeled with *Page Break*, as shown in Figure 10.18.

FIGURE 10.18

A manual page break appears in Normal view as a dotted line with the words Page Break on it.

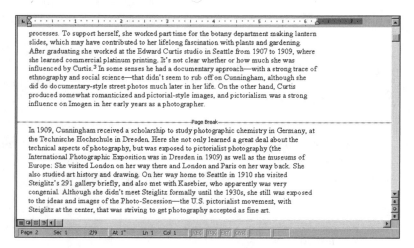

If you revise text above a manual page break, you likely will end up bumping the break into the wrong place in your document. If this happens, just delete it and reinsert it in the desired location.

To delete a manual page break in Normal view, click on the break and press Delete, or, if your insertion point is just past the break, press Backspace. If you're in Print Layout view, press Delete if your insertion point is immediately above the break, and Backspace if your insertion point is just after it.

Varying the Page Formatting in Your Document

Word automatically applies all page formatting to your entire document. In many cases, you need to alter this behavior. For example, you may have a table in a long report that you have to print in landscape orientation to fit all of the columns on the page, but you want the other pages to print in portrait orientation. Or you might want to vertically center the text on your title page, but not on the remaining pages. To make these kinds of changes, you have to divide your document into multiple *sections* by inserting *section breaks* at the appropriate spots. After you've done this, you can apply different page formatting in each section, independent of the others.

Word lets you create four kinds of section breaks:

- Next page—This section break is like a page break and a section break combined. It both breaks the page and starts a new section. An appropriate place to use a next page section break would be at the end of a title page.

- Continuous—This section break does not break the page. Once in a while, you may need to apply different page formatting on the same page. For example, if you want to format your document text in two columns, but want the title to be centered in the middle of the page, you can insert a continuous section break directly under the title. This enables you to keep the title and document text on the same page, but use the default single-column format for the title, and a two-column format for the text.

- Even page—This type of section break is most useful for longer documents that are divided into multiple parts, especially those that are bound. It forces the text in the new section to begin on the next even page.

- Odd page—This is the same as an even page section break, but it forces the text in the new section to begin on the next odd page.

To Do: Insert a Section Break

It's easiest to work with section breaks in Normal view because the breaks are labeled onscreen. To insert a section break, follow these steps:

1. Choose View, Normal if you aren't already using Normal view.
2. Move the insertion point to the location where you want to insert the section break.
3. Choose Insert, Break to display the Break dialog box (see Figure 10.19).

10

▼ To Do

FIGURE **10.19**

Use the Break dialog box to insert a section break.

4. Under Section Break Types, mark the desired option button.

 5. Click OK.

After you've inserted one or more section breaks in your document, you can use the status bar to keep track of which section you are in. Figure 10.20 shows a next page section break in Normal view. Note that the section break is labeled `Section Break (Next Page)`, and the insertion point is below the break, so the status bar indicates *Sec 2*.

FIGURE **10.20**

The status bar tells you in what the section the insertion point is.

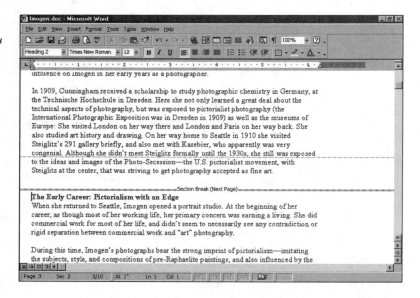

When your document has more than one section, all of the formatting options in the Page Setup dialog box are by default applied to the section containing the insertion point. To apply page formatting to the entire document, change the setting in the Apply To list from This Section to Whole Document.

To delete a section break, use the same methods as the ones you use to delete manual page breaks (see the preceding section). To change a section break from one type to another, delete the old break, and then insert the new one.

Summary

You now have a solid foundation in Word's formatting techniques. By mixing and matching the formatting options you learned in this hour and the two previous ones, you can create documents that are easy to read and pleasing to the eye. In the next hour, you learn to collect font and paragraph formatting into styles, which you can apply to your documents to give them a consistent look.

Q&A

Q I want to adjust the distance between the page border and the edge of the page. Does Word let you do this?

A Yes. In the Page Border tab of the Borders and Shading dialog box, click the Options button to display the Border and Shading Options dialog box. Change the values in the Top, Bottom, Left, and Right text boxes to adjust the distance. You can also clear the Surround Header and Surround Footer text boxes if you want the header and/or footer text to appear outside of the page border.

Q I want every section in my report to begin on a new page. Do I have to insert a manual page break above the heading for each section?

A That is one way to handle it. The other option is to format the headings with the Page Break Before option that you learned about in the last hour. (Click in the heading, choose Format, Paragraph, click the Line and Page Breaks tab, mark the Page Break Before option button, and click OK.)

10

HOUR 11

Working with Styles

A *style* is a collection of formatting options to which you assign a name. For example, you could create a style called *Title* that contains all the formatting—font, font size, alignment, and so on—that you normally apply to the titles of your reports. When you apply a style to text, the text takes on all the formatting that the style contains. As you'll see, using styles can greatly speed up the formatting process. If you apply a lot of formatting in your documents, you will likely come away from this hour a true believer in the value of styles.

The highlights of this hour include

- Applying styles to your text
- Creating your own styles
- Modifying styles
- Chaining styles together
- Viewing styles onscreen

Understanding Styles

If you know a bit about how styles can benefit you, what kinds there are, and where they are stored, you will feel confident about creating and using them in your documents.

The Advantages of Using Styles

Styles are advantageous for several reasons:

- They let you apply formatting quickly. Instead of applying several formatting options one at a time, you can apply them all at once by applying a style that contains all the options.

- They let you modify your formatting quickly. If you decide to make a formatting change to some element of your document (for example, you decide that all your headings should be boldface instead of italic), you need to update only the style you applied to that element, and the affected text throughout your document reformats instantly.

- They let you create a consistent look for all the documents that you and your coworkers create.

- If you use *heading styles* (styles that are designed specifically for formatting headings) to format the different levels of headings in a document, you can take advantage of two handy features—the Document Map and Outline view—that help you navigate in and reorganize structured documents. (You'll learn about these features in Hour 15, "Working with Long Documents.")

Styles Come in Two Flavors

Word lets you create two types of styles:

- Character styles
- Paragraph styles

Character styles can contain only font formatting, and for this reason, they are far less useful than paragraph styles. However, you might occasionally want to create a character style if a word or phrase crops up frequently in your documents and has to be formatted in a particular way. For example, company style might dictate that the name of your company always appear in an Arial, 12-point, bold font.

Paragraph styles can contain both font formatting and paragraph formatting. This makes them much more versatile than character styles. As you might expect, paragraph styles can be applied, at a minimum, to a single paragraph. In this hour, you will focus on working with paragraph styles.

You Can Store Styles in Documents or Templates

If you create a style that will be useful only in a particular document, you can store it in that document only. It will always be available in that document, but not in any others. If, on the other hand, you want to use a style in all the documents based on a particular template, you can store the style in the template itself. You'll learn how to specify where to store your styles in "Creating Your Own Styles" later in this hour.

Applying Styles

The styles that are available in your document are listed in the Style list at the left end of the Formatting toolbar (see Figure 11.1).

FIGURE 11.1

The Style list gives you access to your available styles.

Style list

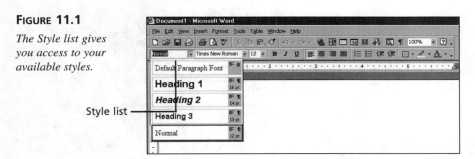

The style names appear with the font formatting that is specified in the style. To the right of each style name is a small gray box that shows you the alignment and font size in the style. In addition, the upper-right corner of the gray box contains an "a" if it's a character style, or a paragraph symbol (¶) if it's a paragraph style.

The styles in the Style list in Figure 11.1 come with the Normal template. Default Paragraph Font and Normal are the default character and paragraph styles. Heading 1, Heading 2, and Heading 3 are paragraph styles that you can use to format your headings. You'll learn more about them in "Applying Styles to Your Headings" later in this hour.

To Do: Apply a Style

To apply a character or paragraph style, follow these steps:

1. To apply a character style, select the text. To apply a paragraph style, click in the paragraph, or select multiple paragraphs to apply the style to all of them.

2. Click the Style list drop-down arrow in the Formatting toolbar, scroll down the list, and click the style that you want to apply.

▼ To Do

11

You can also apply styles with keyboard shortcuts or toolbar buttons. In "Creating Your Own Styles" later in this hour, you learn how to assign a keyboard shortcut to a style. In "Creating a Toolbar for Your Styles" at the end of this hour, you learn how to create a toolbar with buttons for your styles.

To check what style you've applied in a particular location, just click in the text. The Style list in the Formatting toolbar displays the style in effect at the location of the insertion point. In Figure 11.2, the insertion point is in a paragraph formatted with the Heading 1 style, so this style name appears in the Style list.

The paragraph containing the insertion point is formatted with the Heading 1 style.

FIGURE 11.2

To check what style you've applied, click in the text and look at the Style list.

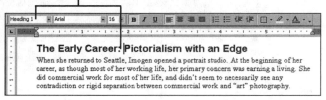

Word Creates Styles On-the-Fly

If you glance at the Style list occasionally as you're typing a document, you may notice new styles suddenly appearing in the list. By default, Word creates styles for you based on the formatting that you apply in your document. Although this might be helpful for people who don't want to pay any attention to styles, it can be annoying if you want to closely control the styles in your document.

While you're learning about styles, it's a good idea to turn off this feature so that you have to contend only with styles that you've created yourself. You can always turn it back on later if you choose.

To Do: Disable Automatically Defined Styles

To turn off this feature, follow these steps:

1. Choose Tools, AutoCorrect to display the AutoCorrect dialog box.
2. Click the AutoFormat As You Type tab.
3. Clear the Define Styles Based on Your Formatting check box.
4. Click OK.

Creating Your Own Styles

To take full advantage of styles, you need to create your own. This way, you can include the exact formatting you need for the different elements in your documents. For example, if you have to type a weekly calendar of events, you might want to create one style for the names of the events, one for their descriptions, one for the date and time information, and so on. You can create new styles in two ways, as described in the next two sections.

Using the Style List in the Formatting Toolbar

The fastest way to create a style is to use the Style list in the Formatting toolbar (this technique is sometimes called *style by example*). However, using the Style list has a major limitation: Any styles you create this way will be stored only in the document, not in the underlying template, so they won't be available outside of the document. In addition, this method works to create only paragraph styles, not character styles.

To Do: Create a Style Using the Style List in the Formatting Toolbar

To create a style by using the Style list, follow these steps:

1. Format a paragraph with all the options that you want to include in the style. For example, if you are creating a style for your body text, you might format the paragraph with a Verdana 11-point font, left alignment, and 12 points of paragraph spacing after the paragraph (so that you won't have to press Enter to create blank lines between the paragraphs).

2. Make sure your insertion point is in the paragraph, and click whatever style is currently showing in the Style list to select it.

3. Type over the selected style name with the name of your new style (it can include spaces). Figure 11.3 shows the insertion point in the formatted paragraph, and the name *Body* entered in the Style list.

FIGURE 11.3

Type a name for your new style in the Style list.

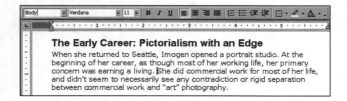

4. Press Enter.

11

Word creates a style that includes all the font and paragraph formatting in the paragraph. In Figure 11.4, note that the new style is now included in the Style list. Try applying your new style to some other paragraphs in your document.

The new style is added to the list.

FIGURE 11.4

When you create a style, Word adds it to the Style list.

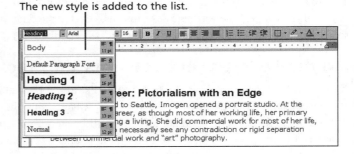

Using the Style Dialog Box

The most flexible way to create styles (either character or paragraph) is to use the Style dialog box. When you use this method, you can instruct Word to save the style in the template so that it will be available to other documents.

To Do: Create a Style Using the Style Dialog Box

To create a style by using the Style dialog box, follow these steps:

1. Choose Format, Style to display the Style dialog box (see Figure 11.5). It doesn't matter where your insertion point is when you issue the command.

FIGURE 11.5

The Style dialog box lets you create and modify styles.

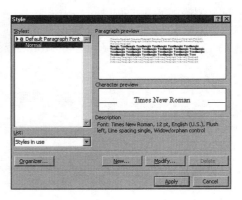

2. In the Styles list on the left side of the Style dialog box, click Normal if it isn't already selected. (Doing this ensures that your new style is based on the

"plain-vanilla" Normal style. You'll learn more about this in "Basing One Style on Another" later in this hour.)

> The option that's selected in the List drop-down list (located in the lower-left corner of the dialog box) controls what's displayed in the Styles list. The All Styles option displays all the styles in all your Word templates. The Styles in Use option displays only the styles that are being used (or were used at some point) in the current document. The User-Defined Styles option displays only the styles you've created yourself. When you highlight a style in the Styles list, the formatting that it contains appears under Description on the right side of the dialog box.

3. Click the New button to display the New Style dialog box (see Figure 11.6).

FIGURE 11.6

Use the New Style dialog box to create a new style.

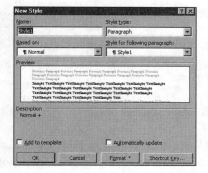

4. Type a name for your style in the Name text box (type over the default name *Style1*). Leave the Style Type option set to Paragraph, unless you want to create a character style. You'll learn about the two remaining text boxes, Based On, and Style for Following Paragraph, later in this hour.

5. Mark the Add to Template check box if you want to add the style to the template underlying the current document. If you do this, the style will be available to other documents based on the template.

11

In general, it's best to leave the Automatically Update check box clear. When it's marked, you can modify a style by revising the formatting in a paragraph to which the style is applied. However, when you modify a style in this way, the modified version is saved in the document only, not in the template. Furthermore, you can easily end up modifying a style when you didn't mean to.

6. Click the Format button to display a list of commands that lead to all the dialog boxes in which you can select font and paragraph formatting (see Figure 11.7).

FIGURE 11.7

Use the Format button to pick and choose the formatting that you want to include in the style.

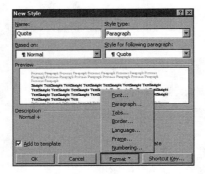

7. Click the command that leads to the dialog box that contains the formatting you want to add. For example, click Font to display the Font dialog box so that you can specify the font formatting for the style. Make your selections in the dialog box, and click OK to return to the New Style dialog box.

8. Repeat steps 6 and 7 to add all the formatting that you want to the style. In Figure 11.8, a new style called *Quote* has been created. It contains a Palatino, 12-point font (specified in the Font dialog box) and left and right indents of 1 inch, justification, and 12 points of paragraph spacing after the paragraph (specified in the Paragraph dialog box).

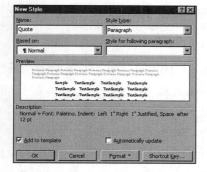

FIGURE 11.8

All the formatting that you've added to the style is listed under Description.

If you want to apply your style with a keyboard shortcut, click the Shortcut Key button in the lower-right corner of the New Style dialog box. In the Customize Keyboard dialog box, press the keyboard shortcut you want to use so that it appears in the Press New Shortcut Key text box. If the shortcut is already assigned to a different command, Word displays a message to that effect. When you have found a shortcut that is currently unassigned, click the Assign button, and then click the Close button.

11

9. Click OK to close the New Style dialog box, and then click the Close button to close the Style dialog box. (Don't use the Apply button to close the Style dialog box. This would apply the new style to whatever paragraph happens to contain the insertion point.)

Your new style now appears in the Style list in the Formatting toolbar.

Creating Styles for Your Headings

If you want to take advantage of two key features for working with documents that contain headings and subheadings—the Document Map and Outline view—you have to apply styles to your headings that tell Word what level each heading should be. You have two options for doing this. The first involves using (and optionally modifying) the default heading styles; the second involves creating your own:

- Apply the default heading styles that come with the Normal template (Heading 1, Heading 2, and Heading 3). Use Heading 1 for your main headings, Heading 2 for your subheadings, and Heading 3 for your sub subheadings. If you don't like the formatting in these styles, you can modify them (see the next section), but keep the style names the same.

- Create your own heading styles with whatever names you choose (Chapter Heading, Section Heading, and Sub Heading, for example), and include in each style an *outline level* setting that tells Word the style's heading level. See the next set of To Do steps.

To Do: Include Outline Levels in Your Heading Styles

When you are adding the formatting to each style (see steps 6–8 in the preceding section), incorporate these three steps:

1. Click the Format button in the New Style dialog box.
2. Click the Paragraph command to display the Paragraph dialog box.
3. Display the Outline Level drop-down list in the upper-right corner of the dialog box, and choose an outline level (see Figure 11.9). Choose Level 1 as the outline level for your top-level heading style, Level 2 for your next-highest heading style, and so on.

FIGURE 11.9

Assign an outline level to your style if you want to use it as one of your heading styles.

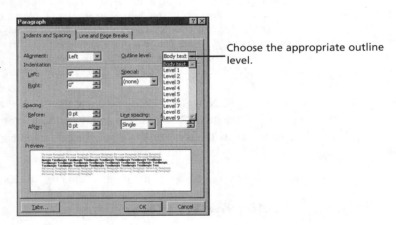

Choose the appropriate outline level.

Modifying Existing Styles

Whether you modify a style that comes with Word or one you created yourself, as soon as you make the change, all the paragraphs formatted with that style in your document automatically update to reflect the new formatting in the style. (Any text formatted with the same style in other existing documents does not get reformatted.)

Using the Style List in the Formatting Toolbar

You can modify a style using the Style list in the Formatting toolbar, just as you can when creating a style. However, the drawback to this method is that the modified style can be stored only in the document itself.

To Do: Modify a Style Using the Style List in the Formatting Toolbar

To modify a style using the Style list, follow these steps:

1. Apply the style to a paragraph, and then modify the formatting of the paragraph so that it looks the way you want it to.

2. Make sure the insertion point is in the paragraph, click the style in the Style list box (don't display the list), and press Enter.

3. Word displays a message asking whether you want to update the style to reflect recent changes or reapply the formatting of the style to the selection (see Figure 11.10). Mark the Update the Style to Reflect Recent Changes option button, and ▲ click OK.

FIGURE 11.10

Mark the first option button to modify the style based on the changes you made to the formatting in the paragraph.

Using the Style Dialog Box

When you modify a style using the Style dialog box, you can save the modified style in the document or in the underlying template.

To Do: Modify a Style Using the Style Dialog Box

To modify a style using the Style dialog box, follow these steps:

1. Choose Format, Style to display the Style dialog box. (It doesn't matter where your insertion point is when you issue the command.)

2. Click the style that you want to modify in the Styles list on the left side of the Styles dialog box. (If you don't see it, choose All Styles in the List drop-down list.)

3. Click the Modify button to display the Modify Style dialog box (see Figure 11.11). Notice that this dialog box is identical to the New Style dialog box shown in Figure 11.6, with the exception of the name in the title bar.

11

Figure 11.11

Use the Modify Style dialog box to modify an existing style.

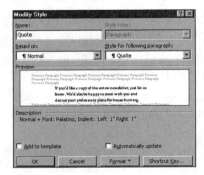

4. Make any changes that you want to the style (see steps 6–8 in "Creating a Style Using the Style Dialog Box" earlier in this hour). If you stored the original style in the template and want the modified style to replace the original in the template, mark the Add to Template check box. (Otherwise, the modified version is stored in the document only; the version in the template remains unchanged.)

5. Click OK to close the Modify Style dialog box, and then click Close to close the Style dialog box.

Chaining Styles Together

If you create documents in which the various text elements always appear in a particular order, you can "chain" them together so that when you press Enter to end a paragraph formatted with one style, Word automatically applies the second style to the next paragraph. Linking styles in this way can save you many trips to the Style list in the Formatting toolbar.

For example, let's say you're creating an instruction manual in which each topic is composed of a heading, an introductory paragraph, and then a numbered list of steps. And let's say you've created styles named Topic, Intro, and Steps for these three elements. You can chain the styles together so that Topic leads to Intro, Intro leads to Steps, and Steps leads back to Topic.

When you're creating or modifying a style, you can specify a style to follow by choosing it from the Style for Following Paragraph list in the New Style or Modify Style dialog box.

Basing One Style on Another

If you're creating a style that is similar to an existing one, you can base the new style on the existing one so that it gains all the formatting in the existing style. Then all you need to do is tweak the new style a little to get the formatting exactly as you want it. To base a style on another one, you select the "based on" style in the Based On list in the New Style or Modify Style dialog box.

Although this method lets you create styles rather quickly, it can cause two problems down the road. First, when you look at the description of a style that's based on another style (in the Description area of the New Style or Modify Style dialog box), it lists the "based on" style plus whatever adjustments you've made to it. For example, in Figure 11.12, the Short Quote style is based on the Quote style, so the description lists `Quote` plus the one modification (the indentation was removed). If you want to see *all* the formatting in the new style, you need to track down the content of the "based on" style—a tedious task. And if the "based on" style is itself based on another style, reach for some coffee or chocolate to cheer yourself up.

FIGURE 11.12

Think carefully before basing one style on another.

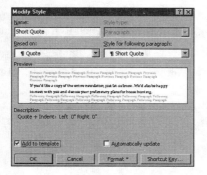

11

Second, if you base several styles on a style and then modify the "based on" style, *all* the other styles will change accordingly. This "ripple effect" can produce some unexpected (and often unwanted) results.

In conclusion, the most straightforward route is to base each style on the Normal style, so you can see exactly what formatting it contains and modify it without affecting other styles.

Viewing the Styles in Your Document

If you work with styles frequently, you'll be glad to know that you can quickly see what styles are applied to your paragraphs as you work. The styles appear in a vertical bar on the left side of the Word window, known as the *style area* (see Figure 11.13). This feature is available only in Normal view.

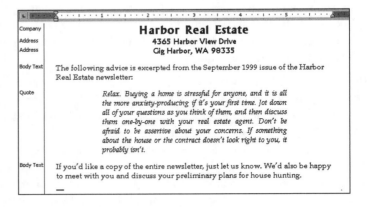

To Do: Display the Styles in Your Document

Follow these steps to open the style area:

1. If you aren't already using Normal view, switch to it now (choose View, Normal).
2. Choose Tools, Options to display the Options dialog box.
3. Click the View tab if it isn't already in front (see Figure 11.14).

4. Set a value in the Style Area Width text box at the bottom of the View tab, such as .5 inch. (You can always adjust it later.)
5. Click OK.

If you want to narrow or widen the style area, just drag the vertical line that separates it from your text. To remove it, drag the line all the way to the left, or repeat these steps and change the value in the Style Area Width text box back to 0.

Creating a Toolbar for Your Styles

Applying styles by clicking toolbar buttons is much faster than accessing them in the Style list in the Formatting toolbar. If you will be using styles extensively, work through this section to create a toolbar that contains buttons for your styles. If you don't think you'll use styles that frequently, feel free to pass by this topic and skip to the summary at the end of this hour.

To Do: Create a Toolbar for Your Styles

Follow these steps to create a toolbar for your styles:

1. Open a document that contains the styles you want to put on the toolbar, and then choose Tools, Customize to display the Customize dialog box.

2. Click the Toolbars tab if it isn't already in front (see Figure 11.15).

FIGURE 11.15

Display the Toolbars tab to create a new toolbar for your styles.

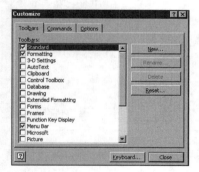

3. Click the New button to display the New Toolbar dialog box.

4. Type a name for your toolbar (you might call it Styles) and specify the template in the Make Toolbar Available To drop-down list (see Figure 11.16). To make the toolbar available to all documents, choose Normal. Click OK.

FIGURE 11.16

Name your toolbar in the New Toolbar dialog box.

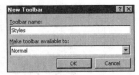

5. Word creates an empty toolbar floating over your document. Click the Commands tab in the Customize dialog box.

6. Scroll down the Categories list on the left side of the dialog box and click Styles to display a list of the styles in the current document in the Commands list on the right.

7. Drag the styles one by one from the Commands list, and drop them onto the new toolbar (see Figure 11.17).

FIGURE 11.17

Drag styles from the Customize dialog box to create buttons for them on your new toolbar.

Drag your styles from the Commands list to the toolbar.

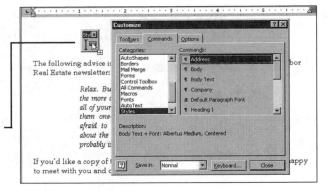

8. The default button names are rather long. To shorten them, right-click each button to display a context menu and edit its name in the Name text box (see Figure 11.18). You can use any name that reminds you which style the button will apply.

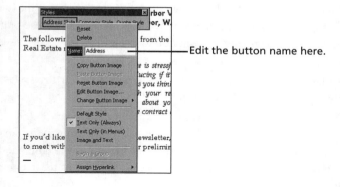

FIGURE 11.18

Shortening the button names lets you fit more buttons on the toolbar.

Edit the button name here.

9. Click the Close button to close the Customize dialog box.

Try applying some styles with your new toolbar. You can move the toolbar wherever you like, and display and hide it as you do all the other toolbars (refer to "Working with Toolbars" in Hour 2, "Getting Acquainted with Word").

Summary

Using styles can greatly reduce the time it takes to format (and reformat) your documents. If you work in an office, you can use styles to standardize the appearance of all the documents you and your coworkers generate. If you expect that styles will improve your quality of life, you will also benefit from the topic of the next hour, creating and modifying templates.

Q&A

Q I created a set of styles that I'd like to share with my coworkers. How do I do that?

A You have to store the styles in a template, not in a document. Then you have to make that template available to your coworkers. See the next hour to learn some strategies for doing this.

Q I created a toolbar for my styles, but there are no lines visually separating the buttons. Can I add them?

11

A Yes. To create separator lines between your toolbar buttons, start with the rightmost button in the toolbar. Hold down the Alt key as you drag the button slightly to the right, away from its neighbor. When you release the mouse button, the line appears. Working button by button to the left, continue this process to create the remaining separator lines.

Q **In this hour, I learned how to create a toolbar for my styles. Can I also create new toolbars for other commands?**

A Yes. You can certainly experiment with creating other toolbars for commands that you use frequently. In the Categories list in the Commands tab of the Customize dialog box, click the various categories to display the commands they contain on the right side of the dialog box. You can drag any of these commands to a toolbar to create a button for it.

HOUR 12

Working with Templates

In Hour 5, "Creating Documents with Templates and Wizards," you learned how to use the templates and wizards that come with Word to create documents with a minimum of fuss. In this hour, you gain more expertise in working with templates. To start with, you'll find out how to personalize Word's templates so that you have less typing and formatting to do in the documents you create with them. You then practice creating and modifying your own templates. Finally, you learn four "bonus point" techniques—changing the template that's attached to a document, copying items from one template to another, making items in one template available to all documents, and sharing your templates with others.

The highlights of this hour include

- Personalizing Word's templates
- Creating your own templates
- Modifying templates
- Attaching a template to the active document
- Copying items from one template to another

- Loading templates globally
- Sharing your templates with others

Understanding Templates

You can think of a template as a big bucket in which you store the things you need to work on a certain type of document. In addition to any formatting and text that you enter directly into a template, it can contain any combination of these items:

- Styles
- AutoText entries
- Toolbars
- Macros

You learned about styles in the last hour—they provide a convenient way of applying consistent formatting in your documents. AutoText entries are covered in Hour 14, "Editing Shortcuts." In a nutshell, AutoText entries let you enter blocks of text automatically. They are a great way of avoiding typing the same text over and over in multiple documents. Toolbars, as you know, let you issue commands with a click of the mouse. In the preceding hour, you found out how to create a toolbar for your styles. If you've experimented a bit (you are certainly encouraged to do so!), you may have discovered that you can use the same basic steps to create toolbars for any commands you use frequently. You are not likely to need the last item, macros, unless you are a true Word nerd, which most of us (thankfully) are not.

The default template, Normal, is unlike other templates in that it is *loaded globally*. This is a geeky way of saying that the styles, AutoText entries, toolbars, and macros stored in the Normal template are available to *all* documents that you create, even if you base them on other templates. In "Loading a Template Globally" at the end of this hour, you learn how to load other templates globally so that you can use the items they contain with other documents.

 In "The Advantages of Using Template or Wizard" in Hour 5, you learned about the advantages of using a template. If you need a refresher on the purpose of using templates, you might want to review that section now.

Personalizing Word's Templates

If you have tried one of the templates that comes with Word and like the look of the finished document, it's probably worth taking a few minutes to make the template your own. Wherever possible, you can replace the "Click here and type" placeholder text with your personal information. For example, if you're revising a letter template, you might fill in your own return address, company name, and signature block. You can also remove any text you don't need, and modify the formatting if desired.

After you've made these changes, creating letters based on the template will be a snap because you will need to fill in only the text that changes from one letter to the next.

To Do: Personalize One of Word's Templates

To personalize one of Word's templates, you create a new template based on Word's template and then modify it, as described in these steps:

1. Choose File, New to display the New dialog box.

2. Click the tab that contains the template you want to modify, and click the template. Under Create New in the lower-right corner of the dialog box, mark the Template option button. This tells Word to start a new template (not a document) based on the selected template (see Figure 12.1). Then click the OK button.

FIGURE 12.1

Word will create a new template based on the Contemporary Fax template.

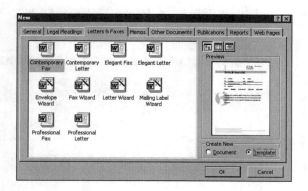

3. Word creates a new template based on the one you selected in the New dialog box. (Notice that the temporary name in the title bar begins with *Template*, not *Document*.) Fill in all the "Click here and type" prompts that should contain your own information, and leave the ones that you will need to change each time you use the template (see Figure 12.2).

FIGURE 12.2

The return address and sender have been filled in.

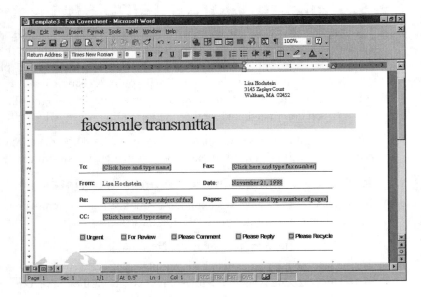

4. Delete or revise text in the template as needed, and make any changes to the formatting that you like. In Figure 12.3, the row of check boxes under the CC line was deleted, the words `facsimile transmittal` were changed to `fax`, and the return address was enlarged.

FIGURE 12.3

Delete, revise, and format the text in the template as needed.

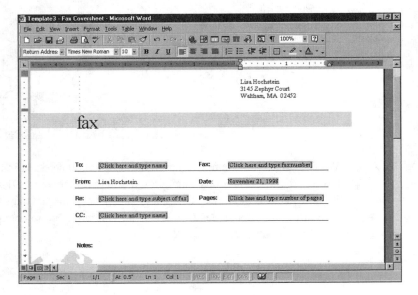

▼

5. Click the Save button in the Standard toolbar to display the Save As dialog box.

6. Because you're saving a template, Word automatically selects the Templates folder in the Save In list. (This folder is a subfolder of C:\Windows\Application Data\Microsoft.) If you save the template in the Templates folder itself, it appears in the General tab of the New dialog box. If this is what you want, skip to step 8.

7. If you want your template to appear in one of the other existing tabs in the New dialog box, create a subfolder of that name under the Templates folder. For example, to make your template appear in the Memos tab, create a Memos subfolder. If your template doesn't belong in any of the existing tabs, you can create a new one. Create a subfolder of the Templates folder with the name that you want to appear on the tab. A tab corresponding to this subfolder appears in the New dialog box the next time you display it. (Refer to "Creating Folders" in Hour 4, "Managing Documents," if you need help creating a subfolder of the Templates folder.) When you've created your subfolder, double-click it.

8. Type a name for the template in the File Name text box (see Figure 12.4), and click the Save button.

▲

FIGURE 12.4

The Lisa's Fax template will appear in the General tab of the New dialog box because it's being saved in the Templates folder itself.

12

You can easily differentiate between Word documents and templates by looking at the extension at the end of the filename. Documents have an extension of .doc, and templates have an extension of .dot. (If you don't see file extensions on your computer and you want to, double-click the My Computer icon on your desktop, choose View, Folder Options, click the View tab, clear the Hide File Extensions for Known File Types check box, and then click OK.)

Your new template now appears in the General tab of the New dialog box, or in another tab if you saved it in a subfolder of the Templates folder. Try using the template to see whether it works as you want it to. If you want to make further changes to it, see "Modifying Your Templates" later in this hour.

An alternative method of personalizing one of Word's templates is to start a new document based on the template and personalize the document. Then choose File, Save As, and specify Document Template in the Save As Type list in the Save As dialog box. Word automatically displays the Templates folder in the Save In list. Save the template in the Templates folder or in a subfolder of this folder.

Creating Your Own Templates

If Word doesn't provide a ready-made template for the type of documents you create, or if you want more control over the appearance of your documents, you will probably want to create a template from scratch. You do this by basing the new template on the "plain-vanilla" Normal template.

To Do: Create a Template from Scratch

To create a template from scratch, follow these steps:

1. Choose File, New to display the New dialog box.

2. In the General tab, make sure the Blank Document icon is selected (this is the Normal template). Under Create New in the lower-right corner of the dialog box, mark the Template option button, and click the OK button.

3. Word starts a new template based on the Normal template. Type and format the text that you want to appear in all documents based on this template. For example, if you're creating a template for business letters, you might include the letterhead, the beginning of the salutation, and the signature block. To make the template easy to use, you might also add placeholders for text that needs to be filled in. Figure 12.5 shows a simple letter template.

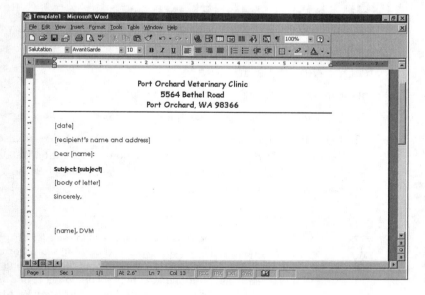

FIGURE 12.5

Type and format the template as desired, and insert placeholders in the appropriate spots.

4. If you want to include styles in the template, create them now (refer to the preceding hour if you need a refresher on creating styles). Because you're working with the template directly, not with a document based on the template, Word saves the styles in the template whether or not you mark the Add to Template check box in the New Style dialog box.

5. When you have completed the template, choose File, Save As, and save the file in the Templates folder or a subfolder of this folder.

▲

12

> If you have an existing document that contains all the text and formatting you want in your template, you can save the document as a template. First remove the text that's specific to that document. (For example, if you're creating a memo template, delete the recipient's name, the body of the memo, and so on.) Then replace the text you deleted with placeholders, and choose File, Save As. Specify Document Template in the Save As Type list in the Save As dialog box, and save the template in the Templates folder or a subfolder of this folder.

Modifying Your Templates

No matter how carefully you originally design your templates, you will sooner or later want to make some improvements.

To Do: Modify a Template

Follow these steps to make changes to a template:

1. Click the Open button in the Standard toolbar.

2. In the Files of Type list at the bottom of the Open dialog box, select Document Templates. Then navigate to the C:\Windows\Application Data\Microsoft\ Templates folder or one of its subfolders and double-click the template that you want to revise (see Figure 12.6).

> Instead of choosing Document Templates in the Files of Type list, which will display only templates, you can also choose All Word Documents. This option displays all manner of Word-related files, including .doc (standard document) and .dot (template) files. If you do select Document Templates, remember to switch back to Word Documents or All Word Documents the next time you want to open a .doc file.

FIGURE 12.6

Select Document Templates in the Files of Type list and double-click the template that you want to modify.

3. Revise your template as necessary.

4. Click the Save button in the Standard toolbar, and then close the template.

The preceding set of steps involves opening a template and making changes to it directly. This is not always necessary, however. When you close a document based on the Normal template after you've added, modified, or deleted any of the items you can store in templates (styles, toolbars, AutoText entries, and macros), Word automatically saves these changes to the template.

 If you want to be prompted to save changes to the Normal template, choose Tools, Options, click the Save tab, mark the Prompt to Save Normal Template button, and click OK.

When you close a document that is based on any template other than Normal, Word first asks whether you want to save changes to the document (if you have unsaved changes). If you have added, modified, or deleted any of the four items you can store in templates, Word then asks whether you want to save changes to the template. Click the Yes button to retain the changes.

Attaching a Template to the Active Document

You may encounter situations in which you need to change the template that's attached to a document. For example, you might click the New button in the Standard toolbar and type for a while in the new document before realizing that you had meant to base the document on a template other than Normal. Or someone may give you a document that is based on an older version of a template, and you want to update the document to the current version. Word lets you change the template that's attached to the active document with a few simple steps.

To Do: Attach a Different Template to the Active Document

To attach a different template to the active document, follow these steps:

1. Open the document to which you want to attach the template.
2. Choose Tools, Templates and Add-Ins to display the Templates and Add-Ins dialog box (see Figure 12.7).

12

▼ To Do

FIGURE 12.7

*Use the Templates and
Add-Ins dialog box
to attach a different
template to the active
document.*

3. The currently attached template is listed in the Document Template text box. To change it, click the Attach button.

4. In the Attach Template dialog box that appears, navigate to the folder that contains the template you want to attach, and then double-click it.

5. Back in the Templates and Add-Ins dialog box, the template you selected is now listed in the Document Template text box. If you want the styles in the document to update to the ones in the newly attached template, mark the Automatically Update Document Styles text box.

6. Click OK.

The styles, toolbars, AutoText entries, and macros in the newly attached template are now available in the active document. However, if the template you attached contains any text, the text will not be copied into the document.

Copying Items from One Template to Another

If you created a style, AutoText entry, toolbar, or macro in one template and now realize that you need it in another, you can copy the item to the other template.

To Do: Use the Organizer to Copy Items Among Templates

To copy an item from one template to another, follow these steps:

1. Choose Tools, Templates and Add-Ins to display the Templates and Add-Ins dialog box.

2. Click the Organizer button to display the Organizer, as shown in Figure 12.8. (An Organizer button is also available in the Styles dialog box—you can use either one.)

FIGURE 12.8

The Organizer lets you copy items among your various templates.

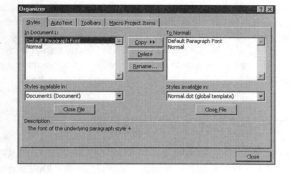

3. Click one of the two Close File buttons (it doesn't matter which one) to close the file whose contents are currently displayed on that side of the Organizer. The button name changes to Open File. Click this button to display the Open dialog box.

4. Navigate to the source template (the one that contains the item you want to copy) and double-click it.

5. Now click the second Close File button, and then click it again when it becomes an Open File button. In the Open dialog box, navigate to and double-click the target template (the one to which you want to copy the item).

6. Now that you have the source and target templates displayed in the Organizer, click each of the four tabs (Styles, AutoText, Toolbars, and Macro Project Items) to see what items each template contains.

7. When you locate the item in the source template that you want to copy, select it and click the Copy button in the middle of the Organizer (see Figure 12.9).

12

FIGURE 12.9

The Body Text style will be copied from the Normal template to the Vet's Letter template.

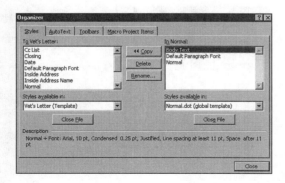

8. The item is copied to the target template. If you want to copy any other items, do so now, and then click the Close button to close the Organizer.

> You can also use the Organizer to copy styles from a document to a template. Just select a document in the Open dialog box in step 4 instead of a template. This is useful if you forgot to mark the Add to Template check box in the New Style or Modify Style dialog box when you were creating or modifying the style, and saved the style in the document instead of the template.

Loading a Template Globally

If you need to make the items in a template available in the active document, but you don't want to attach the template to the document, you can load the template globally. When a template is loaded globally, all the items it contains are available to all documents.

To Do: Load a Template Globally

Follow these steps to load a template globally:

1. Choose Tools, Templates and Add-Ins.
2. Click the Add button in the Templates and Add-Ins dialog box to display the Add Template dialog box.
3. Navigate to the template that you want to add globally and double-click it.
4. In the Templates and Add-Ins dialog box, the template now appears under Checked Items Are Currently Loaded (see Figure 12.10). (You can later clear the check box next to its name if you want to temporarily unload the template, or select it and click the Remove button to permanently unload it.)

FIGURE 12.10

The templates you selected appear in the Checked Items are Currently Loaded list.

5. Click the OK button.

If you want a template to load globally every time you start Word, copy the template to C:\Windows\ApplicationData\Microsoft\Word\Startup.

Sharing Your Template with Others

If you've invested a lot of time creating a spiffy new template, you may want to share this template with other people in your office so that they can use it as well. You can do this in a couple of different ways.

If you're on a network, you might be able to give everyone access to it by copying it to the folder designated in Word as the Workgroup Templates folder. If you aren't sure which folder this is, choose Tools, Options, click the File Locations tab, and look at the location listed to the right of Workgroup Templates. (Ask your network administrator for advice before proceeding.)

If you are not on a network, you can copy the template to the Templates folder (or one of its subfolders) on each of your coworkers' computers. If you use this method, you might want to require a password to modify the template, so people won't change it accidentally. To do so, choose File, Save As, click the Tools button at the top of the Save As dialog box, and choose General Options. In the Save dialog box that appears, enter a password in the Password to Modify text box and click OK to return to the Save As dialog box. Then continue saving as usual. People will be able to create documents based on the template, but they won't be able to modify the template itself.

Summary

Word provides templates for creating all kinds of documents. If you like one in particular, you can tweak it to make it your own. If you don't like Word's templates, or if none are designed for the type of documents you create, you can create a template from scratch so that it contains the exact text and formatting that you need. Templates can also store styles, AutoText entries, toolbars, and macros. Word gives you a variety of ways to access these items, regardless of what template they are stored in. This is the last of the hours on formatting. In the next hour, you move on to spelling and grammar features.

12

Q&A

Q Can I store templates in any folder?

A No. Word expects to find templates in the Templates folder or one of its subfolders, or in the folder designated as the Workgroup Templates folder.

Q I don't see the file extensions .doc and .dot for my documents and templates in the New, Open, and Save As dialog boxes. Why is that?

A By default, Windows hides file extensions for common file types. To display them, choose View, Folder Options in My Computer or Windows Explorer, click the View tab, clear the Hide File Extensions for Known File Types check box, and click OK.

Q I created my own template, and I want to see a preview of it in the New dialog box. Is this possible?

A Yes. Open your template and choose File, Properties. Mark the Save Preview Picture check box at the bottom of the Summary tab in the Properties dialog box, and click OK. The next time you select your template in the New dialog box, a preview of it will appear on the right side of the dialog box.

PART V
Timesavers

Hour

HOUR 13

Checking Your Spelling and Grammar and Using the Thesaurus

For most people, writing is a bear. If you're not wondering whether `vicissitude` has one s or two, you're probably trying to recall what your high school English teacher said about split infinitives, or hunting down a more interesting word to substitute for `interesting`. Although Word can't turn a clunky phrase into elegant prose, it can help you fix most spelling and grammar errors, and it can assist you in tracking down alternative word choices.

The highlights of this hour include

- Fixing flagged spelling and grammar errors
- Using the spelling and grammar checker
- Using the thesaurus

Correcting Spelling Errors Flagged by Word

Word's automatic spell checking monitors the characters you type and marks words that it doesn't find in its dictionary with red wavy lines (see Figure 13.1). This makes it easy to correct your spelling "on-the-fly" as you're typing.

FIGURE 13.1

When Word can't find a word in its dictionary, it marks it with a red wavy line.

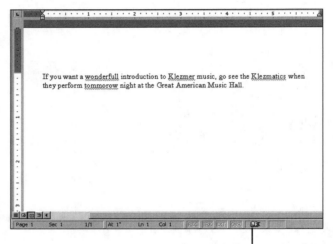

Spelling and Grammar Error Status

You may discover that Word fixes some of your typos automatically. It does this with its AutoCorrect feature, which you'll learn about in "Correcting Text Automatically" in the next hour.

To Do: Correct the Spelling of Words Marked with Red Wavy Lines

To correct the spelling of a word marked with a red wavy line, follow these steps:

1. Right-click the word.

2. A context menu appears with a list of possible spellings (see Figure 13.2). If you see the one you want, click it. Word makes the correction for you.

FIGURE 13.2

Click the correct spelling in the context menu.

3. If the mistake is one that you make frequently, point to AutoCorrect, and click the correct spelling in the submenu that appears to create this AutoCorrect entry, as shown in Figure 13.3. If you do this, Word corrects the spelling automatically from now on.

FIGURE 13.3

Create an AutoCorrect entry for a misspelling so that you don't have to fix it in the future.

4. If a word is spelled correctly and you use it frequently, click Add to add it to the dictionary so that Word won't catch it in the future (see Figure 13.4).

FIGURE 13.4

Add a word to the dictionary if you don't want Word to think it's misspelled in the future.

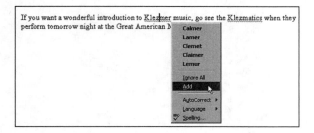

13

5. If a word is spelled correctly but you don't use it that often, choose Ignore All to prevent Word from marking it as a misspelling in this document only (see Figure 13.5).

FIGURE 13.5

If you just want to hide the red wavy line under a word, you can ask Word to ignore it.

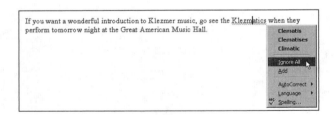

To move quickly from one possible spelling/grammar error to the next, double-click the Spelling and Grammar Error Status icon—the little book in the lower-right corner of the Word window (refer to Figure 13.1). Each time you double-click the icon, Word moves to the next mistake and displays the context menu you normally display by right-clicking the underlined word or phrase.

If you find the red wavy lines distracting, you can turn off automatic spell checking. Choose Tools, Options, click the Spelling & Grammar tab (see Figure 13.6), and clear the Check Spelling As You Type check box. If you just want to hide all the red wavy lines in the current document without turning off the automatic spell checking altogether, mark the Hide Spelling Errors in this Document check box; then click OK.

FIGURE 13.6

If the red wavy lines drive you nuts, you can hide them temporarily or turn them off permanently.

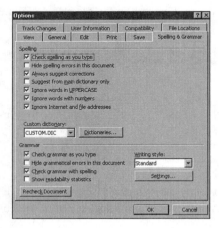

Correcting Grammar Errors Flagged by Word

When Word comes upon what it thinks is a possible grammar error in your document, it marks it with a green wavy line (see Figure 13.7). Depending on the error, it may mark anything from a single space (it catches double spaces between words) to an entire paragraph.

FIGURE 13.7

When Word thinks it's found a grammar error, it marks it with a green wavy line.

Imogen could also have been influenced by the two German photographers Albert Renger-Patzsch and Karl Blossfeldt, both of whom photographed plants extensively. Remember, she both spoke and read German, so their work would have been accessible to her. But her photos seem less "scientific" and "clinical" than theirs, and are also in many cases less straightforward and immediately recognizable, with shadows often playing as important a role as the plants themselves.[6] (See Figure 9, "Sempervivum Percarneum," by Renger-Patzsch.) On the West Coast, Margrethe Mather did plant photographs that Imogen admired greatly. In addition, she befriended James West, a German transplant to the West Coast and an expert in plants (he was instrumental in creating the University of California Botanical Garden[7]). They apparently went on occasional trips together to photograph plants.

To Do: Correct the Grammar of a Phrase Marked with a Green Wavy Line

To correct the grammar of text marked with a green wavy line, follow these steps:

1. Right-click the underlined text.
2. Word displays a context menu with suggested corrections.
3. If you see a correction that makes sense, click it (see Figure 13.8).

FIGURE 13.8

Click the correction that you want to use in the context menu.

4. If you want to leave your text as is, click Ignore.

Although the grammar checking feature is improved in Word 2000, you may find that more often than not, you disagree with its suggestions. If you want to turn off automatic grammar checking, choose Tools, Options, click the Spelling & Grammar tab, and clear the Check Grammar As You Type check box (refer to Figure 13.6). If you just want to hide the green wavy lines in the current document but keep automatic grammar checking enabled, mark the Hide Grammatical Errors in this Document check box. Then click OK.

13

Using the Spelling and Grammar Checker

The spell checker lets you check the spelling (and grammar) of an entire document all at once. You won't really need to use it if you use automatic spelling checking to fix your spelling "on-the-fly." However, if you've disabled automatic spell checking, or if you're working on a rather large document, the spelling and grammar checker comes in handy.

To Do: Check Your Spelling and Grammar with the Spelling and Grammar Checker

1. Press Ctrl+Home to move the insertion point to the top of the document. (The spell check starts at the location of the insertion point.)

2. Click the Spelling and Grammar button on the Standard toolbar (or press F7, or choose Tools, Spelling and Grammar) to start checking your document (see Figure 13.9).

FIGURE 13.9

Click the Spelling and Grammar button in the Standard toolbar to start the spelling and grammar check.

Spelling and Grammar

3. Word displays the Spelling and Grammar dialog box (see Figure 13.10). As soon as you click a button in the dialog box to tell Word how to handle a possible misspelling or grammatical error, it goes on to the next error. When Word finds a spelling error, it highlights it in red in the top half of the dialog box. If you see the correct spelling, click it and click the Change button (or click Change All to change it throughout the document).

If you don't want Word to look for grammatical problems during the spell check, clear the Check Grammar check box in the lower-left corner of the Spelling and Grammar dialog box.

FIGURE 13.10

The Spelling and Grammar dialog box lets you check the spelling and grammar in your document all at once.

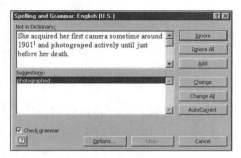

4. Sometimes Word doesn't offer the correct spelling for a misspelled word. If this happens, select the word in the top half of the dialog box, type over it with the correct spelling, and click the Change button.

5. If the word is spelled correctly and you plan to use it often, click the Add button to add it to the dictionary.

6. To leave the word as is, click Ignore to ignore it this once or Ignore All to ignore it throughout the document.

7. When Word has finished the spell check, it displays a message box to inform you of that fact. Click OK.

If you want to exclude a section of your document from the spell check, select the text before running the spell check and choose Tools, Language, Set Language. In the Language dialog box, mark the Do Not Check Spelling or Grammar check box, and click OK.

Editing the Dictionary

If you add a word to the dictionary accidentally, you can remove it so that Word will start flagging it as a possible misspelling again.

By default, when you click the Add command in the context menu that appears when you right-click a possible misspelling, or when you click the Add button in the Spelling and Grammar dialog box, Word adds the word to a dictionary file called Custom.dic. You can open this file in a Word window and revise it to remove, edit, or add words.

To Do: Remove, Edit, or Add Words in Custom.dic

To edit the contents of your dictionary, follow these steps:

1. Choose Tools, Options, and click the Spelling and Grammar tab in the Options dialog box.

2. Click the Dictionaries button to display the Custom Dictionaries dialog box, and click the Edit button.

3. The custom dictionary, Custom.dic, opens in a Word window. This file contains a list of all the words you've added to the dictionary, each one on a separate line. Delete any words that you want Word to flag as possible misspellings in the future. You can also edit the words in the dictionary or add new ones. (Make sure to type each new word on a separate line.)

4. When you have finished, save and close Custom.dic.

13

5. Word disables automatic spell checking when you modify Custom.dic. To turn it on again, choose Tools, Options, click the Spelling and Grammar tab, mark the Check Spelling As You Type check box, and click OK.

Using the Thesaurus

If you find yourself overusing a particular word and want to find a good synonym for it, or if you want to get some ideas for livening up your text, Word's thesaurus can help.

To Do: Use the Thesaurus to Look for Synonyms

To use the thesaurus, follow these steps:

1. Select the word that you want to look up, and press Shift+F7 (or choose Tools, Language, Thesaurus).

2. Word displays the Thesaurus dialog box with the word you selected in the Looked Up list (see Figure 13.11). If the selected meaning in the Meanings list is not the one you need, double-click a different one.

The Thesaurus dialog box lets you hunt for alternative word choices.

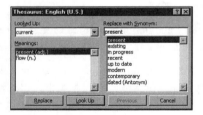

3. If you want to see the synonyms of a word in the Replace with Synonyms list on the right side of the dialog box, double-click the word.

> If you want to look up synonyms for a word that isn't in the Replace with Synonyms list, select the current entry in the Replace with Synonym text box, type over it with the word whose synonyms you want to look up, and click the Look Up button.

4. Word places the new word in the Looked Up list and displays the synonyms for that word. If you want to go back to a previous definition, click the Previous button.

5. When you see the word that you want to use, click it and click the Replace button. Word replaces the selected word in your document with the one you chose.

If you want to quickly look up the synonyms for a word without taking a trip to the Thesaurus dialog box, just right-click the word and point to Synonyms in the context menu to display a list of synonyms. In Figure 13.12, the user right-clicked the word `lifelong`. Click the synonym you want, or click Thesaurus at the bottom of the submenu if you decide to visit the Thesaurus dialog box after all.

FIGURE 13.12

A list of synonyms is a right-click away.

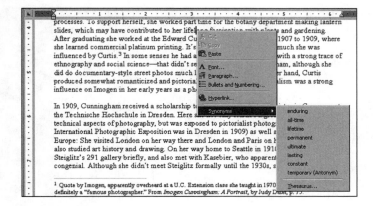

Summary

Word's spelling, grammar, and thesaurus features are no substitute for careful writing and proofreading, but they can definitely help you produce clean and well-written documents. In the next hour, you add to your bag of tricks with several time-saving editing features.

Q&A

Q I told Word to ignore some possible misspellings and now I'm not so sure I was right. How can I get Word to mark these words again?

A You can tell Word to reflag all possible spelling and grammar errors in the current document. Choose Tools, Options, click the Spelling and Grammar tab, click the Recheck Document button, click Yes in the message box that appears, and then click OK.

Q I have used a formal writing style in a document, and Word is suggesting all sorts of grammatical changes to make the prose more casual. Can I tell it that this document is supposed to be formal?

A Yes. You can set the writing style on which Word should base its grammar check. To do this, choose Tools, Options, click the Spelling & Grammar tab, and select the desired style in the Writing Style list. (To see what Word checks for this writing

13

style—and optionally modify the list—click the Settings button to display the Grammar Settings dialog box, and click OK when done.) Then click OK in the Options dialog box.

HOUR 14

Editing Shortcuts

If you type only an occasional short document, you won't have much need for the features discussed in this hour. If, however, you generate a substantial number of documents, the shortcuts you learn here soon become an essential part of your repertoire. As an added benefit, facile use of these features is a surefire way to impress your coworkers or family members.

The highlights of this hour include

- Correcting text automatically
- Inserting standard blocks of text
- Finding and replacing text
- Inserting the date
- Inserting fields
- Inserting symbols
- Sorting lists

Correcting Text Automatically

Word's AutoCorrect feature fixes spelling errors for you automatically. For example, if you type *hte*, AutoCorrect changes it to *the*. By default, AutoCorrect makes corrections based on suggestions from the spell checker. It also has its own list of many commonly misspelled words, and you can add your own favorite typos to the list. In addition, you can use AutoCorrect to automatically enter special symbols, long names, or phrases that you have to type frequently.

To Do: Create an AutoCorrect Entry

Follow these steps to add an entry to the list of words that AutoCorrect corrects automatically:

1. Choose Tools, AutoCorrect to display the AutoCorrect dialog box.

2. Scroll down the list at the bottom of the AutoCorrect tab to see what AutoCorrect knows how to fix. Word replaces the items in the left column with the items in the right column. At the top of the list are symbols, followed by a large number of commonly misspelled words.

3. To add an entry, click in the Replace text box and type the misspelling.

4. Click in the With text box and type the correct spelling (see Figure 14.1).

Type the misspelling in the Replace text box and the correct spelling in the With text box.

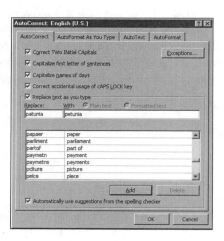

5. Click the Add button. The new entry appears in the list.

 6. Click OK.

Try typing the misspelled word. As soon as you press the Spacebar or Enter, Word replaces it with the correct spelling.

If you add an AutoCorrect entry and later decide to delete it, choose Tools, AutoCorrect, click the entry in the list in the AutoCorrect tab, click the Delete button, and click OK.

If you want to use AutoCorrect to insert a long name or phrase, type an abbreviation for the phrase in the Replace box, and type the full spelling in the With box. For example, you could type *napf* in the Replace box and *National Association of Poodle Fanciers* in the With box.

If you enter an abbreviation for a long name or phrase in the Replace box, choose one that you don't ever want to leave "as is" in your document, because Word changes it to the full "correct" spelling every time you type it. (If AutoCorrect does make a change that you want to undo, however, you can always click the Undo button on the Standard toolbar or press Ctrl+Z to reverse the change.)

Inserting Standard Blocks of Text Automatically

AutoText is an extremely handy feature enabling Word to "memorize" large blocks of text. Once you've created an AutoText entry, you can insert it in your text by simply beginning to type the name of the entry. As soon as you've typed the first few characters, Word's AutoComplete feature takes over and inserts the entire block of text for you.

One of the advantages of using AutoText is that you only have to proofread the block of text once, before you create the AutoText entry. From then on, each time you insert the entry in a document, you can rest assured that it is error-free.

Creating AutoText Entries

Creating an AutoText entry is relatively easy.

To Do: Create an AutoText Entry

1. Type the text that you want Word to "memorize," and then select it.
2. Choose Insert, AutoText, New (or press Alt+F3) to display the Create AutoText dialog box.
3. Type over Word's suggested name with your own name for the entry. (Choose a name that is at least four characters long.) See Figure 14.2.

14

FIGURE 14.2

Type a name for your AutoText entry in the Create AutoText dialog box.

    4. Click OK.

Word comes with an AutoText toolbar (View, Toolbars, AutoText) that contains a New button. If the toolbar is displayed, you can click this button in step 2 to bring up the Create AutoText dialog box.

Inserting an AutoText Entry in Your Document

Word provides several ways of insertion AutoText entries your document. The method described in these steps is the simplest.

To Do: Insert an AutoText Entry

Follow these steps to insert an AutoText entry in your document:

1. Click where you want to insert the entry.
2. Type the first few letters of the name. A ScreenTip appears for your entry (see Figure 14.3).

FIGURE 14.3

As soon as you type the first few letters of an AutoText entry's name, a ScreenTip appears.

    3. Press Enter to insert the entry in your document.

One other convenient way to insert an entry is to type the full name of the entry and press F3 when the insertion point is just past the name.

Revising and Deleting AutoText Entries

If you want to revise the text for an AutoText entry but keep its name the same, type the new version of the text, select it, choose Insert, AutoText, New, type its name in the Create AutoText dialog box and click OK. Word asks whether you want to redefine the AutoText entry. Click the Yes button.

To delete an AutoText entry, choose Insert, AutoText, Autotext to display the AutoText tab of the AutoCorrect dialog box. Click the entry in the middle of the dialog box, click the Delete button, and click OK.

Finding and Replacing Text Automatically

Any time you find yourself about to embark on a time-consuming hunt through a long document for a word or phrase, or for certain formatting, see whether Word's Find and Replace features can do the work for you.

Finding Text

If you frequently type long documents, you have probably had the experience of scrolling through each page trying to find all of the places where you used a particular word or phrase. Word can help you with this process, searching for text much more quickly and accurately than we humans can.

To Do: Find Text

1. Choose Edit, Find (or press Ctrl+F) to display the Find tab of the Find and Replace dialog box (see Figure 14.4).

FIGURE 14.4

Use the Find tab of the Find and Replace dialog box to search for text.

14

2. Type the text that you want to find in the Find What text box.

3. Click the Find Next button. Word highlights the first occurrence of the word.

4. Continue to click the Find Next button to look for more matches.

5. Click OK when Word informs you that it has found all the matches.

6. Click the Cancel button in the Find and Replace dialog box.

If you want to be more specific about what text you're looking for, click the More button to expand the dialog box and display more options (see Figure 14.5). To collapse the dialog box again, click the Less button.

FIGURE 14.5

Click the More button to expand the dialog box, and the Less button to collapse it.

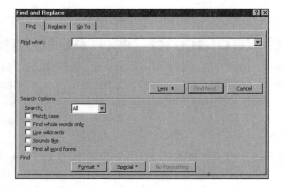

By default, Word searches the entire document for the Find What text. If you want to search up or down from the location of the insertion point, change the option in the Search list from All to Up or Down. The five check boxes work as described here:

- Match Case—Mark this check box if you want to find only occurrences of the word that have the same combination of upper and lowercase letters that you typed in the Find What box.

- Find Whole Words Only—Use this option if you don't want Word to find the search text when it's part of another word. For example, you'd mark this check box if you wanted to find only the word *cat*, not *catch*, *decathlon*, or *scathing*.

- Use Wildcards—Mark this option if you want to use wildcard characters in the Find What text. You can enter wildcards by typing them directly, or by clicking the Special button and choosing them from a list. (To learn more about wildcards, look up information on Find and Replace in Word's help system.)

- Sounds Like—This option finds words that sound like the text you're searching for; use it if you're not sure of the spelling.

- Find All Word Forms—Use this option to find all forms of the word. For example, if you search for *sing*, Word also finds *sings, sang, sung, and singing*.

Replacing Text

Sometimes you not only need to find text, you also have to replace it with something else. Word's Replace feature takes the tedium out of making the same change in several places.

To Do: Replace Text

Follow these steps to search for text and replace it with something else:

1. Choose Edit, Replace (or press Ctrl+H) to display the Replace tab of the Find and Replace dialog box (see Figure 14.6).

To Do

FIGURE 14.6

Use the Replace tab of the Find and Replace dialog box to search for and replace text.

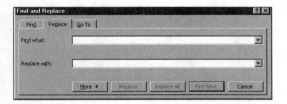

2. Type the text that you want to find in the Find What text box.
3. In the Replace With text box, type the text that you want to replace the Find What text.
4. Click the Find Next button.
5. Word highlights the first occurrence of the word. To replace it, click the Replace button.
6. To skip this instance without making the change, click the Find Next button.
7. Continue this process. If you don't need to confirm every replacement, click the Replace All button.
8. Click OK when Word informs you that it has found all the matches.
9. Click the Close button in the Find and Replace dialog box.

If you change your mind about a replace operation after completing it, you can click the Undo button in the Standard toolbar to undo the replacements one by one if you used the Replace button, or all at once if you used the Replace All button.

If you like, you can customize your find and replace operation by using the options in the expanded version of the Find and Replace dialog box (refer to Figure 14.5) .

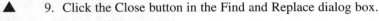

14

Finding and Replacing Formatting

You can use Find and Replace as a quick way to search for and replace formatting in your document.

To Do: Find and Replace Formatting

To modify formatting with Find and Replace, follow these steps:

1. Display the Replace tab of the Find and Replace dialog box, and click in the Find What text box. (If the dialog box isn't already expanded, click the More button.)

2. Click the Format button, and click the command that leads to the formatting option you want to search for. For example, if you want to search for boldface, click the Font command.

3. Select the desired formatting option in the dialog box that appears, and click OK.

4. The formatting is now listed beneath the Find What box.

5. Click in the Replace With text box and use the Format button to specify the formatting that you want to replace the Find What formatting (see Figure 14.7). If you want to strip off the Find What formatting without replacing it, choose the default formatting. For example, to remove boldface, you would choose Not Bold in the Font Style list in the Font dialog box.

FIGURE 14.7

Use the Format button to select the formatting to find and replace.

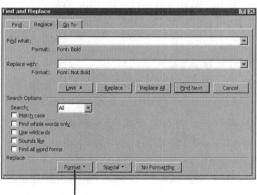

Click to select formatting.

6. Continue with the usual replace procedure.

To remove formatting from the Find What or Replace With text boxes when you perform future find and replace operations, click in the appropriate text box and click the No Formatting button.

If you like, you can combine formatting and text in the Find and Replace dialog box. For example, you could type the words *Puget Sound* in the Find What text box, and then type *Puget Sound* in the Replace With text box and specify a single underline. This would search for and underline every instance of *Puget Sound* in your document.

Finding and Replacing Special Characters

In addition to finding and replacing regular text and formatting, you can also work with special characters. This enables you to do such things as searching for manual page breaks and fields, removing extra blank lines, and so on. As you'll see, Word uses a code that consists of the caret symbol (^) followed by a single letter to represent each special character. For example, the code for a paragraph mark is ^p. Fortunately, you don't have to memorize these—you can simply select the special characters from a list.

To Do: Find and Replace Special Characters

Follow these steps to search for and replace special characters:

1. Display the Replace tab of the Find and Replace dialog box, and click in the Find What text box. If the dialog box isn't already expanded, click the More button.

2. Click in the Find What text box, click the Special button to display a list of special characters, and click the one you want. Depending on what you're doing, you may need to enter more than one symbol in the text box. For example, if your goal is to remove the tabs at the beginning of each paragraph and separate the paragraphs with blank lines instead, you would enter ^p^t in the Find What text box to search for a paragraph mark (which ends each paragraph) followed by a tab character (which begins the next paragraph).

3. Click in the Replace With text box and use the Special button to insert the characters replacing the ones in the Find With text box. Using the same example, you would enter ^p^p in the Replace With text box to replace each instance of a paragraph mark followed by a tab with two paragraph marks, thus removing the tab and adding a blank line (see Figure 14.8).

▼ To Do

14

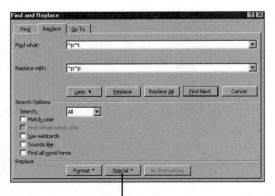

Click to select special characters.

After you have learned the codes that Word uses for the various special characters, you can type them directly into the Find What and Replace With text boxes instead of using the Special button.

▲ 4. Continue with the usual replace procedure.

You can combine text and symbols in the Find What and Replace With text boxes if you like. For example, you could search for the word *Part* wherever it follows a manual page break by typing ^mPart in the Find What box. (The symbol for a manual page break is ^m.)

Inserting the Date

Your computer has a clock that keeps track of the date and the time. Instead of typing the entire date yourself, you can have Word take this information from the computer and insert it for you.

To Do: Insert the Date by Starting to Type It

Follow these steps to insert the date:

1. Begin typing today's date. After you type the month and a space after it, a ScreenTip containing the completed date appears (see Figure 14.9).

FIGURE 14.9

A ScreenTip appears after you type the month in the current date.

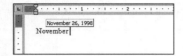

 2. Press Enter to let Word fill in the rest of the date for you.

> Whenever you start typing a month that is longer than five letters, a ScreenTip containing the completed month appears. Press Enter to insert the month quickly.

You can also insert the date as a *field*, which lets Word update it to the current date for you when you open the document in the future. Inserting a date as a field is useful in documents that you open frequently because the date is always current. The drawback to doing this is that you don't have a date within the document that verifies when the document was first created and saved.

To Do: Insert the Date As a Field

If you want to insert the date as a field, follow these steps:

1. Choose Insert, Date and Time to display the Date and Time dialog box (see Figure 14.10).

FIGURE 14.10

The Date and Time dialog box enables you to insert the date as a field.

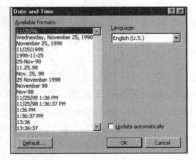

2. Mark the Update Automatically check box.

3. Click the date format that you want to use.

4. If you want to use this format all of the time, click the Default button, and then click Yes in the message box that appears.

5. Click OK in the Date and Time dialog box.

14

The keyboard shortcut for inserting the date as a field is Alt+Shift+D.

To delete a date that you've inserted as a field, select it first (it appears as white text on a gray background when it's selected), and then press Delete or Backspace.

 If Word inserts the wrong date in your document, you have to correct your computer's clock. Double-click the time at the right end of the taskbar to display the Date/Time Properties dialog box. Specify the correct date in the Date & Time tab, and click OK.

Inserting Other Fields

You already know how to insert page number and date fields. Word lets you insert many other types of fields as well. For example, you can insert the FileName field in the footer so that the document's file name prints at the bottom of every page, or you can add the UserAddress field to the top of a letter to quickly insert your return address. You may not need to use any of these other fields, but it's worth poking around a bit to see if some of them might make your life easier. As you work with fields, these tips may come in handy:

- To force a field to update, select it and press F9. If you want to update all of the fields in your document, select the entire document and press F9.
- To see the underlying field code instead of the result of the code, select the field and press Shift+F9. To switch back to seeing the results of the code, press Shift+F9 again.
- To control whether fields appear gray in your documents, choose Tools, Options, click the View tab, and display the Field Shading list. If you only want them to turn gray when they're selected, choose When Selected. If you want them to always be gray, choose Always. If you don't want them to ever appear gray, choose Never. Then click OK. The gray shading just makes it easier for you to differentiate between fields and regular text onscreen—it doesn't print.
- To convert a field to regular text so that it won't update automatically, select the field and press Shift+Ctrl+F9. If you do this, you can't convert it back to a field again.
- To delete any field, select it and then press Delete or Backspace.

To Do: Insert a Field

Follow these steps to insert a field in your document:

1. Move the insertion point to the location where you want to insert the field. In many cases, you want to insert the field in the header or footer. (See "Creating Headers and Footers" in Hour 10 if you need help.)

2. Choose Insert, Field to display the Field dialog box (see Figure 14.11).

FIGURE 14.11

The Field dialog box enables you to insert all kinds of fields in your document.

3. Click various categories in the Categories list on the left. The fields in the selected category appear in the Field Names list on the right.

> Some of the categories containing fields that are useful to average (not nerdy) Word users are Date and Time, Document Information, and User Information.

4. When you find the field that you want to insert, click it in the Field Names list. It appears in the Field Codes text box.

5. Customize the field with switches if you like (see the remainder of this section), and click OK to insert the field in your document.

You can modify many fields with switches. A *switch* is an optional instruction telling Word to revise the format of the field in some way. Some switches are general (meaning you can use them with any field), while others are specific to individual fields. All switches begin with a backslash (\), followed by a symbol or a lowercase letter. As an example of a useful switch, you can add the \p switch to the FileName field to include the path in the filename. If you use \p, the field not only displays the name of the document itself, such as *resume.doc*, it also displays the location of the file, as in *c:\my documents\job search\resume.doc*.

14

To Do: Modify the Formatting of a Field

To add one or more switches to your field, follow these steps:

1. Follow the first four steps in the "Insert a Field" steps.

2. Click the Options button in the lower-left corner of the Field dialog box to display the Field Options dialog box (see Figure 14.12).

FIGURE 14.12

Use the Field Options dialog box to add switches to your field.

3. If you want to add a general switch to your field, click it in the General Switches tab and click the Add to Field button.

4. If you want to add a switch that's particular to your field, click the Field Specific Switches tab, and click the switch you want to add in the Switch list. If you aren't sure what a switch does, select it and read the description at the bottom of the dialog box (see Figure 14.13).

FIGURE 14.13

Use the Field-Specific Switches tab to add a switch that is specific to your field.

5. Click OK, and then click OK in the Field dialog box to insert the field in your document.

If you know the switch that you want to use, you can just type it after the field name in the Field Codes text box at the bottom of the Field dialog box. (Make sure to include a space between the field name and the first switch. If you are including more than one switch, you do not need spaces between them.)

Inserting Symbols and Special Characters

Many everyday documents, such as letters and memos, require special characters here and there. For example, you might need to use the trademark symbol (™), a long dash (—), or the ellipsis (…). Word inserts many of these symbols for you automatically as you type. If it doesn't insert the one you need, you can likely find it in the Symbol dialog box.

To see what symbols Word inserts automatically, first choose Tools, AutoCorrect to display the AutoCorrect dialog box, and click the AutoCorrect tab. As you saw in "Correcting Text Automatically" earlier in this hour, when you type the characters in the left column, Word replaces them with the symbols on the right. Next, click the AutoFormat As You Type tab. The Replace As You Type options in the middle of the dialog box insert many symbols for you as well (see Figure 14.14). Click the Cancel button to close the AutoCorrect dialog box.

FIGURE 14.14

The Replace As You Type options insert many symbols for you as you type.

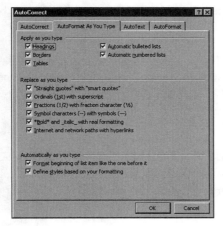

14

To Do: Insert Symbols Yourself

To insert a less commonly used symbol, follow these steps:

1. Click where you want the symbol to go, and choose Insert, Symbol (see Figure 14.15).

FIGURE **14.15**

The Symbol dialog box lets you insert all sorts of symbols.

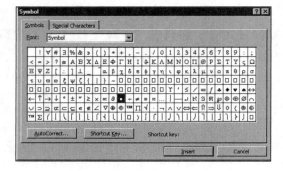

2. Click the Symbols tab if it isn't already in front. Look through the symbols in the grid. If you want to see one more clearly, click it to magnify it.

3. If you don't see the symbol you want, display the Font drop-down list, and choose a different font set. (The Webdings and Wingdings sets include a lot of fun symbols.)

 4. To insert a symbol, double-click it, and then click the Close button.

You can enlarge symbols that you've inserted in your document just like regular text. Drag over a symbol to select it, and then choose a larger point size from the Font Size drop-down list in the Formatting toolbar.

Sorting Lists

Many people aren't aware that Word enables you to sort lists in alphabetical order, or by number or date. Remember this feature the next time you have to type up a phone list!

Sort a List

To sort a list, follow these steps:

1. Select the entire list.

2. Choose Table, Sort to display the Sort Text dialog box (see Figure 14.16).

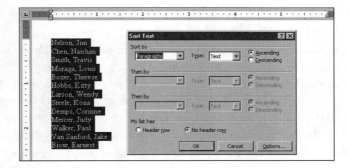

FIGURE 14.16

Select all of the paragraphs you want to sort, and then display the Sort Text dialog box.

3. By default, Word assumes you want to sort your paragraphs alphabetically, so Text is selected in the Type box. (If you want to sort by numbers or by date instead, choose Numbers or Date in the Type list.)

4. Click OK to sort the list.

> You can also use the Sort Text dialog box to sort rows in a table. You'll learn how to do this in Hour 16, "Columns and Tables."

Summary

You can create perfectly respectable documents without using anything that you learned about in this hour. But if you do use even a few of these editing shortcuts, you can greatly reduce, or even eliminate, the tedious and repetitious typing that often goes along with word processing. In the next hour, you learn a variety of techniques for working with long documents.

Q&A

Q I created some AutoText entries that I want to share with my coworkers. How do I do that?

A AutoText entries are stored in templates, so you need to give your coworkers access to the template containing the entries you created. Refer to "Copying Items from One Template to Another" in Hour 12, "Working with Templates," if you have to move your AutoText entries to the template. Review "Sharing Your Templates with Others" in Hour 12 if you need suggestions for ways to share your template.

14

Q **The Insert, AutoText contains categories such as Attention Line, Closing, and Header/Footer. What are these?**

A Each of these menu items leads to a submenu of "prefabricated" AutoText entries that come with Word. To use one of these entries, simply click in the desired location and choose it from the submenu. If you create your own entries, they also appear in the Insert, AutoText menu, under the category Normal (for the Normal style). The exception to this is if the first paragraph in an entry is formatted with another style. In this case, the entry is listed under that style.

Q **As I'm using the Find and Replace dialog box, I frequently spot things in my text that I want to edit. Do I have to close the dialog box before making these changes?**

A No. The Find and Replace dialog box is one of the few dialog boxes that can remain open while you edit your text. Just drag the dialog box's title bar to move it out of the way, and then click in your text to deactivate the dialog box and activate your document. When you want to go back to using the dialog box, click its title bar to activate it.

Hour 15

Working with Long Documents

If you have to type long documents—reports, proposals, school papers, journal articles, and manuals—you will probably appreciate the features discussed in this hour. Although you can use all these features with documents of any length, they come into play most frequently with documents that are at least a few pages long.

The highlights of this hour include

- Creating footnotes and endnotes
- Using the Document Map to navigate among headings
- Modifying the heading structure of your document
- Creating a table of contents
- Bookmarking specific locations in your document
- Adding hyperlinks to your text

Inserting Footnotes and Endnotes

Word does a great job of handling footnotes and endnotes. It inserts the reference mark (usually a number) in the text for you, separates the footnotes or endnotes from the document text with a thin horizontal line, and keeps the numbering sequential. With footnotes, Word adjusts the automatic page breaks to make room for the footnote text. In case you're not clear about the distinction between a footnote and an endnote, a footnote appears at the bottom of the page that contains the reference mark (see Figure 15.1) and an endnote appears at the end of the document.

FIGURE 15.1

These footnotes were added with Word's Footnotes and Endnotes feature.

Adding footnotes is a snap.

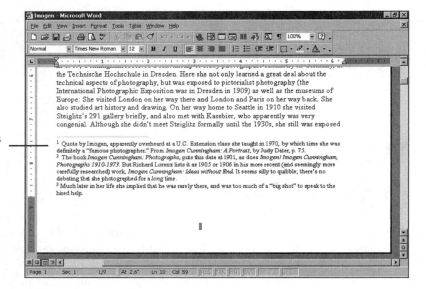

To Do: Insert a Footnote or Endnote

Follow these steps to insert a footnote or endnote:

1. Choose View, Print Layout if you aren't already in Print Layout view.
2. Click where you want to insert the reference mark for the footnote.
3. Choose Insert, Footnote to display the Footnote and Endnote dialog box (see Figure 15.2).

FIGURE 15.2

Use the Footnote and Endnote dialog box to insert footnotes or endnotes in your document.

4. If you want to insert an endnote, mark the Endnote option button. Otherwise, leave the Footnote option button marked. (The remaining steps assume you're inserting a footnote, but the process is virtually identical.)

5. By default, your footnotes will be numbered beginning with 1, and will appear at the bottom of the page. If these settings are okay, skip to step 6. If you want to change them, click the Options button to display the Note Options dialog box (see Figure 15.3).

FIGURE 15.3

The Note Options dialog box lets you customize the appearance of your footnotes and endnotes.

6. Make any changes you like in this dialog box, and click OK.

7. Click OK in the Footnote and Endnote dialog box.

8. Word inserts reference marks for the footnote in the text and at the bottom of the page, adds a horizontal line above the footnote, and places the insertion point immediately to the right of the reference mark in the footnote. Type your footnote text.

If you are using Normal view when you insert a footnote, Word opens a special footnote pane at the bottom of the document window. When you are finished typing the footnote, click the Close button at the top of the footnote pane.

15

> The keyboard shortcut to insert a footnote is Alt+Ctrl+F. The shortcut for inserting an endnote is Alt+Ctrl+D. Both of these bring you to step 7 in the previous set of steps, bypassing the Footnote and Endnote dialog box altogether.

To quickly view your footnote, rest your mouse pointer over the reference mark in the text. A ScreenTip with the footnote text appears, as shown in Figure 15.4. You can also see your footnotes in the bottom margin as they will appear when printed in both Print Layout view and Print Preview (as shown earlier in Figure 15.1). A quick way to jump to a particular footnote is to double-click its reference mark.

FIGURE 15.4

Word displays your footnote text in a ScreenTip when you rest the mouse pointer over a footnote reference.

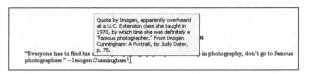

If you need to move a footnote's reference mark in the text, select it and then cut and paste it (either with drag and drop or the Cut and Paste commands) to the new location. If you move the reference mark to a different page, the footnote text automatically moves to that page. By the same token, if the text containing a reference mark shifts onto another page as you're editing your document, the footnote text moves with it as well. To delete a footnote, select its reference mark and press Delete. The footnote text is automatically deleted

Navigating with the Document Map

Word 97 comes with a feature called Document Map, which lets you view an outline of your document onscreen as you work and quickly navigate among headings. This feature works properly only if you have applied heading styles or outline levels to your headings. (See "Creating Styles for Your Headings" in Hour 11, "Working with Styles," to review options for doing this.)

To Do: Use the Document Map

Follow these steps to use the Document Map:

1. Click the Document Map button in the Standard toolbar.

15

2. An outline of your document appears in a pane on the left side of the Word window, as shown in Figure 15.5. The document in the figure contains two heading levels, formatted with the Heading 1 and Heading 2 styles. To navigate to another section of your document, click the desired heading in the Document Map.

FIGURE 15.5

Click the Document Map button in the Standard toolbar to display the Document Map to the left of your document.

Document Map ———

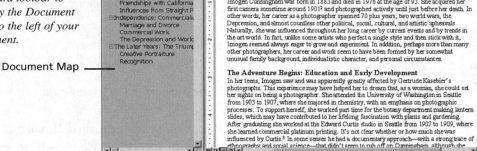

3. You can expand and collapse the outline in the Document Map by right-clicking the Document Map and clicking the heading level that you want to view in the context menu. In Figure 15.6, the Document Map has been collapsed to show only the top-level headings, and the context menu is displayed.

FIGURE 15.6

Click the heading level that you want to display in the context menu.

4. To expand an individual heading in the Document Map to display its subheadings, click the plus sign next to its name. The plus sign changes to a minus sign. To collapse the heading again (thus hiding its subheadings), click the minus sign.

5. To close the Document Map, click the Document Map toolbar button again.

Organizing Your Outline

If you have applied heading styles (or outline levels) to the headings in your document, you can use Outline view to examine and modify the heading structure of your document.

To Do: Work with Your Document in Outline View

To use Outline view, follow these steps:

1. Choose View, Outline, or click the Outline View button in the lower-left corner of the Word window.

2. Word switches to Outline view and displays the Outlining toolbar. Headings that contain subheadings and/or body text have plus signs to the left of their names. Those that are currently empty have minus signs. To collapse the outline down to your top-level headings, click the Show Heading 1 button in the Outlining toolbar (see Figure 15.7).

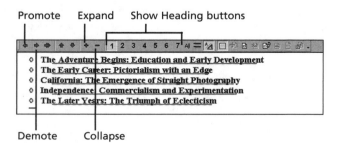

Promote   Expand   Show Heading buttons

Demote   Collapse

3. To further expand the view of your outline, click the desired Show Heading button. (For example, to display the top three heading levels in your document, click the Show Heading 3 button.)

4. To expand an individual heading to see all of its subheadings, click the plus sign to its left to select it (the mouse pointer changes to a four-headed arrow when you point to the plus sign), and then click the Expand button in the Outlining toolbar. To collapse the view of a heading, select it and click the Collapse toolbar button.

▼

5. To restyle a heading to demote it one level or promote it one level, select it and then click the Promote or Demote buttons in the Outlining toolbar. Word applies the appropriate heading style. For example, if you demote a heading formatted with the Heading 2 style, Word reformats it with the Heading 3 style.

6. To move a heading (along with all the subheadings and body text it contains) to a new location in the document, drag its plus sign. As you drag, a horizontal line indicates where the heading will appear. When the line is in the right place, release the mouse button.

7. When you're finished using Outline view, use the View menu or the View buttons to go to another view.

▲

If you want to print an outline of your document, switch to Outline view, collapse your outline to the level that you want to print, and click the Print button in the Standard toolbar.

Generating a Table of Contents

Rather than painstakingly typing a table of contents yourself, and then retyping it whenever the page numbers or headings change, you can have Word handle this for you.

As with the Document Map and Outline view, you have to apply heading styles before creating a table of contents. Word uses heading styles to locate your headings and decide how to format them in the table of contents it generates. Asking Word to create a table of contents for you has three advantages:

- The table of contents is actually a field, so you can update it at any time to reflect changes in your document. Word can update both the headings and page numbers or just the page numbers.

- Each heading in the table of contents is a hyperlink that leads to that heading in the document text. The hyperlinks let your table of contents double as a navigation tool. (You'll learn more about hyperlinks in "Inserting Hyperlinks" at the end of this hour.)

- Most importantly, you don't have to type the whole thing yourself.

To Do: Create a Table of Contents

To create a table of contents, follow these steps:

1. Click at the location where you want the table of contents to appear. If you want it to be on a separate page, insert manual page breaks before and/or after it as necessary. (See "Controlling Page Breaks" in Hour 10, "Formatting Pages," if you need help.) If you like, you can also type the title *Table of Contents* at the top of the page.

2. Choose Insert, Index and Tables to display the Index and Tables dialog box, and click the Table of Contents tab (see Figure 15.8).

FIGURE 15.8

Use the Table of Contents tab in the Index and Tables dialog box to create a table of contents.

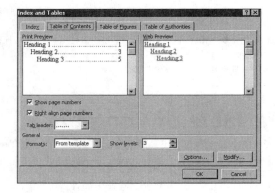

3. Experiment with different "looks" in the Formats drop-down list (Classy, Fancy, Modern, and so on) to find one that you like.

4. Specify the number of heading levels that you want in the table of contents in the Show Levels text box.

5. When you've made your selections, click the OK button.

6. In a moment, the table of contents appears (see Figure 15.9). It may appear light gray to indicate that it's a field. (As mentioned earlier in this hour, the gray shading will not print.)

7. Try pointing to a heading in the table of contents. The mouse pointer becomes a pointing hand. When you click, Word jumps to the associated heading in the text.

FIGURE 15.9

This table of contents was created by using the Formal format, with two heading levels showing.

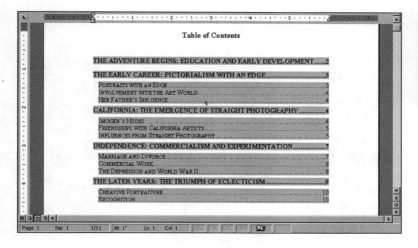

After you revise your headings or the pagination changes, you need to update the table of contents. To do so, right-click anywhere in it and choose Update Field in the context menu. (You can also click to the left of the table to select it and then press F9.) Word displays the Update Table of Contents dialog box (see Figure 15.10) to ask whether you want to update only the page numbers or the entire table (the page numbers and the headings). Mark the desired option button, and click OK. (Remember to update the table of contents right before you print.)

FIGURE 15.10

The Update Table of Contents dialog box asks how you want to perform the update.

To delete a table of contents, select it by clicking to the left of the table, and then press Delete.

Bookmarking Locations in Your Document

If you're working on a long document, you might find it handy to "bookmark" a particular spot so that you can get back to it easily. You could bookmark a section that still needs work or one that's missing information, for example. And as you'll see in the next section, you can use a bookmark as the target of a hyperlink.

To Do: Insert a Bookmark

Follow these steps to insert a bookmark:

1. Click at the location where you want to insert the bookmark.
2. Choose Insert, Bookmark (or press Shift+Ctrl+F5).
3. In the Bookmark dialog box, type a name for the bookmark (see Figure 15.11). Bookmark names cannot include spaces.

FIGURE 15.11

Type a name for your bookmark in the Bookmark Name text box.

4. Click the Add button to add the bookmark and close the dialog box.

To navigate to a bookmark, display the Bookmark dialog box and double-click the bookmark in the list in the middle of the dialog box. When you're finished using the Bookmark dialog box, click its Close button.

To delete a bookmark, select it in the Bookmark dialog box and click the Delete button.

Inserting Hyperlinks

A *hyperlink* is a "clickable" piece of text or a graphic that leads to another location (the *target* of the hyperlink). With Word's Hyperlink feature, you can create links to other documents on your computer or network, to specific locations within a document, or to Web pages. Keep in mind that hyperlinks are useful only if your readers will view the document onscreen.

Figure 15.12 shows a hyperlink that points to an Excel spreadsheet. Note that when you point to a hyperlink, its target appears in a ScreenTip.

If you create a hyperlink to a document on your own computer network, make sure the document is in a folder that your readers can access.

FIGURE 15.12

You can see where a hyperlink will take you by pointing to it.

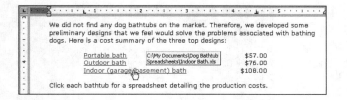

Linking to Another Document

If you add hyperlinks to other documents, you can lead your readers to associated information without cluttering up your own document. If you want people to review several documents stored in different locations on your network, you can make it easy for them by giving them a short Word document that contains only hyperlinks to these documents. In this case, the Word document would function as a sort of table of contents.

To Do: Insert a Hyperlink to a Document

Follow these steps to insert a hyperlink to a document on your own computer or network:

1. Select the word or phrase in your document that you want to become the hyperlink text.

2. Click the Insert Hyperlink button in the Standard toolbar or press Ctrl+K (see Figure 15.13).

FIGURE 15.13

Click the Insert Hyperlink button in the Standard toolbar to insert a hyperlink in your document.

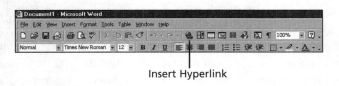

Insert Hyperlink

3. In the Insert Hyperlink dialog box, click the File button under Browse For (see Figure 15.14).

4. In the Link to File dialog box, navigate to and select the target document (see Figure 15.15), and click OK.

5. The address of the document now appears in the Type the File or Web Page Name text box in the Insert Hyperlink dialog box. Click OK.

FIGURE 15.14

Use the Insert Hyperlink dialog box to specify the target of your hyperlink.

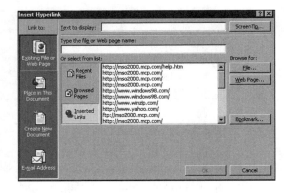

FIGURE 15.15

Select the target of the link in the Link to File dialog box.

The hyperlink text is now colored and underlined. When you point to it, the address of the target document appears in a ScreenTip. Click the hyperlink. In a moment, Word displays the document. If the document was created in another application, it launches that application and opens the document within it. When you're finished viewing the document, close it.

Whenever you click a hyperlink in a Word document, the Web toolbar appears. This toolbar has buttons similar to those in a browser window. You'll learn more about the Web toolbar in Hour 24, "Word and the Web." If you find it distracting, choose View, Toolbars, Web to hide it.

Linking to a Specific Location in a Document

If you've written a long Word document that people will view onscreen, consider adding some hyperlinks at the top of it that point to the main sections within the document. (You can also create hyperlinks in the main sections that lead back to the top of the document.)

To Do: Insert a Hyperlink to a Specific Location in the Current Document

Follow these steps to insert a hyperlink to a heading or a bookmark in the current document:

1. Select the word or phrase in your document that you want to become the hyperlink text.

2. Click the Insert Hyperlink button in the Standard toolbar or press Ctrl+K.

3. In the Insert Hyperlink dialog box, click the Bookmark button.

4. In the Select Place in Document dialog box that appears, you can specify the top of the document, a heading, or a bookmark as the target of the hyperlink. Click the plus signs next to Headings and Bookmarks to display the headings and bookmarks in the document. Select the desired location (see Figure 15.16), and click OK.

FIGURE 15.16

Use the Select Place in Document dialog box to specify a heading or bookmark as the target of the link.

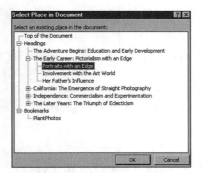

5. The location now appears in the Type the File or Web Page Name text box in the Insert Hyperlink dialog box, preceded by a pound (#) sign. Click OK.

Word creates the colored and underlined hyperlink. When you point to it, the ScreenTip lists the specific location in the document. Click the hyperlink to test it.

You can also create a link to a bookmark in another document. (You can't create a link to a heading in another document. If you want the link to point to a heading, insert a bookmark at that heading.) To do so, first use the File button in the Insert Hyperlink dialog box to select the file, and then use the Bookmark button to select the bookmark in that file.

Linking to a Web Page

If you like, you can create hyperlinks that lead to Web pages. You might want to point your readers toward Web sites (or Web pages on your company intranet) that contain information related to topics in your document.

To Do: Insert a Hyperlink to a Web Page

To add a hyperlink to a Web page, follow these steps:

1. Select the word or phrase in your document that you want to become the hyperlink text.

2. Click the Insert Hyperlink button in the Standard toolbar or press Ctrl+K.

3. Click the Web Page button in the Insert Hyperlink dialog box. Alternatively, you can type the full address of the target Web page (including the `http://` in the Type the File or Web Page Name text box and skip to step 5.

4. Your browser window opens, and you are prompted to connect to the Internet if you aren't already online. Navigate to the target Web page, and then click the Word document's taskbar button to switch back to it.

5. The address of the document or Web page now appears in the Type the File or Web Page Name text box. Click OK.

The hyperlink text is now colored and underlined. When you point to it, the address of the target Web page appears in a ScreenTip. Try clicking the hyperlink. In a moment, Word displays the target Web page. (You may be prompted to connect to the Internet if you disconnected after following steps 3 and 4 in the previous list.) When you're finished viewing the Web page, close your browser.

Modifying or Deleting a Hyperlink

If you want to modify a hyperlink, right-click it and choose Hyperlink, Edit Hyperlink in the context menu to display the Edit Hyperlink dialog box. This dialog box looks just like the Insert Hyperlink dialog box. Make any changes you like to the hyperlink, and click OK.

To remove a hyperlink (thus converting the hyperlink text to regular text), right-click it and choose Hyperlink, Remove Hyperlink in the context menu.

15

Summary

Tasks that used to be complex and cumbersome—such as adding footnotes, reorganizing your outline, and creating a table of contents—are now a breeze. And in addition to these more prosaic features, you can take advantage of slick navigation features such as the Document Map, bookmarks, and hyperlinks to jump from one location to another with a click of the mouse.

Q&A

Q **I've added a table of contents, but I also need to create an index at the end of the document, and cross-references within the text. I want both the index and the cross-references to update when the pagination changes. Can I do this in Word?**

A Yes. The general steps for creating an index involve marking the words that will be indexed in your text, and then generating the index (by choosing Insert, Index and Tables). To create cross-references, choose Insert, Cross-reference. To find out more about these features, ask the Office Assistant to search for information on *index* and *cross-reference* in the help system.

Q **Is it possible to change the ScreenTip that appears when you point to a hyperlink?**

A Yes. Click the ScreenTip button in the upper-right corner of the Insert Hyperlink or Edit Hyperlink dialog box, edit the ScreenTip text in the Set Hyperlink ScreenTip dialog box, and click OK.

PART VI
Columns, Tables, and Graphics

Hour

HOUR 16

Columns and Tables

Now that you know all the basic formatting techniques, you're ready to add some flair to your documents. In this hour, you learn how to format text in columns and tables. Then in the following two hours, you get the rundown on graphics. If you combine the skills you learn in these three hours, you will be fully equipped to design anything from professional reports to eye-catching flyers and brochures.

The highlights of this hour include

- Creating columns
- Modifying columns
- Creating tables
- Typing, navigating, and selecting in tables
- Changing the structure of a table
- Formatting a table
- Sorting text within a table

Working with Columns

If you plan to produce newsletters, bulletins, journal articles, and so on, you'll appreciate Word's capability to format text in multiple columns. When you use this feature, the text snakes from column to column (see Figure 16.1). After you've formatted your text in columns, changing the number of columns is a breeze.

FIGURE 16.1

This document is for-matted in two columns.

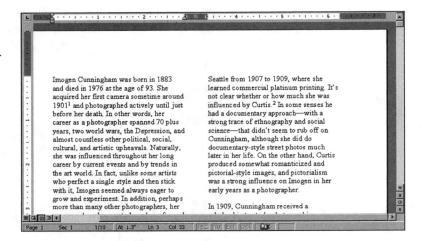

 If you want to create columns of text that *do not* wrap from one column to the next, use either custom tabs (see Hour 9, "Formatting Paragraphs") or a table.

Creating Columns

Columns fall into the page formatting category. As with other page formatting, columns apply to your entire document unless you insert *section breaks* around the text that you want in columns. For example, you might do this is if you want a title above the columns that is centered in the middle of the page (see Figure 16.2). To do this, you need to insert a continuous section break between the title and the remainder of the document.

Column Width marker

FIGURE 16.2

A continuous section break separates the title from the rest of the text.

There is a continuous section break here.

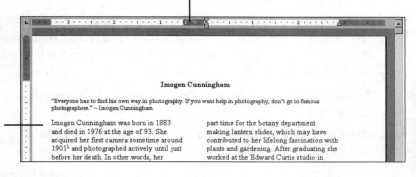

16

You can then leave the default (single) column formatting in the first section, and apply two or more columns to the rest of the text. If you need help with section breaks, see the section "Varying the Page Formatting in Your Document" in Hour 10, "Formatting Pages."

To Do: Apply Column Formatting

▼ To Do

Follow these steps to format your text in columns.

1. Make sure you're using Print Layout view (choose View, Print Layout). Columns don't display accurately in Normal view.

2. If you have inserted section breaks, make sure your insertion point is in the section where you want to apply the columns. If you're applying columns to the entire document, your insertion point can be anywhere in the text.

3. Click the Columns button on the Formatting toolbar, and click the number of columns that you want in the grid that drops down (see Figure 16.3).

▲

FIGURE 16.3

Click the number of columns that you want in the grid attached to the Columns button in the Formatting toolbar.

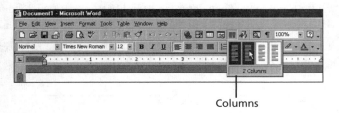

Columns

Word creates the number of columns that you specified. If you decide to change the number of columns in your document, follow these steps again. To remove columns, click the leftmost column in the grid in step 3.

Modifying Columns

In addition to the standard font and paragraph formatting you learned about in Hours 8, "Formatting Characters," and 9, "Formatting Paragraphs," Word gives you a few other choices for formatting text in multiple columns. Try some of the options described here and see what works well in your documents.

To Do: Adjust Column Width and Add a Vertical Line Between Columns

Follow these steps if your columns need to be a specific width or if you want to add a vertical line between the columns:

1. Click anywhere in the multiple-column text, and choose Format, Columns to display the Columns dialog box (see Figure 16.4).

FIGURE 16.4

You can make changes to your column formatting in the Columns dialog box.

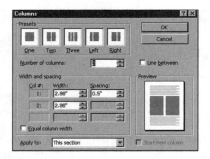

2. If you see a format under Presets at the top of the dialog box that matches what you want, click it.

3. If you have specific requirements for column widths, first clear the Equal Column Width check box. Then enter the desired settings for each column under Width and Spacing. (*Spacing* refers to the amount of space between columns.)

4. To add vertical lines between your columns, mark the Line Between check box.

5. When you have made all your selections, click OK.

To quickly adjust column width, drag the Column Width marker (see Figure 16.2). If you want to see their precise widths, hold down the Alt key as you drag.

Columns sometimes look better if the text is justified so that it has a straight right edge. If you do justify your text, it will probably look best if you hyphenate it as well to reduce gaps between words. To apply hyphenation, choose Tools, Language, Hyphenation, mark the Automatically Hyphenate Document check box, and click OK.

If you need to force a column to break in a particular place, move the insertion point there, choose Insert, Break, mark the Column Break option button, and click OK.

> To balance the length of your columns on the last page of a document, insert a continuous section break at the very end of the document. (Press Ctrl+End to move to the end of the document, choose Insert, Break, mark the Continuous option button, and click OK.)

16

Working with Tables

Word's table feature gives you a wonderfully flexible way of aligning text in a grid of rows and columns. You enter text into the individual boxes in the grid, which are referred to as *cells*. You can create a table that looks table-ish, like the one shown in Figure 16.5.

FIGURE 16.5

This table doesn't disguise its true nature.

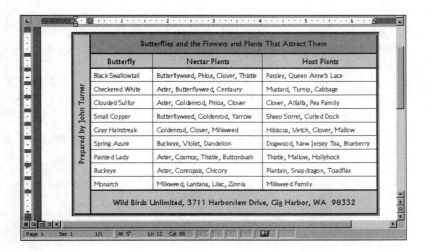

But you can also create tables that are "invisible" by hiding the gridlines between cells. The résumé shown in Figure 16.6 is actually typed in a table, but the gridlines have been hidden so that it's not obvious.

FIGURE 16.6

Tables don't have to look like they belong in a scientific paper.

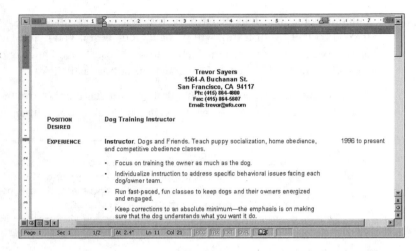

Creating a Table

Word gives you two methods for creating tables. With the standard method, you tell Word to create a table with a particular number of rows and columns, and then revise it from there. With the second method, you "draw" the table with your mouse. The first method is a little faster, but the second is better for creating a more complex table such as the one shown earlier in Figure 16.5.

Using the Standard Method

To create a table using the standard method, you can either use the Insert Table button on the Standard toolbar or choose Insert, Table; the end result is the same. In these steps, you use the Insert Table toolbar button because it's a little more efficient.

To Do: Create a Table with the Standard Method

Follow these steps to insert a table with the standard method:

1. Move the insertion point to the place where you want to insert the table.

2. Click the Insert Table button on the Standard toolbar.

3. The squares in the grid that drops down represent cells. Drag through the approximate number of rows and columns that you want (see Figure 16.7), and then release the mouse button.

Insert Table

FIGURE 16.7

Drag through the number of rows and columns that you want to start off with.

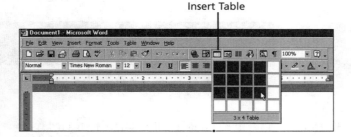

16

A table appears in your document. To change the number of rows and columns, see "Adding and Deleting Rows and Columns" later in this hour.

> If you start a table at the very top of a document and then decide that you want to insert text above the table, click at the far-left edge of the upper-left cell in the table and press Enter. Word inserts a blank line above the table; you can now click in the blank line and type your text. (If the table isn't at the top of the document, pressing Enter adds a blank line to the cell.)

Drawing a Table

To draw a table, you use the Draw Table button on the Tables and Borders toolbar. (This tool is available in Print Layout view; it isn't in Normal view.) Although you can start by drawing a single cell and then add on, it's usually more straightforward to draw the outline of a table and then fill in the rows and columns. This method of creating a table is extremely flexible; if you can envision a design for your table, you can almost certainly create it.

To Do: Create a Table with the Drawing Method

To draw a table, follow these steps:

▼ To Do

1. Make sure you're in Print Layout view, and then click the Tables and Borders button on the Standard toolbar (see Figure 16.8) to display the Tables and Borders toolbar.

▼

FIGURE 16.8

Use the buttons on the Tables and Borders toolbar to help create a table.

Tables and Borders

2. Click the Draw Table button if it isn't already selected (pushed in). Your mouse pointer now looks like a small pencil when it's over your document.

3. Display the Line Style list and choose a line style for the outside border of your table.

4. Display the Line Weight list and choose a line weight for the outside border of your table.

5. Click the Border Color button and click a color for the outside border of your table in the drop-down palette.

6. Starting in the upper-left corner, drag diagonally down and to the right, releasing the mouse button when the outline is the right size (see Figure 16.9). Word creates the outside border of your table.

Draw Table   Line Style   Border Color

FIGURE 16.9

Drag until the outline of your table is approximately the right size.

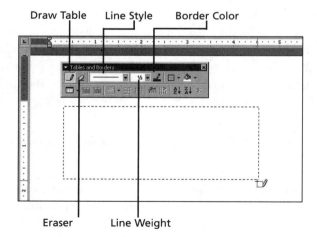

Eraser   Line Weight

7. Now repeat steps 3–5 to choose what kind of inside lines you want, and draw them with the Draw Table tool (see Figure 16.10). If you want to remove a line, click the Eraser toolbar button and then draw over the line. When you release the mouse button, the line disappears.

▼

FIGURE 16.10

Draw the inside lines in your table.

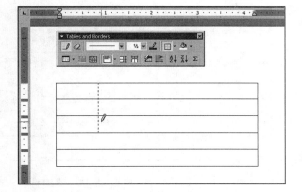

> You can draw lines to divide up the inside of the table however you like. You are not restricted to a standard grid. You can create cells of different sizes depending on what you're using the table for. Word even lets you draw diagonal lines.

8. Click the Draw Table button to turn it off, and enter the text in the table (see the next section).

> If you inserted a table accidentally and want to start over, make sure that the insertion point is in the table, and choose Table, Delete, Table.

Typing, Navigating, and Selecting in a Table

Typing, navigating, and selecting in a table works much like you might expect, with a few twists.

Typing Text in a Table

When you type text in a cell, if the entry is too wide to fit in the cell, Word automatically wraps the text to the next line and increases the row height. In Figure 16.11, the text was allowed to wrap within cells, and the row height adjusted accordingly.

Pressing Enter in a cell ends the paragraph and adds a blank line to that row. (If you accidentally press Enter, press Backspace to remove the blank line.)

FIGURE 16.11

Unlike in a spread-sheet program, Word wraps text in cells automatically.

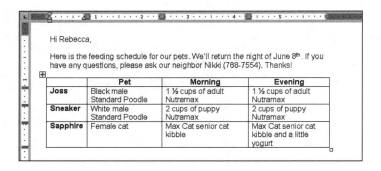

If you want to insert a tab within a cell, press Ctrl+Tab instead of Tab. (Pressing the Tab key by itself just selects the contents of the cell to the right.)

Navigating in a Table

Navigating in a table with the mouse is just a matter of clicking in the cell you want to move to. To navigate with the keyboard, refer to Table 16.1.

TABLE 16.1. KEYBOARD TECHNIQUES FOR MOVING THE INSERTION POINT IN A TABLE

Navigation Technique	Moves the Insertion Point
↓	Down one row
↑	Up one row
→	One cell to the right, or character by character to the right if the cell contains text
←	One cell to the left, or character by character to the left if the cell contains text
Tab	One cell to the right; if the cell to the right contains text, it will be selected
Shift+Tab	One cell to the left; if the cell to the left contains text, it will be selected

Selecting Parts of a Table

Selecting is a big deal in a table. In many cases, you have to select the part of the table that you want to affect before issuing a command. For this reason, it's worth taking a few moments to practice the various selection techniques outlined in Table 16.2. Before you do, check to make sure the Draw Table and Eraser buttons in the Tables and Borders toolbar are turned off.

TABLE 16.2. SELECTION SHORTCUTS IN A TABLE

Amount Selected	Technique
One cell	Point just inside the left edge of the cell. When the mouse pointer becomes a black arrow (see Figure 16.12), click once.
A group of cells	Select the first cell and then drag over the additional adjacent cells.
One row	Rest the mouse pointer outside of the left border of the table—it should be a white arrow angled toward the table, as shown in Figure 16.13. Click once. (If you've increased the row height or you drew your table, only the top of each cell in the row becomes highlighted. Don't worry; the row is selected.)
Multiple rows	Select the first row and then drag straight up or down to add rows to the selection.
One column	Rest the mouse pointer on the top border of the column. When it changes to a small downward-pointing arrow (see Figure 16.14), click once. You can also Alt+click anywhere in the column.
Multiple columns	Select the first column and then continue dragging to the right or left to add columns to the selection.
Entire table	Click the four-headed arrow icon just outside the upper-left corner of the table (see Figure 16.15). (This icon appears only when the Draw Table and Eraser tools are turned off.)

Double-clicking the four-headed arrow icon displays the Table Properties dialog box, which lets you set a variety of options for your table.

FIGURE 16.12

Click at the left edge of a cell to select the cell.

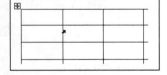

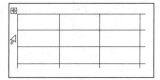

FIGURE 16.13

Click to the left of a row to select the row.

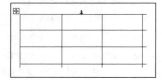

FIGURE 16.14

Click the top edge of a column to select the column.

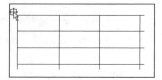

FIGURE 16.15

Click the four-headed arrow icon to select the table.

Changing the Structure of a Table

As you enter text in a table, you will almost certainly need to change its structure. Here you learn the most common adjustments that you'll need to make. As you experiment with these techniques, keep in mind that Word does not prevent you from making a table too wide to fit on the page. If you're adding columns and increasing column widths, check periodically to make sure that table isn't running off the page. (You have to check in Print Layout view or Print Preview—Normal view won't do the trick.)

> Most of the commands in the Table menu are active only when the insertion point is in a table. If you notice that the commands are dim, it's a sign you accidentally clicked outside the table. Click inside the table and then display the Table menu again.

Adding and Deleting Rows and Columns

If you want to add a row at the end of the table, click anywhere in the lower-right cell in the table, and press the Tab key.

To add a row in the middle of the table, select the row below the location of the new one, and click the Insert Rows button on the Standard toolbar. (The Insert Table button turns into Insert Rows when a row is selected.) If you want to add two or more rows, select that number of rows before clicking the Insert Rows button.

To insert a column, select the column to the right of where the new one will go, and click the Insert Columns button on the Standard toolbar. (The Insert Table button turns into Insert Columns when a column is selected.) Again, you can add two or more columns at once by selecting that number before clicking the Insert Columns button.

If you want to delete a row or column, select it first, and then choose Table, Delete, Rows or Table, Delete, Columns (or right-click the selected row or column and choose Delete Rows or Delete Columns).

16

Merging and Splitting Cells

When you merge cells, they become one larger cell. You might, for example, merge all the cells in the top row of a table to create a large cell in which to type a centered title. You can merge cells that are horizontally or vertically adjacent to one another. To merge cells, first select them, and then click the Merge Cells button in the Tables and Borders toolbar (see Figure 16.16).

Split Cells

FIGURE 16.16

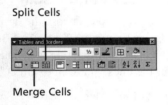

The Merge Cells and Split Cells buttons in the Tables and Borders toolbar give you a quick way to merge and split cells.

Merge Cells

Merging cells is not the same as hiding the lines that separate them. When you merge cells, they become one. When you hide the lines, the cells remain separate.

You can also split a cell into two cells. To do so, click in the cell and then click the Split Cells toolbar button.

Another way to merge cells is to erase the lines between them with the Eraser tool in the Tables and Borders toolbar. And you can split a cell by drawing a line through it with the Draw Table tool.

Formatting a Table

Formatting a table can take far longer than creating it in the first place. Try not to overdo it. If your table is plastered with wild colors, fancy lines, and flamboyant fonts, the text it contains will be almost impossible to read. Also, be careful to select the exact cells that you want to format before issuing a command, and remember that you can always use Undo if you make a change that you don't like.

At the risk of stating the obvious, you can apply all the regular font and paragraph formatting in a table. Select the part of the table that you want to affect, and then use the familiar options in the Formatting toolbar, Font and Paragraph dialog boxes, and so on. The next four sections describe formatting that's specific to tables.

Changing the Appearance of Lines and Adding Shading

To change the appearance of the lines in your table, choose the desired options in the Line Style, Line Weight, and Border Color lists in the Tables and Borders toolbar. (If you want to hide the lines, choose No Border in the Line Style list.) Then turn on the Draw Table tool, if necessary, and draw over the lines you want to affect.

To apply shading, select the desired part of the table, display the Shading Color list in the Tables and Borders toolbar (see Figure 16.17), and click the desired color.

FIGURE 16.17

Click a color in the Shading Color palette to shade the selected cells.

Shading Color

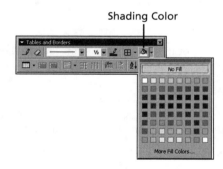

The most recently selected color appears on the face of the Shading Color button. If you want to apply this color, just click the button itself instead of choosing a color from the palette.

Resizing Columns, Rows, and the Entire Table

To adjust a column's width, drag its right border. To adjust a row's height, drag its bottom border. (When you point to any line in a table, the mouse pointer changes to a double-headed arrow to remind you that you can drag to resize.)

16

If you want to make multiple rows the same height, or multiple columns the same width, select the rows or columns, and then click the Distribute Rows Evenly or Distribute Columns Evenly button on the Tables and Borders toolbar (see Figure 16.18).

Distribute Rows Evenly.

FIGURE 16.18

The Distribute Rows Evenly and Distribute Columns Evenly buttons let you quickly even out your rows and columns.

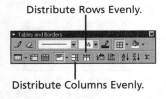

Distribute Columns Evenly.

To proportionally resize the entire table, make sure the Draw Table and Eraser tools are turned off, and point to the small square just outside the lower-right corner (refer to Figure 16.11). Then drag diagonally up and to the left to shrink the table, or down and to the right to enlarge it. If you don't see this square, make sure the Draw Table and Eraser tools are turned off, and rest the mouse pointer inside the table.

Adjusting the Position of the Table on the Page

To move your table around on the page, drag the four-headed arrow icon located just outside the upper-left corner of the table (refer to Figure 16.11).

Aligning Text and Changing Its Direction

To change the vertical/horizontal alignment of text in your table, select the cells whose alignment you want to change, display the Align list, and click the desired option. To change the direction of text from the default left-to-right to either bottom-to-top or top-to-bottom, select the cell and then click the Change Text Direction button one or more times (see Figure 16.19).

FIGURE 16.19

Use the Align and Change Text Direction tools to play with the appearance of text in a table.

Sorting Rows in a Table

The fastest way to sort rows in a table is to use the Tables and Borders toolbar. Click in the column that you want to sort by, and click the Sort Ascending or Sort Descending button (see Figure 16.20). Word assumes that you want to sort all rows but the first. (In Figure 16.20, the last row was added after sorting by the Name column to prevent it from being included in the sort.) If you want to include the first row, click in the column to sort by, choose Table, Sort, mark the No Header Row option button, and click OK.

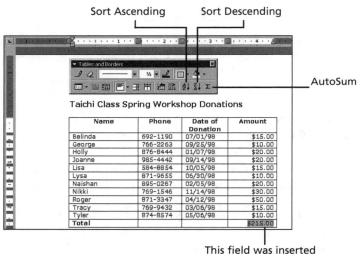

FIGURE 16.20

Click the Sort Ascending or Sort Descending button in the Tables and Borders toolbar to sort by the column containing the insertion point.

This field was inserted with the AutoSum tool.

If you have entered numbers in a column, you can have Word total them automatically. Click in the last cell in the column and then click the AutoSum toolbar button to insert a field that sums the numbers above. If you later change some of the numbers, remember to update the field. (It won't update automatically.)

Summary

The Columns feature is the way to go if you want your text to wrap from one column to the next. For all other documents in which you want text to line up in columns, use custom tabs (described in Hour 9) or tables.

Q&A

16

Q I want to center my table exactly in the middle of the page. How do I do that?

A Double-click the four-headed arrow icon outside the upper-left corner of the table to display the Table Properties dialog box. In the Table tab, click Center, and click OK.

Q I have a table that takes up five pages and I want the first row, which contains labels, to repeat at the top of each page. Can you do this?

A Yes. Select the first row, and choose Table, Heading Rows Repeat.

Q I want to use precise measurements in inches for my column width and row height. How do I do that?

A Select the rows or columns you want to resize, and then choose Table, Table Properties to display the Table Properties dialog box. If you want to set row height and column width for the entire table, double-click the four-headed arrow icon to both select the table and display the Table Properties dialog box. In the Row tab, choose Exactly in the Row Height Is list, and type a value in inches in the text box. In the Column tab, mark the Preferred Width check box, and type a value in inches in the text box. Then click OK.

HOUR 17

Inserting Graphics, Drawing Shapes, and Creating Text Effects with WordArt

One of the perks of using a powerful word processing program is that you get to put pictures in your documents. Graphics help break up the text, convey meaning, and grab the reader's attention. Plus they are just plain fun to work with. In this hour, you start by learning how to insert an image in your document. This could be a piece of clip art, a photograph or image that you've scanned, a drawing you created in another program, or an image you found on the Web. You then learn how to draw shapes (this isn't as boring as it sounds) and use WordArt to create special effects with text.

The highlights of this hour include

- Inserting images from the Clip Gallery
- Inserting images from other places
- Inserting scanned images or digital photographs
- Drawing shapes with the drawing tools
- Dressing up your text with WordArt

Inserting Images

Word lets you insert images from a variety of sources. You can pull them from the Clip Gallery, or from any folder on your own computer or network. And if you have a scanner or digital camera, you have the option to import images directly from the scanner or camera software into Word.

Inserting Images from the Clip Gallery

The Microsoft Office CD contains a Clip Gallery of stock clip art images you can use in your documents. Although functional, they are nothing to write home about. However, you can also use the Clip Gallery as a jump-off point to browse a larger gallery of clip art at Microsoft's Web site, and you can use it to catalog all the images you gather from various sources, so you have them all in one place.

To Do: Insert Clip Art from the Clip Gallery

To insert a piece of clip art from the Clip Gallery, follow these steps:

1. Move the insertion point to the approximate place where you want to insert the graphic.

2. Place the Microsoft Office CD in your CD-ROM drive, and choose Insert, Picture, Clip Art to display the Insert ClipArt dialog box (see Figure 17.1). If the Drawing toolbar is displayed, you can click its Insert Clip Art button as well.

3. In the Pictures tab, scroll through the categories of images and click one that you want to browse.

4. To return to the list of categories, click the All Categories button. To move backward and forward among categories you've already browsed, click the Back and Forward buttons.

5. If you know what type of image you're looking for, type a descriptive word or two in the Search for Clips text box, and press Enter. Word displays the images that most closely match your keywords.

Forward
Back　　All Categories

FIGURE 17.1

The Insert ClipArt dialog box lets you browse the images in the Clip Gallery and insert them into your document.

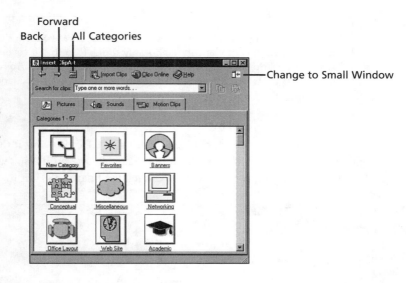

Change to Small Window

6. When you find an image that you want to use, click it.

7. A small toolbar appears above the image. Click the Insert Clip button (see Figure 17.2). (You can also right-click the image and click Insert in the context menu.)

FIGURE 17.2

Click the image that you want to insert, and then click the Insert Clip toolbar button.

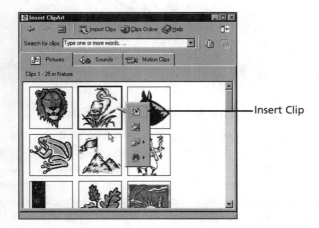

Insert Clip

8. Insert additional images if you like (you may have to drag the dialog box out of the way to see the images in your document), and then click the Close button in the upper-right corner of the Insert ClipArt dialog box.

17

If you like leaving the Insert ClipArt dialog box open as you work on your document, you might want to temporarily shrink it so that it covers less of the Word window. Click the Change to Small Window button. To return the dialog box to its full size, click the same button (now labeled Change to Full Window).

The graphic is inserted in your document (see Figure 17.3). Don't worry if the image is not the right size. You'll learn how to resize it in the next hour. You'll also learn how to use the Picture toolbar, which appears when you click the image to select it.

FIGURE 17.3

After you've got the image in your document, you'll have to do a little tinkering to get its size, position, and appearance just right.

Searching for Clip Art Online

If you don't find a suitable clip-art image in the Insert ClipArt dialog box, you can click the Clips Online button at the top of the dialog box to connect to Microsoft's Clip Gallery Live Web site. After you click this button, you may see a message box telling you to click OK if you have access to the Web and want to browse additional clips. And, depending on your Internet connection, you may also be prompted to connect. Word then launches your browser and takes you to the site.

The first Web page you'll see at the site is an end-user license agreement for using the images at the site. Click the Accept button. You can then browse Microsoft's collection of images and download them for free. This set of images is continuously updated, so you might want to check back periodically to see what's new.

Importing Images to the Clip Gallery

You can use the Clip Gallery as a "binder" of sorts to collect all your images in one place. Word gives you three options for how you want to import an image to the Clip Gallery:

- Leave the image in its current location and copy it to the Clip Gallery. Use this option if you want to be able to access the image in its current folder on your computer or network.

- Move the image to the Clip Gallery. You might choose this option if you are short on disk space. This option is not available if the image is on a network drive.

- Leave the image in its current location and ask the Clip Gallery to retrieve it from that location when you issue the command to insert the image. Use this option if you frequently access the image in its current location, but want to be able to access it from the Clip Gallery once in a while.

17

To Do: Import an Image to the Clip Gallery

Follow these steps to add an image to the Clip Gallery:

1. Choose Insert, Picture, Clip Art to display the Insert ClipArt dialog box.
2. Click the Import Clips button at the top of the dialog box.
3. In the Add Clip to Clip Gallery dialog box, choose one of the three option buttons at the bottom of the dialog box.
4. Navigate to and select the image (see Figure 17.4), and click the Import button.

FIGURE 17.4

Select the image that you want to add to the Clip Gallery in the Add Clip to Clip Gallery dialog box.

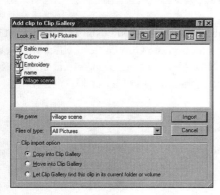

5. The Clip Properties dialog box appears (see Figure 17.5). Type a short description of the image in the Description of This Clip text box. This description is used to label the image in the Clip Gallery.

FIGURE 17.5

*Use the Description
tab to enter a name to
identify your image in
the Clip Gallery.*

6. Click the Categories tab, and mark the categories in which you want this image to
   appear (see Figure 17.6). To create a new category, click the New Category button,
   type the name of the category in the New Category dialog box, and click OK.

FIGURE 17.6

*Use the Categories tab
to categorize your
image in the Clip
Gallery.*

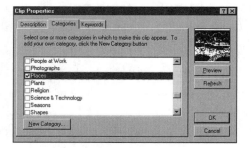

7. Click the Keywords tab. You use this tab to enter the keywords that will pull up this
   image when you perform a search in the Clip Gallery. Click the New Keyword button, enter a keyword in the New Keyword dialog box, and click OK. Repeat this
   step if you want to add more keywords (see Figure 17.7).

FIGURE 17.7

*Use the Keywords tab
to enter keywords you
can use to search for
this image in the Clip
Gallery.*

8. Click OK in the Clip Properties dialog box.

The image now appears in the Clip Gallery. If you want to change any of the information that you entered in steps 5–7, right-click the image and choose Clip Properties in the context menu. To remove the image from the Clip Gallery, right-click the image and choose Delete.

Inserting Images from Other Locations

If the graphic that you want to use is not in the Clip Gallery, but is sitting in a folder on your computer or network, you can insert it in your document. Word can handle graphics files in all sorts of formats, including (but not limited to) BMP, EMF, EPS, PNG, GIF, JPG, PCX, PICT, PING, and WMF. (If these formats don't mean anything to you, don't worry about it. Chances are, Word will be able to use your graphics file without a problem.)

To Do: Insert an Image from Another Location

If you want to insert a graphic from a folder on your hard disk or network instead of from the Clip Gallery, follow these steps:

1. Move the insertion point to the approximate place where you want to place the image.

2. Choose Insert, Picture, From File. (Or, if the Picture toolbar is showing, click the Insert Picture toolbar button.)

3. In the Insert Picture dialog box, navigate to and select the desired graphics file (see Figure 17.8). You might want to display the Views list and choose Preview to display a preview of the selected image in the right side of the dialog box.

To Do ▼

17

FIGURE 17.8

Select the graphics file that you want to insert in the Insert Picture dialog box.

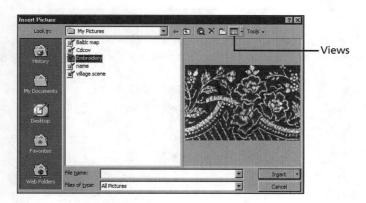

Views

▼

> By default, Office 2000 creates a My Pictures subfolder of My Documents to give you a handy place to store images. The Insert Picture dialog box automatically points to this folder, but you can navigate to any other folder that you like.

4. Click the Insert button to insert the image in your document.

Inserting Scanned Images and Digital Photographs

Word knows how to "talk" to the software that manages scanners and digital cameras. If you have one of these gadgets (they are known as TWAIN devices), you can easily insert a scanned image or digital photograph into your Word document, without first saving it as a separate graphics file on disk.

To Do: Insert a Scanned Image or Digital Photograph

To insert a scanned image or digital photograph from the scanner or camera, follow these steps:

1. Choose Insert, Picture, From Scanner or Camera.

> If you don't have a scanner or digital camera, don't even bother with these steps. If you try to issue this command, Word displays a message telling you that it can't find any TWAIN devices connected to your computer.

2. In the Insert Picture from Scanner or Camera dialog box (see Figure 17.9), select the camera or scanner that you want to use in the Device list.

FIGURE 17.9

If you have more than one TWAIN device, select the one you want to use.

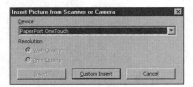

3. Depending on the software that runs your scanner or camera, the Insert button and the associated Web Quality and Print Quality option buttons may be active or dim. If they're active, the software knows how to send an image to Word with no more participation from you after this dialog box. Select Web Quality (poorer) or Print

▼   Quality (better), click the Insert button, and wait for the image to appear in your document. If these buttons are dim, as they are in Figure 17.9, continue with the next two steps.

   4. Click the Custom Insert button to launch the software you use for your scanner or camera.

   5. Issue the command to scan the image or import it from the camera. Figure 17.10 shows the main program window for software that runs a scanner. Unless you're using the exact same software program (PaperPort), your window will look differ-

▲   ent.

FIGURE 17.10

Use the software that manages your TWAIN device to scan or import the image.

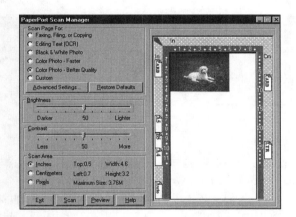

After a moment, the image appears in your document (see Figure 17.11).

FIGURE 17.11

The image appears in your document as soon as it's scanned or imported.

17

Deleting Images

To delete an image, click it to select it and then press the Delete key. When an image is selected, small squares (called *selection handles*) appear around its edges. Depending on the situation, the squares are either black, as they are in Figure 7.12, or white. (You'll learn more about this in the next hour.)

Drawing Shapes

Sometimes you don't need a complex graphic in your document—you just need something simple, such as an arrow or a box. Word's Drawing toolbar lets you quickly draw all manner of arrows, rectangles, ovals, callouts, banners, and so on. (You can also create text boxes, which are discussed at the end of this section.) Figure 17.13 shows one example of a drawing you can create with Word's drawing tools. After you have inserted a drawing object, you can modify the image in a variety of ways, as you'll see in the next hour.

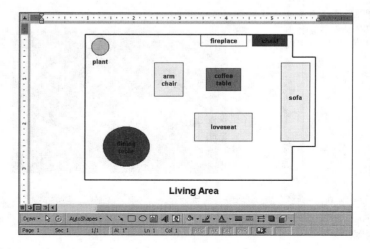

To Do: Draw a Shape

▼ TO DO

1. Click the Drawing button on the Standard toolbar.

2. The Drawing toolbar appears docked at the bottom of the Word window by default. In Figure 17.14, it has been moved and is floating over the Word window.

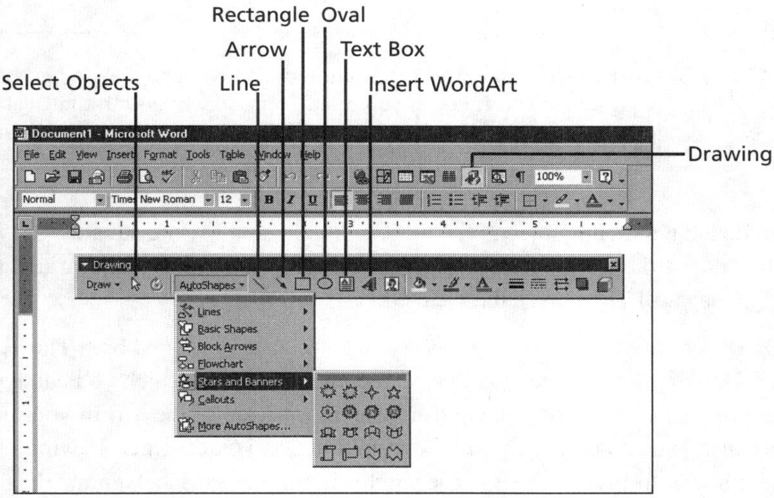

Rectangle Oval

Arrow   Text Box

Select Objects   Line   Insert WordArt

FIGURE 17.14

Click the Drawing button on the Standard toolbar to display the Drawing toolbar.

Drawing

17

3. Click the drawing tool that you want to use. The tools for basic shapes (lines, arrows, boxes, and so on) are available directly on the toolbar. If you want a more unusual shape, click the AutoShapes button, point to the category that you want to use, and click the shape in the submenu. In Figure 17.14, the Stars and Banners submenu is displayed.

4. Point with the crosshair mouse pointer to the upper-left corner of the area where want to draw the shape, and drag diagonally down and to the right (see Figure 17.15).

FIGURE 17.15

Drag to create the shape.

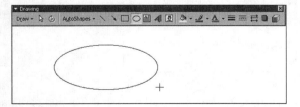

▲ 5. Release the mouse button to finish drawing the shape.

If you plan on drawing several objects using the same tool (for example, you want to draw several lines), *double-click* the button in step 3. It will stay turned on as long as you want to use it. When you're finished, click it again to turn it off. (This does not work for the tools in the AutoShapes menu.)

If you are using the Rectangle tool and want to draw a perfect square, hold down the Shift key as you drag. This also works with the Oval tool to get a perfect circle, the Star tool to get a perfectly proportioned star, and so on.

To delete a drawing object, click it. It will gain small white squares (selection handles). (If it doesn't, click the Select Objects button in the Drawing toolbar and then click the object again.) Then press the Delete key.

One drawing object that deserves special attention is the text box. The Text Box tool on the Drawing toolbar lets you draw a rectangular box in which you can type text. Putting text in a text box gives you control over the position of the text in your document because you can drag the text box around just as you do other drawing objects (see the next hour). In Figure 17.13 earlier in this hour, the text labels in the diagram were all created with text boxes. (Their borders were removed, and they were placed on top of other drawing objects.)

To create a text box, click the Text Box tool, drag to create a rectangle of about the right size, and then release the mouse button. An insertion point appears in the box to let you type text (see Figure 17.16).

FIGURE 17.16

When a text box is selected, an insertion point appears in it to let you type.

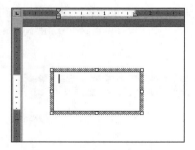

After you've typed your text, you can apply all the usual font and paragraph formatting to it. In addition, you can format the box itself, adjusting the appearance of the borders, changing the fill color, and so on. (You'll learn these techniques in the next hour.)

In addition to creating text boxes with the Text Box tool, you can type text into any drawing object (with the exception of lines and arrows) by right-clicking it and choosing Add Text in the context menu. An insertion point appears in the object. Type the text as you would in a text box.

Creating Special Effects with WordArt

When you add graphics to a document, you aren't limited to working with images separate from your text. WordArt lets you add flair to your text itself. It's perfect for creating splashy headings and titles. You start with a basic "look" for your word or phrase, and then tweak it to get the exact effect you want. After you've added a WordArt image, you can resize it, add borders, and so on (see the next hour). Figure 17.17 shows a heading created with WordArt.

FIGURE 17.17

You can create a variety of effects with WordArt.

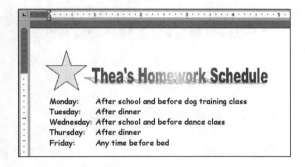

To Do: Create WordArt

To create a WordArt image, follow these steps:

1. Click where you want the WordArt image to go.

2. Choose Insert, Picture, WordArt. (If your Drawing toolbar is displayed, you can also click the Insert WordArt button on this toolbar.)

3. The WordArt Gallery dialog box opens (see Figure 17.18). Click the look that you want to start with, and click the OK button.

4. The Edit WordArt Text window appears.

5. Type the text for your WordArt image, replacing the *Your Text Here* dummy text (see Figure 17.19). Your text won't take on the look you chose in step 3 until it's inserted in the document.

FIGURE 17.18

Choose the WordArt style that most closely matches what you want.

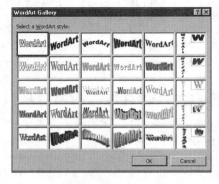

FIGURE 17.19

Type the text that you want to use in the Edit WordArt Text window.

6. Use the Font and Size lists and the Bold and Italic buttons to make additional adjustments to the text.

7. Click the OK button.

The WordArt image appears in your document. To revise the WordArt text or change its appearance after you've created the image, use the WordArt toolbar. This toolbar appears as soon as you insert a WordArt image. If you don't see it, choose View, Toolbars, WordArt. (You'll learn more about this in the next hour.)

Summary

You can insert existing images into your documents—via the Clip Gallery or from another location on your computer or network—or you can create new images with the drawing tools or WordArt. After an image is in your document, you have to adjust its size, position, and relationship to the surrounding text, and otherwise alter its appearance. You'll learn how to make these kinds of changes in the next hour.

Q&A

Q Are there other places to find clip art on the Internet? I'm not enthralled with what I see at the Microsoft's Clip Gallery Live Web site.

A Yes. There are literally hundreds of sites on the Internet that offer free clip-art images. A good way to start looking is to visit Yahoo! (www.yahoo.com) and search for the keyword *clip art*.

Q I need to create several identical drawing objects. Do I have to draw each one separately?

A No. Draw the first one, click it to select it, and click the Copy button in the Standard toolbar (or press Ctrl+C). Then click the Paste button in the Standard toolbar (or press Ctrl+V) to paste a duplicate of the image. The copy appears on top of the original image. Continue with the next hour to learn how to move it to a new location.

17

HOUR 18

Manipulating Graphics

Putting a graphic in your document is a bit like bringing a new piece of furniture home. After you get it in the door, you have to play around a bit to make it blend in with its surroundings. Word lets you modify graphics (pictures, drawing objects, and WordArt) in a myriad of ways. In this hour, you'll try out quite a few techniques for manipulating graphics. You should also feel free to experiment more on your own, and remember that if you botch something badly, you can always click the Undo button.

The highlights of this hour include

- Resizing and moving images
- Controlling the way that text wraps around an image
- Cropping out part of an image
- Making your image look good
- Working with multiple images

Resizing an Image

After you've placed a graphic in your document, one of the first adjustments you'll probably want to make is to change its size.

To Do: Resize an Image

To resize an image, follow these steps:

1. Click the graphic to select it. As you learned in the last hour, when a graphic is selected, selection handles appear around it. (These handles may be black or white. You can resize the image either way.)

2. Point to a selection handle. The mouse pointer becomes a diagonal double-headed arrow.

3. Drag to enlarge or shrink the image (see Figure 18.1). As you drag, you'll see the sizing pointer, a crosshair, and an outline that indicates how big the image will be. Release the mouse button when the image is the right size.

▲

FIGURE 18.1

As you drag, an outline shows how large the image will be when you release the mouse button.

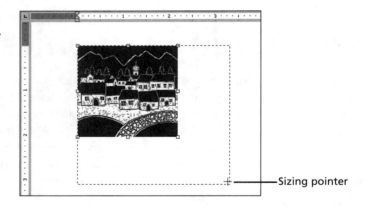

Sizing pointer

If you are resizing a picture, you can keep the height and width proportional by dragging a corner selection handle (as shown in Figure 18.1). If you drag a side selection handle, you will skew the image. Drawing objects and WordArt images work a little differently. By default, when you drag a corner selection handle of one of these image types, the height/width ratio is not maintained. If you want to preserve the image's proportions, hold down the Shift key as you drag a corner selection handle.

Moving an Image

By default, Word places pictures (most of the images that you insert with Insert, Picture, Clip Art or Insert, Picture, From File) *inline*, meaning that they are in the same "layer" of the document as the text. You can, as you saw in the previous section, resize an image when it's inline. However, if you want to move an image, it's much easier if you first set a *text wrapping* option, which takes the image out of the text layer. You'll learn more about text wrapping options in the next section. For now, note that you can choose any text wrapping option you like before moving the image—you can always change it later.

> You can tell when an image is inline because it has black selection handles. As soon as you remove it from the text layer, it gets white selection handles.

To Do: Move an Image

Follow these steps to move an image:

1. Select the image. If it is inline (has black selection handles), click the Text Wrapping button in the Picture toolbar and click Square, as shown in Figure 18.2. (If you don't see the Picture toolbar, choose View, Toolbars, Picture.)

FIGURE 18.2

Choose the Square text wrapping option for now (you can always change it later).

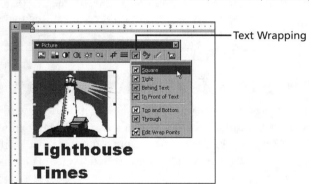

Text Wrapping

18

> Drawing objects and WordArt images, unlike pictures, have a text wrapping option (In Front of Text) turned on by default. So if you're moving one of these image types, you can skip step 1.

▼   2. The graphic's selection handles are now white. Point to the middle of the graphic and drag the image to the desired location (see Figure 18.3). As you drag, you'll see the moving pointer, which looks like a four-headed arrow, and an outline of the image.

FIGURE 18.3

Drag your image to the desired location.

Moving pointer

▲   3. Release the mouse button when the outline is in the right place.

To position a graphic precisely on the left margin, in the horizontal center of page, or at the right margin, make sure it has a text-wrapping option turned on, and then right-click the image. If it's a picture, choose Format Picture. If it's a drawing object, choose Format AutoShape. If it's a WordArt image, choose Format WordArt. In the dialog box that appears, click Layout tab, mark the Left, Center, or Right option button under Horizontal Alignment, and click OK.

Controlling the Text Flow Around an Image

Word gives you six options for controlling how text flows around your image. The same options are available for all graphics. To set a text-wrapping option, select the image, click the Text Wrapping button on the Picture toolbar (or the WordArt toolbar), and click one of the options in the menu. Here is a description of what each option does:

- Square—Wraps the text in a square shape around the image.
- Tight—Wraps the text right up to the outside edges of the image.
- Through—Same as Tight, but text also flows through any open areas inside the image. If there are no open areas, it will look the same as Tight.
- Behind Text—Doesn't wrap the text at all; the image is sent behind the text so that the text flows over the image.

- In Front of Text—Doesn't wrap the text; the image appears in front of the text so that the text is not visible behind it.
- Top and Bottom—Wraps the text above and below the image, but not along its sides.

With the Tight and Through options, you can control exactly how close the text wraps to the image. Select the image, click the Draw button at the left end of the Drawing toolbar, point to Text Wrapping, and click Edit Wrap Points. A dashed red line appears around the image to indicate the wrapping boundary. Drag any of the small black squares on the red line to adjust the boundary. When you're finished, click outside the image.

Figure 18.4 shows an example of each text-wrapping option. Note that the Through option looks the same as Tight because the dragon clip art doesn't contain any open areas.

18

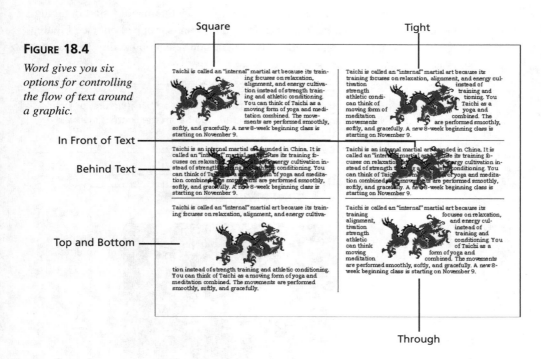

FIGURE 18.4

Word gives you six options for controlling the flow of text around a graphic.

> If you want to make your picture or WordArt image inline with the text, right-click it, choose Format Picture (or Format WordArt), click the Layout tab, mark the Inline with Text option under Wrapping Style, and click OK. This option is not available with drawing objects.

Cropping a Picture

You can crop a picture to remove a portion of it. Cropping doesn't resize the image or change its proportions—it just lops part of it off. You can't crop drawing objects or WordArt images.

To Do: Crop a Picture

Follow these steps to crop a picture:

1. Select your picture.
2. Click the Crop button on the Picture toolbar.
3. You will see a special cropping pointer. Point to a selection handle, start dragging, and release the mouse button when the desired portion is cropped out (see Figure 18.5). (If you want to crop one side only, drag a side selection handle. To drag two sides at once, drag a corner selection handle.)

> If you don't see the Picture toolbar, choose View, Toolbars, Picture, or right-click the picture and choose Show Picture Toolbar in the context menu.

FIGURE 18.5

Drag a selection handle with the cropping pointer to cut out a part of the image.

Crop

Cropping pointer

4. Click the Crop button again to turn it off.

Changing the Appearance of an Image

This is the part of working with graphics that can gobble up as much time as surfing the Web. As you're fiddling with an image, save frequently, be patient, and don't be obsessed with getting it perfect.

In general, the Picture, Drawing, and WordArt toolbars are designed to work with their respective image types. However, you can "mix and match" in many cases. For example, you can use the Text Wrapping button on the Picture toolbar to set a text wrapping option for a drawing object, or use the Line Color button on the Drawing toolbar to add a colored border around a picture. If you aren't sure whether a particular toolbar button works with the selected graphic, try it out. The worst thing that will happen is nothing.

Adding or Modifying the Borders of an Image

Adding borders around the edge of an image gives it definition, and removing borders makes it blend into the surrounding text. You can add borders around pictures, drawing objects, and WordArt images. (With WordArt images, the border appears around the outside edge of each letter.)

To Do: Add or Modify a Border

To add or modify a border, follow these steps:

1. Select the image.

2. If you haven't yet done so, set a text-wrapping option. (You can't add borders to inline images.)

3. Display the Line Style menu in the Drawing (or Picture) toolbar, and choose the desired line style.

4. If you want a colored border, keep the image selected, display the Line Color menu in the Drawing toolbar, and choose the desired color (see Figure 18.6).

18

▼ To Do

▲

FIGURE **18.6**

The border around this photograph was added with the Line Style and Line Color tools.

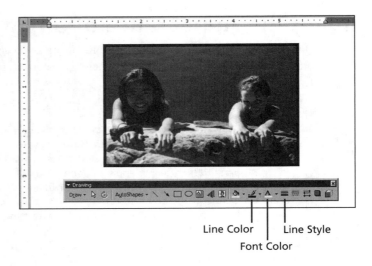

Line Color | Line Style
Font Color

Word adds a border to the image. You may want to click outside of the image to deselect it so that you can see the border more clearly.

To remove a border, select the image, click the Line Style button in the Drawing (or Picture) toolbar, and choose More Lines to display the Colors and Lines tab of the Format Picture (or Format AutoShape or Format WordArt) dialog box. Display the Color list under Line, choose No Line, and then click OK.

Adding or Modifying the Fill Color of an Image

If an image has a background, you fill it in with color. You can also use fill color to color drawing objects such as rectangles and ovals. When you apply a fill color to a WordArt image, it colors the inside portion of each letter. If your image doesn't have any background areas, nothing will happen when you apply a fill color.

To Do: Add or Modify the Fill Color of an Image

To add or modify a fill color of an image, follow these steps:

1. Select the image.

2. Display the Fill Color menu in the Drawing toolbar (see Figure 18.7) and click the desired color.

FIGURE 18.7

The fill color is the background color behind the sheets of music.

Fill Color

Rotating a Drawing Object or a WordArt Image

You can rotate a drawing object or WordArt image (you can't rotate a picture). The image stays the same—you just adjust its angle on the page.

To Do: Rotate a Drawing Object or a WordArt Image

Follow these steps to rotate a drawing object or WordArt image:

1. Select the image.

2. Click the Free Rotate button in the Drawing or WordArt toolbar.

3. The image gains rotate handles (small circles) around its edges. Point to one of them. When you do, you get a special rotate pointer. Drag until the image is rotated the right amount (see Figure 18.8), and then release the mouse button.

18

Rotate handle

FIGURE 18.8

Drag a rotate handle to rotate the image.

Rotate pointer

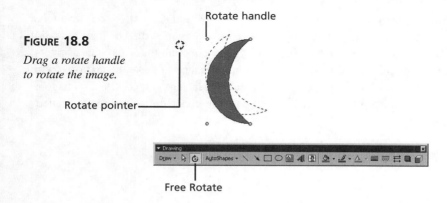

Free Rotate

> If you want to rotate the image in standard increments, select the image, click the Draw button at the left end of the Drawing toolbar, point to Rotate or Flip, and click Rotate Left, Rotate Right, Flip Horizontal, or Flip Vertical.

Formatting the Text in a Text Box

You can format text in a text box with all the standard font and paragraph options in the Formatting toolbar. In addition, you can change its color with the Font Color button, which appears in both the Formatting toolbar and the Drawing toolbar (refer to Figure 18.6). Finally, you can change the text direction. When a text box is selected, a small Text Box toolbar appears, which contains a Text Direction button. Click the button one or more times to change the orientation of your text.

> If you don't see the Text Box toolbar, you can also choose Format, Text Direction. The Text Direction command appears in the Format menu when a text box is selected.

Before issuing a command to format a text box, either select the entire text box to format all the text it contains, or drag over a portion of the text to format just that amount.

Turning an Image into a Watermark

The text wrapping option Behind Text sends an image behind the text of your document, but it doesn't alter the colors of the image, so the text on top of it may be hard to read. If you want your image to appear behind the text, you might want to format it as a watermark. When you do this, Word mutes the colors in the image to make the text on top of it legible. Figure 18.9 shows two copies of an announcement. In both copies, the image's text-wrapping option is set to Behind Text, but only the image on the right is formatted as a watermark.

FIGURE **18.9**

The text over the watermark on the right is much easier to read.

University Place Book Club

Join us for a discussion of Into Thin Air by Jon Krakauer. Sunday, December 27 from 3:00 to 5:00 p.m. Snacks will be served. Please bring a copy of your book.

Image Control

To Do: Create a Watermark

Follow these steps to create a watermark:

1. Select the image, click the Text Wrapping button in the Picture toolbar (or Drawing toolbar) and choose Behind Text.

2. Click the Image Control button in the Picture toolbar (refer to Figure 8.9), and click Watermark.

> When an image is behind text, it can be hard to select. If you're having trouble, click the Select Objects button on the Drawing toolbar (the white mouse pointer) and then click the image. When you're finished using the Select Objects button, click it again to turn it off.

18

If you want a watermark to appear on every page of a multiple-page document, follow the previous steps, but insert the image in the header or footer. (Choose View, Header and Footer and click in the header or footer area before inserting the graphic.) The graphic can be much bigger than the default header or footer area. In fact, you can drag it out of the header or footer area so that it appears over the document text. In Figure 18.10, the selected clip art is formatted with the Behind Text and Watermark options. The image is still inserted in the header, even though it has been dragged down underneath the header area.

Figure 18.11 shows the same document in Print Layout view so that you can see how the watermark will look when the document is printed.

FIGURE 18.10

Put the watermark in the header or footer if you want it to print on every page.

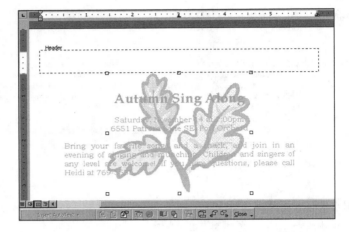

FIGURE 18.11

The watermark in this figure was placed in the header.

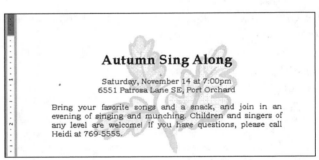

Adjusting Brightness and Contrast

If you have a picture with brightness or contrast problems—maybe it looks washed out or it's too dark—try using the More Contrast, Less Contrast, More Brightness, and Less Brightness buttons on the Picture toolbar (see Figure 18.12). Select the image and then click the desired button one or more times until you see the desired effect. These tools are especially useful for photographs.

FIGURE 18.12

This photograph was darkened with the Less Brightness tool.

Modifying a WordArt Image

As you've seen, many of the tools you can use with pictures and drawing objects also work with WordArt images. However, the WordArt toolbar also contains four tools that are specific to modifying WordArt images (see Figure 18.13). The WordArt toolbar appears automatically when a WordArt image is selected, but you can display it at any time by choosing View, Toolbars, WordArt.

FIGURE 18.13

WordArt comes with some special tools.

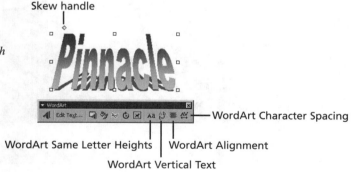

The names of the WordArt tools give you a good idea of what they do. Use WordArt Same Letter Heights if you want the lower- and uppercase letters in your WordArt text to be the same height. Click WordArt Vertical Text to stack the letters in your WordArt image vertically. Click the WordArt Alignment button if your WordArt image has two or more lines of text and you want to change their alignment. Use the WordArt Character Spacing button to adjust the amount of space between the letters.

You may have noticed the two small yellow diamonds that appear when a WordArt image is selected. These are skew handles; you can drag either one of them to skew the image.

18

Working with Multiple Images

When you are creating a drawing made up of multiple drawing objects, or if you have more than one picture on a page, you may need to stack images on top of one another, group them together to treat them as a unit, or align them. You accomplish all these tasks with commands in the Draw menu on the Drawing toolbar.

Ordering Images

If you have moved images on top of one another, you can reorder them however you like. Select the image in the stack that you want to move, click the Draw button on the Drawing toolbar, point to Order, and choose Bring to Front or Send to Back to bring it to the top of the stack or send it to the bottom. To move it up or down one level at a time, click Bring Forward or Send Backward. (The last two options, Bring in Front of Text and Send Behind Text, don't work unless the text wrapping option for the object is Behind Text or In Front of Text.) Figure 18.14 shows two copies of a stork and frog pair. On the left, the frog image is in front. On the right, it has been sent to the back.

FIGURE 18.14

You can order stacked images however you like.

This frog is hiding.

Selecting Multiple Images

When you're working with multiple images, you have to be able to select more than one at a time. When multiple images are selected, you move them as a unit, apply the same formatting to all of them, copy or delete all of them at once, and so on.

To select multiple images, click the first one, and then Shift+click the additional ones. If you need to select a large number of images, click the Select Objects button in the

Drawing toolbar, and then drag to draw a large rectangle around all the images. When you release the mouse button, they will all be selected. To remove one image from a selection, Shift+click it again. If you want to deselect all the images, click anywhere else in the document.

If you frequently handle the same set of images together, consider grouping them as described in the next section.

Grouping Images

When you group two or more images, Word treats them as a single object. This makes it easy to maintain the same spatial relationships between them when you move them around. To group images, select them all, click the Draw button in the Drawing toolbar, and click Group. When the images are grouped, you will see only one set of selection handles around all of them, as shown in Figure 18.15.

FIGURE 18.15

These three photographs are grouped together.

18

To ungroup images, select the group and choose Ungroup in the Draw menu. As soon as they are ungrouped, they all get their own selection handles. If you ungroup a set of images to manipulate one of the images in the group independently and then want to group them again, make sure one of the members of the group is selected and choose Regroup in the Draw menu. Word remembers which objects were originally in the group and includes them again.

Aligning and Distributing Images

If you want to align two or more images with each other, select them all, click the Draw button, point to Align or Distribute, and choose any of the alignment options in the sub-menu that appears. (The last two commands, Distribute Horizontally and Distribute Vertically, put an even amount of space between the selected images.) In Figure 18.16, the two photographs have been aligned on the left.

FIGURE **18.16**

These two photographs are aligned on the left.

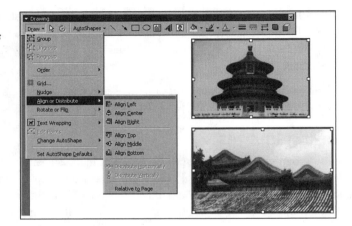

Summary

If you're at all visually oriented, you'll get a kick out of working with graphics. In addition to adjusting the size and position of an image, you can also crop portions out, change the way text flows around it, and tweak its appearance in many other ways. And if you have several images overlapping or in close proximity to one another, you can change the way they are arranged and aligned. In the next hour, you switch gears and start learning how to generate mass mailings in Word.

Q&A

Q I've aligned several drawing objects along their top edges, and now I want to shift one to the right. How can I drag it without accidentally moving it out of vertical alignment with the other images?

A If you hold down the Shift key as you drag an image, Word lets you move it only vertically or horizontally, but not both. This lets you maintain an image's alignment with other images as you drag.

Q I want to have finer control over resizing, moving, cropping, and images. Is this possible?

A Yes. When you drag to resize, move, or crop an image, Word uses invisible gridlines to respond to your mouse movements. By default, the gridlines are 0.13 inch apart. If you reduce this amount to, say, 0.02 to 0.05 inch, you will have much finer control. To do this, click the Draw button in the Drawing toolbar, and click Grid to display the Drawing Grid dialog box. Under Grid Settings, decrease the values in the Horizontal Spacing and Vertical Spacing text boxes, and then click OK.

Q **I rotated a drawing object and now I want to get it back to its original orientation. How do I do this?**

A Right-click the object and choose Format AutoShape (or, if it's a WordArt image, choose Format WordArt). Then click the Size tab, change the setting in the Rotation text box back to 0, and click OK.

Q **I resized and cropped a picture, and now I want to get it back to its original state. What do I do?**

A Right-click the picture and choose Format Picture. To reset the size, click the Size tab, and then click the Reset button. To reset cropping and any changes you made to the picture's brightness and contrast, click the Picture tab and click the Reset button. Then click OK.

18

PART VII
Mail Merge

Hour

HOUR 19

Generating a Mass Mailing

When you want to send a letter to a large number of people, Word's mail merge feature lets you sidestep the mind-numbing task of personalizing the document for each recipient. You prepare two documents: the form letter and a list of the recipients' names and addresses. Word then "merges" the information from the list into the form letter to generate the mass mailing. In this hour, you step through the standard mail merge procedure from start to finish, and then you explore some alternate routes that may come in handy occasionally. In the next hour, you learn how to merge envelopes or labels to go with your letters, and you explore other options for customizing a mail merge.

The highlights of this hour include

- Understanding mail merge terminology
- Starting your form letter
- Creating your list of recipient data

- Finishing your letter
- Merging the letter and the data
- Running future mail merges with the same documents
- Editing your recipient data

Understanding Mail Merges

Before you start your "training run" through the mail merge process, you need to understand the two documents that make up a mail merge:

- Main document—This is the actual document that you are producing. It can be a form letter, label, envelope, or catalog. (See the "Q&A" section at the end of this hour if you're curious about what a catalog is.) The main document contains the text and formatting that stays the same for each copy of the letter, as well as *merge fields*, which "hold places" that tell Word where to insert individual pieces of information from the *data source*.
- Data source—This is the file that contains the data you will merge into the main document. It is organized into *records*, one for each recipient. Each record is composed of individual fields for specific pieces of information, such as first name, last name, address, and so on.

It's easiest to learn how to do a mail merge if you work through the next five sections in one sitting. So make sure you have a full hour, grab your coffee, and plow in.

Starting the Main Document

In this first phase of the mail merge process, you tell Word which document you want to use as the main document.

To Do: Start Your Main Document

Follow these steps to start your main document:

1. If you have an existing letter that you want to use for your form letter, open it now, and delete any parts of it (such as the name and address) that you don't want to include in the form letter. If you want to start a letter from scratch, start a new, blank document.

2. Save the document (use File, Save As if you've opened an existing document) with a name such as *Form Letter - Main* to remind you that it is a main document.

> If you perform a lot of mail merges, you might want to create a separate
> folder for all your main documents and data source files to store these spe-
> cialized documents separately from your other files. You could name this
> folder something like *Mail Merge Documents.*

3. Choose Tools, Mail Merge to display the Mail Merge Helper dialog box.

4. Click the Create button, and click Form Letters in the drop-down list (see Figure 19.1).

FIGURE 19.1

Use the Mail Merge Helper dialog box to start your mail merge.

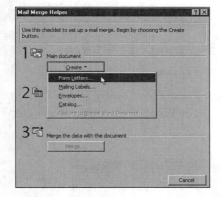

5. Word displays a message box asking whether you want to use the active document as your main document or start a new document. Click the Active Window button (see Figure 19.2).

19

FIGURE 19.2

Click the Active Window button to use the active document as your main document.

The Mail Merge Helper dialog box appears again with information about the main document listed under the Create button. Continue with the next section.

Creating and Saving the Data Source

In this second phase, you tell Word which document you want to use as your data source. You can either create a new one or open an existing one. You learn how to create a new one in this hour. In "Merging Envelopes and Labels" in the next hour, you learn how to open an existing data source.

The key step in creating a data source is telling Word which fields you want to use. Typical fields are first name, last name, company, address, city, state, zip code, and so on. Include a field for any piece of information that you might want to include in your main document. For example, if you want to refer to the recipient's job title in your form letters, be sure to include a job title field. (When you are entering your records, as described in the next section, you can always leave a field blank if you don't have that piece of data for a particular recipient.)

To Do: Create and Save the Data Source

Follow these steps to create and save the data source:

1. Click the Get Data button in the Mail Merge Helper dialog box, left open from the previous section, and choose Create Data Source in the drop-down list (see Figure 19.3).

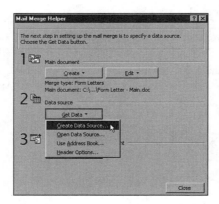

2. The Create Data Source dialog box appears (see Figure 19.4). To remove a field that you don't want, click it in the Field Names in Header Row list, and then click the Remove Field Name button.

▼

FIGURE 19.4

Use the Create Data Source dialog box to define the fields you want to use in your data source.

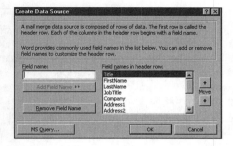

3. To add a field, first replace the contents of the Field Name text box with the name of the field you want to add. Then click the Add Field Name button to add the name to the Field Names in Header Row list. (This button becomes active as soon as you type text in the Field Name text box.) No spaces are allowed in field names.

> The order of the fields in the Field Names in Header Row list determines the order in which they will appear when you enter the data later on. If you want to adjust the position of a field in the list, click it and then use the Move arrows to the right of the list to move it up or down.

4. When your list of fields is the way you want it, click OK. In Figure 19.5, the Title, JobTitle, Address2, Country, HomePhone, and WorkPhone fields have been removed, and a Salutation field has been added. (The Salutation field was added to the end of the Field Names in Header Row list, so it is scrolled out of view in the figure.)

19

FIGURE 19.5

You can remove fields you won't use in your mail merges and add those you will.

▼

> If your mailing list contains a lot of addresses with building or department
> names, suite numbers, and so on, keep the Address2 field to use for this
> information. The Salutation field is a good one to add to a data source. Use
> it to store the name that will appear after *Dear* in the letter. This lets you
> adjust the way you address a letter depending on the recipient. For exam-
> ple, if a person's FirstName field contains *Elizabeth* and the LastName field
> contains *Larson,* you can enter *Liz* in the Salutation field if you know the
> recipient well, or *Ms. Larson* if you want to be more formal.

    5. Word displays the Save As dialog box to let you save your data source (see
       Figure 19.6). Save it with a name that will remind you that it's a data source, such
       as *Mailing List and Data Source.*

FIGURE 19.6

*Choose a name and
location for your data
source.*

    6. When Word asks what you want to do next, click the Edit Data Source button (see
       Figure 19.7).

FIGURE 19.7

*Click the Edit Data
Source button to start
typing data in your
data source.*

The Data Form appears to let you enter data in your new data source. Continue with the
next section.

If you already have a table of names and addresses in a database program such as Access, you may be able to use that table as your data source. In step 1 in the previous list, click Open Data Source instead of Create Data Source, display the Files of Type list in the Open Data Source dialog box, and click the appropriate file format. Locate and select your database, and then click the Open button.

Entering Records into the Data Source

In this third phase, you enter the records in your data source. Luckily, you have to do this only once—in the future, you can use the same data source with other main documents.

To Do: Enter the Data in Your Data Source

1. The blank Data Form that appeared at the end of the previous section contains text boxes for all the fields that you defined for your data source (see Figure 19.8).

FIGURE 19.8

The Data Form gives you an easy interface for entering your records.

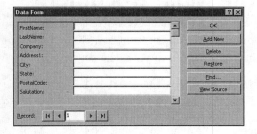

2. Enter the information for the first person in your mailing list, using the Tab key to move from field to field.

3. Click the Add New button to add the next record (see Figure 19.9).

FIGURE 19.9

Add your records one by one to your data source.

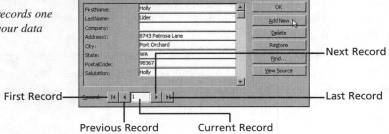

Next Record

First Record

Last Record

Previous Record   Current Record

▼

 Be careful not to click the OK button at this point. If you do, Word assumes you are finished entering records and closes the Data Form. If this happens, click the Edit Data Source button at the far-right end of the Mail Merge toolbar to redisplay the Data Form (see Figure 19.13 in the "Running the Merge" section later in this hour).

4. Word clears the Data Form to let you enter record 2. Continue entering records.

5. The Record arrows let you move forward and back in your data source so that you can review and revise records you've already entered.

▲ 6. When you've finished entering all the records, click the OK button.

Your main document appears onscreen. Continue with the next section.

Completing the Main Document

In this fourth phase, you finish the main document. This entails typing and formatting the text (if you started your main document from scratch) and inserting the merge fields that tell Word where to insert the data from your data source.

To Do: Complete the Main Document

Follow these steps to complete the main document:

1. Word has displayed your main document. Notice the Mail Merge toolbar directly under the Formatting toolbar. This toolbar automatically appears in main documents—you'll learn how to use many of its buttons in the remainder of this hour and the next.

2. Type and format the text that stays the same in all the form letters, including the letterhead (unless you're using preprinted letterhead), the body of the letter, and so on. If you opened an existing document in "Starting the Main Document," confirm that you've deleted all the personal data (the name, address, salutation, and any text in the body of the letter that's specific to the recipient).

3. Place the insertion point on the line where the address block will go, and click the Insert Merge Field button in the Mail Merge toolbar. In the list that appears, click the first field in the address block, usually Title or FirstName (see Figure 19.10).

▼

▼

FIGURE 19.10

The Insert Merge Field button lists all the fields in the attached data source.

Mail Merge toolbar

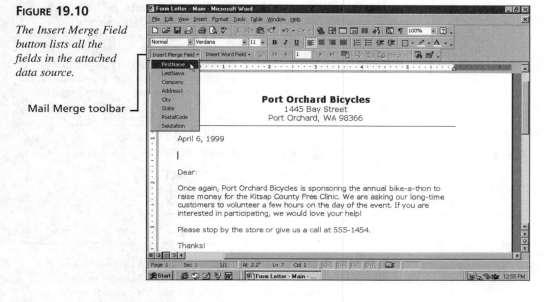

4. Word inserts the merge field surrounded by chevron brackets. Insert the remaining merge fields in the address block, pressing Enter and adding spaces and commas where necessary. If you have a salutation field, add it after *Dear*, and follow it with a colon or comma (see Figure 19.11).

FIGURE 19.11

Add all of your merge fields to your main document.

Merge fields

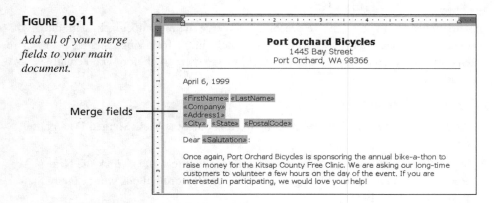

19

▲ 5. Save the main document, and leave it open for the next section.

When you close the main document (either before or after performing the merge), Word may ask whether you want to save the data source attached to the main document (see Figure 19.12). You'll see this message box if you have any unsaved changes in your data source. Click the Yes button. Otherwise, you'll lose any changes you've made to your data source (this could mean hours of typing if you've added a lot of records). If you have unsaved changes in your main document, you will then be asked to save it as well. Click Yes again.

Figure 19.12

If you are asked to save the data source attached to your main document, click Yes.

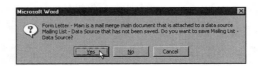

If you later want to convert your main document back to a normal Word document, open it, choose Tools, Mail Merge. In the Mail Merge Helper dialog box, click the Create button, and choose Restore to Normal Word Document. In the message box that appears, click the Yes button, and then click the Close button in the Mail Merge Helper dialog box.

Running the Merge

In this final phase of the mail merge process, you merge the main document with the data source to produce your letters. The first two steps in the following list are optional—they let you confirm that the data will merge correctly before you actually perform the merge.

To Do: Run the Merge

1. After completing step 5 in the previous section, click the View Merged Data button on the Mail Merge toolbar.

2. Word displays the data from the first record (see Figure 19.13). Click the Next Record button on the Mail Merge toolbar. (These Record buttons work exactly like those in the Data Form.)

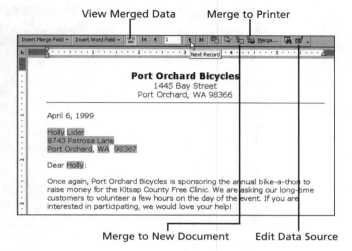

FIGURE 19.13

Optionally use the View Merged Data button to check for errors in your data and merge fields.

View Merged Data   Merge to Printer

Merge to New Document   Edit Data Source

3. Word displays the data from the next record. Look at a few more to see whether the data is merging correctly. If you find any mistakes in the data, click the Edit Data Source button to display the Data Form, revise the data, and then click OK. When you're finished, click the View Merged Data button again to turn it off.

4. Click the Merge to New Document button on the Mail Merge toolbar to merge the documents.

> If you're merging a large number of letters, you may want to click the Merge to Printer button instead. This button also performs the merge, but the letters are sent directly to the printer instead of appearing onscreen in a new document. (A document containing hundreds of merged letters would be hundreds of pages long, and if your computer doesn't have much memory, it may balk at the task of displaying the document onscreen.)

19

5. The merged letters appear in a document entitled *Form Letters1* (see Figure 19.14). Scroll down the document. The letters print on separate pages because Word separates them with next page section breaks. (If your main document is a multiple-page letter, the section break comes at the bottom of the last page of each letter.) Click the Print button in the Standard toolbar to print the letters.

FIGURE 19.14

The Form Letters document contains all your merged letters, separated by next page section breaks.

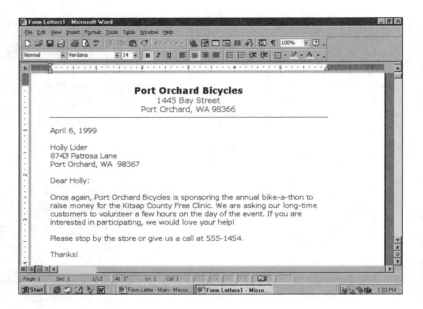

6. Close the *Form Letters1* document without saving it. (You don't usually need to save the merged letters because you can always run the merge again.) Then click the taskbar button of the main document to switch to it if necessary, and close it as well.

That's it! Everything else you can do with mail merge builds on the procedure you've just completed.

Running Future Merges

When you want to merge the same main document and data source in the future, just open the main document with the usual File, Open command, and click the Merge to New Document or Merge to Printer button in the Mail Merge toolbar. That's all there is to it.

If you want to merge an existing main document with a different data source than the one you used with it previously, you can attach a new data source. Open the main document, choose Tools, Mail Merge, and click the Get Data button.

Then, if you want to create the new data source from scratch, choose Create Data Source and continue with the steps described earlier in this hour to run the merge (starting with "Creating and Saving the Data Source").

If you want to attach an existing data source, click Open Data Source, select the data source in the Open Data Source dialog box, and click the Open button. Back in the Mail Merge Helper dialog box, click the Merge button, and then click the Merge button again in the Merge dialog box to run the merge.

> If you attach a data source that has different field names than the ones referenced in the merge fields in your main document, you'll get errors when you try to run the merge. To prevent this from happening, check the merge fields in your main document. If they don't match the data source, delete them and insert them again using the Insert Merge Field toolbar button (this button always displays the merge fields in the currently attached data source).

Editing Your Data Source

The easiest way to edit an existing data source is to open it through the main document to which it is attached.

To Do: Edit Your Data Source

Follow these steps to edit your data source:

1. Open the main document.
2. Click the Edit Data Source button at the far-right end of the Mail Merge toolbar to display the Data Form.
3. Edit the records. You can revise and delete existing records, and add new ones.
4. When you're finished, click OK.
5. Save the main document, and click Yes when Word asks whether you want to save the data source.

The one drawback to this method is that it's easy to forget to save the data source in step 5. If this feels risky and you want more control over saving the data source, you can open and edit your data source directly instead of using the Data Form.

Word actually stores your data source in a Word table. To view this table, click the View Source button in Data Form (refer to Figure 19.8), or choose File, Open and open your data source file.

In a data source table, each field is a column, and each record is a row (see Figure 19.15). Word provides the Database toolbar at the top of data source files to let you easily revise your data.

To Do

19

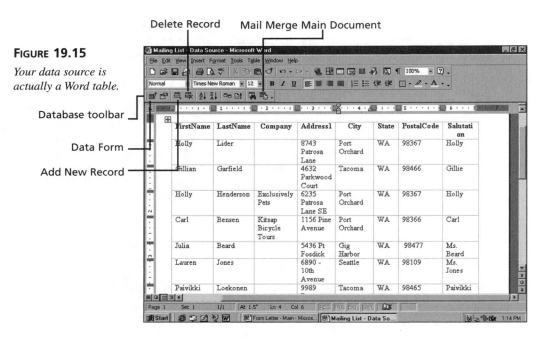

FIGURE 19.15

Your data source is actually a Word table.

Delete Record   Mail Merge Main Document

Database toolbar

Data Form

Add New Record

You can add or delete a record by adding a row and filling in the data for the record, or selecting the row that contains the record and deleting it. (If you need to review how to add and delete rows in a table, review Hour 16, "Columns and Tables.") However, it's a little faster to use the Add New Record and Delete Record toolbar buttons. When you click the Add New Record button, Word automatically adds a blank row at the bottom of the table. When you click the Delete Record button, Word deletes the row containing the insertion point.

If you like entering data through the Data Form better than typing it directly in the data source table, click the Data Form toolbar button. If you want to view the main document to which the data source is attached, click the Mail Merge Main Document toolbar button.

In Hour 16, you learned how to sort rows in a table. The Database toolbar provides the same Sort Ascending and Sort Descending buttons as those in the Tables and Borders toolbar. You can use them to sort your table by the field (column) in which you want the merged letters to appear the next time you run your merge. (You'll learn a faster way to sort your data source in the next hour.)

If you make changes in your data source table, remember to save it before closing.

Summary

You should now have a good overall feel for how to run a merge, although it will probably take a little practice to feel completely comfortable with the process. If you veer off the beaten path and get perplexed, come back to the procedure described here to solidify your understanding of the basic steps before continuing with the next hour.

Q&A

Q I put a merge field in the wrong place in my main document. How do I get rid of it?

A Delete a merge field just as you delete all other fields: Select it and press the Delete key.

Q I used the Merge to Printer button to merge a data source with hundreds of records, only to realize that the main document contained a typo. I wasted more paper than I want to admit. How can I avoid this in the future?

A One option if you're planning to use the Merge to Printer button to print a large number of letters is to create a small data source of only ten or so records. Merge your main document with that data source as a "test run." If everything looks okay, then merge the main document with your complete data source.

Q What is a catalog main document?

A It's like a form letter, but the records are not separated by next page section breaks, so information from multiple records can print on the same page. People usually use catalog main documents to create things such as membership directories and product catalogs.

19

HOUR 20

More on Mass Mailings

In the last hour, you learned the basic skills required to prepare and merge a
form letter. Here, you have a chance to broaden your mail-merge repertoire:
You learn how to merge envelopes and labels, how to sort merged records in
a particular order, and how to merge only a selected group of records in your
data source. In this hour, you will use the data source you created in your
mail-merge "trial run" in the last hour to practice the skills you learn here.

The highlights of this hour include

- Merging envelopes and labels
- Merging records in a particular order
- Merging only selected records

Merging Envelopes and Labels

Chances are that you usually need to print labels or envelopes to go with your form letters. When you merge addresses onto labels or envelopes, the five basic steps of performing a mail merge (described in the previous hour) stay the same. However, two aspects of the process are slightly different:

- The main document is a label or an envelope instead of a form letter.
- It's easier to merge labels and envelopes from the Mail Merge Helper dialog box than from the Mail Merge toolbar in the main document.

In the "Running Future Merges" section in the previous hour, you learned about one other situation in which you run the merge from the Mail Merge Helper dialog box—when you're attaching a different data source to the main document.

Before you practice these steps, note that if you have an envelope tray on your printer that holds a stack of envelopes, it will be much simpler for you to merge labels. (To merge envelopes without an envelope tray, you would have to feed each envelope manually.)

To Do: Merge Envelopes

Follow these steps to merge envelopes:

1. Start a new document, and save it with a name such as *Envelopes - Main*. This is your main document.
2. Choose Tools, Mail Merge to display the Mail Merge Helper dialog box.
3. Click the Create button under Main Document, and then choose Envelopes (see Figure 20.1).

FIGURE 20.1

Choose Envelopes to start setting up your main document.

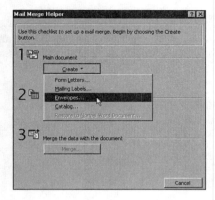

4. Word asks what document you want to use as your main document. Because you've already started the main document, click the Active Window button (refer to Figure 19.2 in Hour 19, "Generating a Mass Mailing").

5. Click the Get Data button, and then click Open Data Source. In the Open Data Source dialog box, navigate to and select your data source, and then click the Open button.

6. When Word informs you that it needs to set up the main document, click the Set Up Main Document button (see Figure 20.2).

FIGURE 20.2

The next step is to finish setting up your envelopes.

7. Word displays the Envelope Options dialog box (see Figure 20.3). Change the envelope size if necessary (see "Printing Envelopes" in Hour 7, "Viewing and Printing Your Documents"), and then click OK.

FIGURE 20.3

Use the Envelope Options dialog box to tell Word what kind of envelopes you're using.

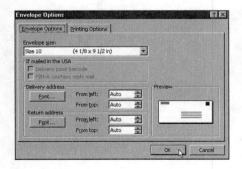

20

8. Word displays the Envelope Address dialog box to let you insert the merge fields in the envelope. Use the Insert Merge Field button to insert all the fields in their proper positions, pressing Enter at the end of the lines, and inserting commas and spaces as necessary (see Figure 20.4). Then click OK.

FIGURE 20.4

Insert the merge fields that you want to use on your envelope.

If you want to use a different font for your envelopes, select all the fields in the Sample Envelope Address area of the Envelope Address dialog box, right-click the selection, and click Font to display the Font dialog box. Select the desired font, and click OK. (In the future, you can revise the formatting of the envelope by opening and editing the main document directly.)

9. Word redisplays the Mail Merge Helper dialog box, and the Merge button is now active (see Figure 20.5). You'll also see the envelope appear in the Word window behind the dialog box. Click the Merge button to display the Merge dialog box.

FIGURE 20.5

The Merge button in the Mail Merge Helper dialog box becomes active after you've set up your main document.

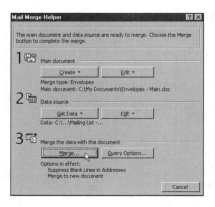

▼ 10. Be sure New Document is selected in the Merge To list, as shown in Figure 20.6, unless you want to merge directly to the printer, and click the Merge button to run the merge.

FIGURE 20.6

By default, Word merges to a new document.

11. Word merges the envelopes into a document named *Envelopesl*, shown in Figure 20.7 in Print Layout view. Scroll through the envelopes to make sure there aren't any problems, make sure your envelopes are properly loaded in your printer, and then print using the standard methods. You can close this document without saving it. (To generate the envelopes again, just rerun the merge.)

12. Click the taskbar button of the main document (your envelopes) if necessary to switch to it. Then save and close it.

▲

FIGURE 20.7

The merged envelopes appear onscreen after you run the merge.

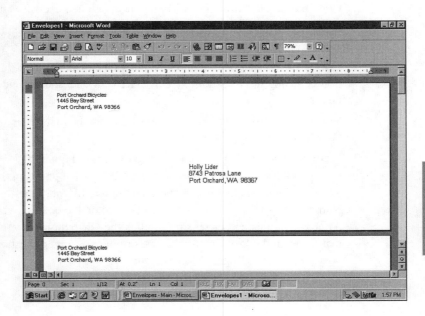

20

> Word automatically prints the return address on merged envelopes. If you want to omit it, use either of these rather clunky workarounds: Before you run the merge, choose Tools, Options. Click the User Information tab. Delete the address under Mailing Address, and click OK. After you've merged and printed the envelopes, retype the address in the User Information tab. Alternatively, you can click Cancel in step 9 to close the Mail Merge Helper dialog box before clicking the Merge button. Delete the return address from the main document, and choose Tools, Mail Merge to go back to the Mail Merge Helper dialog box. Click the Merge button and continue with the steps.

To Do: Merge Labels

Follow these steps to merge mailing labels. You'll notice that they are similar to the steps for merging envelopes:

1. Start a new document. This document will be your main document (a page of labels). Save it and give it a descriptive name such as *Labels - Main*.
2. Choose Tools, Mail Merge to display the Mail Merge Helper dialog box.
3. Click the Create button under Main Document, and choose Mailing Labels.
4. Word asks what document you want to use as your main document. Click the Active Window button.
5. Click the Get Data button, and then click Open Data Source. In the Open Data Source dialog box, navigate to and select your data source, and click the Open button.
6. When Word informs you that it needs to set up the main document, click the Set Up Main Document button.
7. Word presents the Label Options dialog box (see Figure 20.8). Use the Tray list to specify which printer tray will hold the labels. The options in this list are specific to your printer. Then select the product number of your labels in the Product Number list. (This number should be printed on the box that your labels came in.) After you've made your selections, click the OK button. (If you're printing labels that aren't in the Product Number list or you have other questions about this dialog box, refer to "Printing Labels" in Hour 7.)

FIGURE 20.8

Use the Label Options dialog box to tell Word about your labels.

8. Word displays the Create Labels dialog box to let you insert the merge fields telling Word where to place the information from the data source. Click the Insert Merge Field button, and insert the fields that you want to include in the address block (see Figure 20.9). When you're finished, click OK.

FIGURE 20.9

Insert the merge fields that you want to use on your labels.

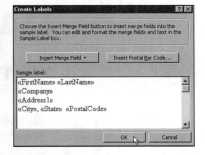

If you want to use a different font for your labels, select all the fields in the Sample Label area of the Create Labels dialog box, right-click the selection, and click Font to display the Font dialog box. Select the desired font, and click OK.

20

9. Word redisplays the Mail Merge Helper dialog box, and the Merge button is now active. Click the Merge button to display the Merge dialog box.

10. Be sure the option New Document is selected in the Merge To list, and click the Merge button to run the merge.

11. Word merges the labels into a document (a Word table, actually) named *Labels1*, shown in Figure 20.10 in Print Layout view. Scroll through the labels to see how they look. Make sure the label paper is in the proper paper tray, and print the labels using one of the standard printing methods. You can then close this document without saving it.

12. Click the taskbar button of the main document (your page of labels) if necessary to switch to it. Then save and close it.

FIGURE 20.10

The merged labels appear onscreen after you run the merge.

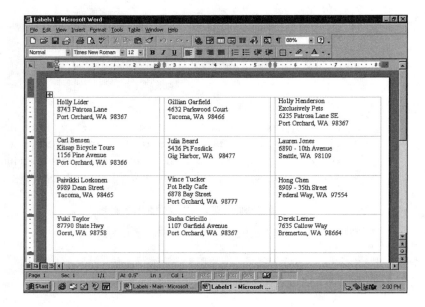

If you notice any problems with your merged envelopes or labels, close the Envelopes or Labels document without saving it and fix the problem in either the main document or the data source. The main document will be open after you run the merge (click its taskbar button to switch to it). To edit the data source, click the Edit Data Source button at the right end of the Mail Merge toolbar in the main document.

You don't have to repeat these same steps each time you want to merge the same main document (your envelopes or labels) with the same data source in the future. All you need to do is open the main document and click the Merge to New Document button in the Mail Merge toolbar.

Sorting Records in a Merge

Sometimes you have to print your merged documents in a particular order. For example, you might want to print your form letters in alphabetical order, or, if you're doing a bulk mailing, you might need to print labels in zip code order. Word allows you to sort the records in the data source before running the merge.

You can sort using up to three fields. So you could, for example, sort your records in zip code order, within zip code by last name, and within last name by first name.

To Do: Sort the Records in a Merge

1. Follow steps 1–9 in the steps for merging envelopes or labels in the preceding section to display the Merge dialog box.

> If you want to sort records when merging a form letter, open the form letter main document, and click the Merge button in the Mail Merge toolbar (see Figure 20.11) to display the same Merge dialog box.

FIGURE 20.11

From a main document, you can click the Merge toolbar button to get to the Merge dialog box.

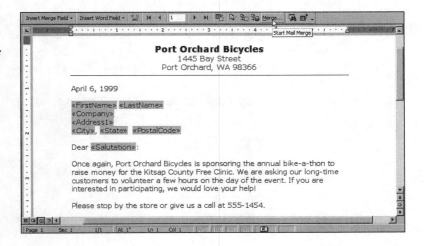

2. Word displays the message No query options have been set in the lower-left corner of the Merge dialog box (see Figure 20.12). This message will change as soon as you define a sort order. Click the Query Options button to display the Query Options dialog box. (You can also get to the Query Options dialog box by clicking the Query Options button in the Mail Merge Helper dialog box.)

20

FIGURE 20.12

Click the Query Options button to define a sort order for your merge.

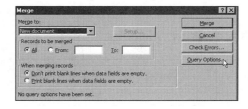

3. Click the Sort Records tab, if it isn't already in front.

4. Display the Sort By list, and click the field you want to use for the sort. To further refine the sort, display the first Then By list, and select the field you want to sort on when Word finds more than one record containing the same value in the first sort field. Then use the second Then By list to define a third field to sort on. In the example shown in Figure 20.13, Word will sort all the records by city, within the same city by last name, and within the same last name by first name. When you've defined the sort order, click the OK button to return to the Merge dialog box.

FIGURE 20.13

You can sort on up to three fields.

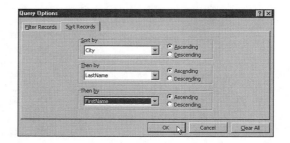

5. The Merge dialog box now displays the message Query options have been set. If you want to merge directly to the printer, choose Printer in the Merge To list. Otherwise, leave the default setting of New Document, and click the Merge button to perform the merge.

The merged documents (form letters, envelopes, or labels) are sorted in the order you defined. In Figure 20.14, the labels are sorted first by city, then by last name, and then by first name.

FIGURE 20.14

These labels are sorted by city, last name, and then first name.

Derek Lerner	Hong Chen	Julia Beard
7635 Callow Way	8909 - 35th Street	5436 Pt Fosdick
Bremerton, WA 98664	Federal Way, WA 97554	Gig Harbor, WA 98477

Yuki Taylor	Carl Bensen	Sasha Ciricillo
87790 State Hwy	Kitsap Bicycle Tours	1107 Garfield Avenue
Gorst, WA 98758	1156 Pine Avenue	Port Orchard, WA 98367
	Port Orchard, WA 98366	

Holly Henderson	Trudy Henderson	Holly Lider
Exclusively Pets	2113 Sidney	8743 Patrosa Lane
6235 Patrosa Lane SE	Port Orchard, WA 96782	Port Orchard, WA 98367
Port Orchard, WA 98367		

Annette Tucker	Vince Tucker	Lauren Jones
Pot Belly Café	Pot Belly Cafe	6890 - 10th Avenue
6878 Bay Street	6878 Bay Street	Seattle, WA 98109
Port Orchard, WA 98777	Port Orchard, WA 98777	

Gillian Garfield	Paivikki Loekonen	
4632 Parkwood Court	9989 Dean Street	
Tacoma, WA 98466	Tacoma, WA 98465	

The options you set in the Query Options dialog box remain in effect until you clear them. So if you establish a particular sort order and then add records to the data source, Word automatically sorts the new records into the existing sort order when you next run a merge. To clear the sort order so that new records are not automatically sorted, display the Query Options dialog box and click the Clear All button.

Filtering Records in a Merge

At times you may want to print form letters, labels, or envelopes for some of the people in your data source, but not others. If you want to send a form letter to clients who live in Seattle, for example, you can tell Word to merge only those addresses that contain *Seattle* in the City field. You indicate which group of records you want to merge by defining a *filter*.

To Do

To Do: Merge Only a Selected Group of Records

Follow these steps to merge only some of the records in your data source:

1. Follow steps 1–9 in the steps for merging envelopes or labels earlier in this hour. After clicking the Merge button in step 9, you see the Merge dialog box.

If you want to filter records when merging a form letter, open the form letter main document, and click the Mail Merge button in the Mail Merge toolbar to display the same Merge dialog box.

20

2. If no sort order or filter has been set, the message No query options have been set appears in the lower-left corner of the dialog box. This message will change as soon as you define a filter. Click the Query Options button to display the Query Options dialog box.

3. Click the Filter Records tab if it isn't already in front.

4. Display the first Field list, and click the field that you want to use to filter the records.

5. If necessary, display the list of choices under Comparison. If you want to look for records that contain one particular value in a field (94367 in the PostalCode field or *Port Orchard* in the City field, for example) you can leave this option set to Equal To.

> Many of the choices in the Comparison list are useful only for number or date fields. For example, if you have a Salary field and you want to send a letter to only those employees who earn over a particular amount, you would first select the Salary field in step 4. Then select Greater Than in the Comparison list, and type the cut-off salary in the Compare To box.

6. In the Compare To box, enter the value you are looking for. In Figure 20.15, Word will merge only records that contain *Port Orchard* in the City field. Click the OK button to return to the Merge dialog box.

FIGURE 20.15

Define your filter in the Filter Records tab.

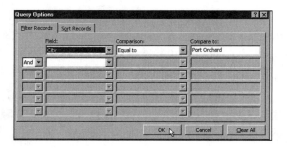

7. The Merge dialog box now displays the message Query options have been set. If you want to merge directly to the printer, choose Printer in the Merge To list. Otherwise, leave the default setting of New Document, and click the Merge button to perform the merge.

Word merges only the records that conform to the filter you defined. In Figure 20.16, only the records that have *Port Orchard* in the City field were merged. A sort order was also defined to sort by last name, and then by first name, so the results of this merge are both filtered and sorted.

FIGURE 20.16

Word merged only those records that contain Port Orchard in the City field.

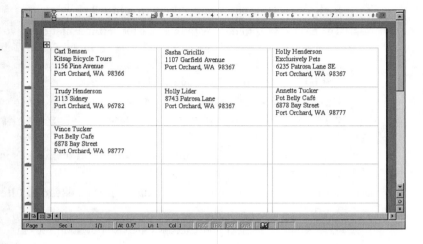

If you like, you can use additional rows in the Filter tab of the Query Options dialog box to set up a more complex filter. You have to connect multiple rules by selecting And or Or from the list at the left edge of the dialog box. If you aren't sure how to use And/Or operators, use the Office Assistant to search for topics related to "Rules for selecting data records from a data source."

Remember that the options you set in the Query Options dialog box remain in effect until you clear them. This is especially important to remember if you've set filter options, because until you clear the options (by clicking the Clear All button in the Query Options dialog box), you won't be able to merge all the records.

20

Summary

In this hour, you learned some key skills for fine-tuning your mail merges. You can now merge both your form letters and the envelopes or labels to go with them, and you can merge your documents in a particular order, or merge only a selected group of records. In the next hour, you explore Word's plentiful collaboration features.

Q&A

Q **The addresses on my merged labels are printing too close to the left edge of each label. How can I move them in a little?**

A The easiest way to do it is to increase the left indentation of your labels. Open the main document (your page of labels), choose Table, Select, Table to select the entire table, and then choose Format, Paragraph. Increase the setting in the Left text box under Indentation, and click OK.

Q **I'm using an Access table for my data source. If I want to sort my merged documents, do I sort the records in Access or follow the steps under "Sorting Records in a Merge"?**

A If you're using an Access table, it's easiest to sort the records in Access before running the merge in Word.

Q **Can I use an Access query as my data source instead of filtering the records in Word?**

A Yes. When you select your Access database (an .mdb file) in the Open Data Source dialog box and click Open (refer to the tip at the end of the "Creating and Saving the Data Source" section in the previous hour), Word enables you to choose which table or query in the database you want to use as your data source.

PART VIII

Collaboration and Integration

Hour

HOUR 21

Collaborating on Documents

Now that networks and email are commonplace, companies are equipped to let people collaborate on documents without printing them out. For example, you can write the rough draft of a document and send it to a colleague for review. This person edits the document onscreen and then sends it to a second person, who adds more revisions before emailing the document back to you. After you receive the edited copy, you incorporate your colleagues' suggestions and finalize the document. In this hour, you learn how to use Word's collaboration tools and a few related features that come in handy when working on documents with other people.

The highlights of this hour include

- Using the highlighter to call attention to text
- Inserting comments in a document
- Tracking the changes made to a document
- Protecting your document from revisions

- Saving multiple versions of a document
- Ensuring that your Word documents are compatible with older versions of Word

Using the Highlighter

Word's highlight feature lets you mark up your document onscreen just as you would use a highlighter pen to mark up a printed document. Highlighting is designed for use on documents that you'll edit onscreen, but it will also print out. If you don't have a color printer, highlighting prints in a shade of gray.

To Do: Highlight Text

To use the highlighter, follow these steps:

1. Click the down arrow to the right of the Highlight button on the Formatting toolbar, and click the color that you want to use in the palette that appears (see Figure 21.1).

Highlight

FIGURE 21.1

You can choose among many highlighter colors.

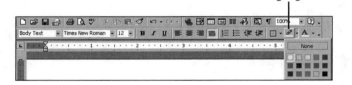

2. The I-beam takes on the shape of a highlighter pen. Drag across the text that you want to highlight, and then release the mouse button.
3. The text is now highlighted with the color you chose (see Figure 21.2). Highlight any other text you like, and then click the Highlight button again to turn the feature off.

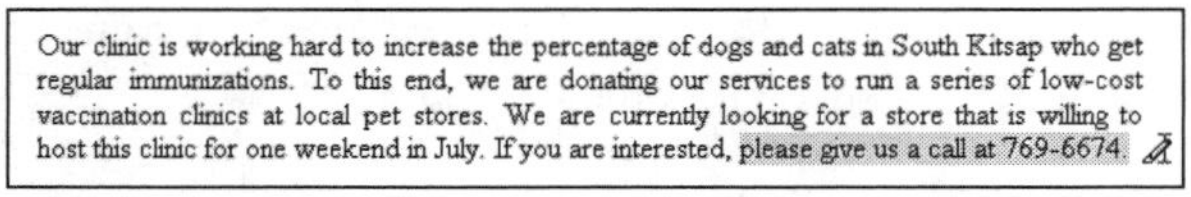

FIGURE 21.2

Highlight text to call attention to it.

> Our clinic is working hard to increase the percentage of dogs and cats in South Kitsap who get regular immunizations. To this end, we are donating our services to run a series of low-cost vaccination clinics at local pet stores. We are currently looking for a store that is willing to host this clinic for one weekend in July. If you are interested, please give us a call at 769-6674.

The Highlight button shows the color that you most recently selected from the palette. If you want to use that color, click the button itself in step 1 instead of choosing a color in the palette.

> Another way to apply highlighting is to select the text and then click the Highlight button (or display the palette and choose a different highlight color).

To remove highlighting, select the text, display the Highlight palette, and choose None.

Working with Comments

You may, at times, want to write notes in a document (either to yourself or to other authors) that don't print out. Word's Comment feature lets you add comments that reference particular blocks of text, and track comments from multiple authors.

If you work extensively with comments, you'll appreciate the buttons in the Reviewing toolbar (choose View, Toolbars, Reviewing), shown in Figure 21.3.

FIGURE 21.3

The Reviewing toolbar contains buttons for working with comments.

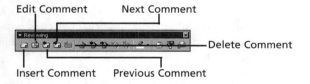

Edit Comment Next Comment

Delete Comment

Insert Comment Previous Comment

To Do: Insert a Comment

To add a comment to a document, follow these steps:

1. Select the text that you want to comment on.

2. Click the Insert Comment button in the Reviewing toolbar. (You can also choose Insert, Comment or press Alt+Ctrl+M.)

3. Word highlights the text you selected, opens the comment pane at the bottom of the document window, and inserts a reference mark for the comment in the document and in the comment pane. Type your comment in the comment pane (see Figure 21.4).

4. Click the Close button at the top of the comment pane.

To Do

21

FIGURE 21.4

Type your comment about the highlighted text in the comment pane.

Comment pane ———

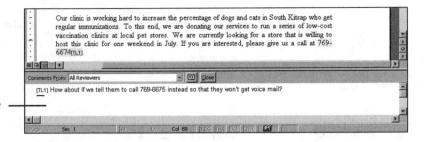

The reference mark is made up of your initials and a sequential number. It is formatted as *hidden text*, so it appears onscreen only when the comment pane is showing or the Show/Hide button in the Standard toolbar is turned on. The dotted underline under reference marks (see the reference mark [TL1] in Figure 21.4) just indicates that it's hidden text.

Word closes the comment pane. When the Show/Hide button is turned off, the reference mark is hidden from view. You can tell where the comment is, however, because the text that you selected is still highlighted.

To read a comment, rest the mouse pointer over the highlighted text. In a moment, a ScreenTip appears with the name of the person who wrote the comment and the comment itself (see Figure 21.5).

FIGURE 21.5

Rest your mouse pointer over high-lighted text to read the associated comment.

To move from one comment to the next in a document, click the Next Comment and Previous Comment buttons in the Reviewing toolbar.

To edit your comments, click the Edit Comment button in the Reviewing toolbar (or right-click the highlighted text of any comment and choose Edit Comment in the context menu). Word opens the comment pane to let you revise the comment text. When you are finished, click the Close button at the top of the comment pane.

To delete a comment, click to the left of the comment and click the Delete Comment button in the Reviewing toolbar (or right-click the highlighted text and choose Delete Comment from the context menu).

Tracking Changes to a Document

The cornerstone of Word's collaboration features is *track changes*. This feature lets you track the revisions (insertions, deletions, and a few formatting changes) that are made to a document. When the feature is turned on, any text you insert in the document is displayed in color with an underline. Text you delete is shown in color with strikethrough. If more than one person edits a document, each person's changes show up in a different color. When you are ready to finalize a document, you can go through and accept or reject each tracked change.

As you work with tracked changes, you may want to use the buttons in the Reviewing toolbar, as shown in Figure 21.6.

Previous Change   Accept Change

FIGURE 21.6

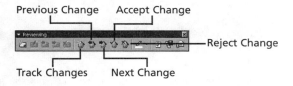

Reject Change

The Reviewing toolbar contains buttons for working with tracked changes.

Track Changes   Next Change

Tracking Your Changes

To turn track changes on (or off), click the Track Changes button in the Reviewing toolbar. The TRK indicator in the status bar at the bottom of the Word window is dark when track changes is turned on. (You can also double-click the TRK indicator, press Ctrl+Shift+E, right-click the TRK indicator and choose Track Changes from the context menu, or choose Tools, Track Changes, Highlight Changes, and mark or clear the Track Changes While Editing check box.)

After you've turned on track changes, revise your text as you normally do. If more than one person has edited a document and you want to see who made a particular change, rest your mouse pointer over the revision. A ScreenTip appears that lists the name of the person who made the edit, and the date on which it was made (see Figure 21.7).

21

FIGURE 21.7

When you rest your mouse pointer over a tracked change, Word tells you who made the change and when.

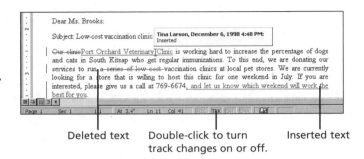

Deleted text   Double-click to turn   Inserted text
track changes on or off.

One of the advantages of using track changes is that you can hide the changes to see how the text would flow if you accepted all of them. To do so, choose Tools, Track Changes, Highlight Changes to display the Highlight Changes dialog box (see Figure 21.8), clear the Highlight Changes on Screen check box, and click OK.

FIGURE 21.8

Clear the Highlight Changes on Screen check box to hide the tracked changes.

Figure 21.9 shows the same text as you saw in Figure 21.7, but the tracked changes are hidden. Hiding changes does not turn off the track changes feature. If you like, you can edit the document while changes are hidden, and Word continues to track your edits. When you next mark the Highlight Changes on Screen check box, you will see all the revisions you made when changes were visible and when they were hidden.

FIGURE 21.9

Hiding tracked changes is a great way to see how the text would read if the changes were all accepted.

Dear Ms. Brooks:

Subject: Low-cost vaccination clinic

Port Orchard Veterinary Clinic is working hard to increase the percentage of dogs and cats in South Kitsap who get regular immunizations. To this end, we are donating our services to run vaccination clinics at local pet stores. We are currently looking for a store that is willing to host this clinic for one weekend in July. If you are interested, please give us a call at 769-6674, and let us know which weekend will work the best for you.

Understanding the Colors of Tracked Changes

By default, Word assigns a different color to each person (*author*) who edits a document. To see how this works, choose Tools, Options to display the Options dialog box, and click the Track Changes tab (see Figure 21.10).

FIGURE 21.10

The Track Changes tab of the Options dialog box lets you change the settings for track changes.

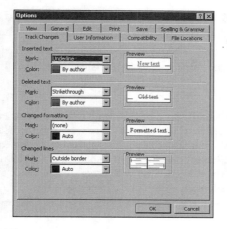

For the colors to work properly, you have to use the default setting of By Author in the Color lists under Inserted Text and Deleted Text. You can't choose a particular color for your revisions; when you edit a document with track changes turned on, Word assigns you the next available color in its color palette. If you choose a specific color in the Color lists, all authors' edits will appear in that color, which defeats the purpose of using track changes.

Helping Word Recognize Different Authors

Word recognizes the different authors who work on a document by checking the name that's listed in the Name text box in the User Information tab of the Options dialog box (choose Tools, Options), as shown in Figure 21.11.

FIGURE 21.11

Make sure your user information is current before using track changes.

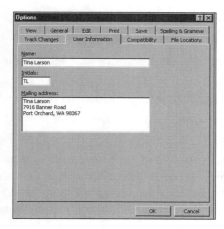

21

Before you use track changes, you should check the User Information tab and make sure that your name is entered correctly. If it isn't and you revise a document with track changes turned on, other people who review the document after you will assume that your edits were made by whoever happens to be listed in the User Information tab.

If you start editing a document on your computer, and then move to a different computer that has someone else's name in the User Information tab, Word assumes that the edits you made after switching computers were made by a different person, and it displays these revisions in a different color. If you share a computer with other people, make sure to update the User Information tab before using track changes.

In some cases, you may need to edit a document twice. If you want your edits on separate passes to appear in different colors, change the name in the User Information tab before you begin your second pass. For example, you could enter *Tina Larson (first pass)* in the User Information tab before beginning your first pass, and then change it to *Tina Larson (second pass)* before beginning your second pass.

Accepting and Rejecting Tracked Changes

When you have finished editing a document with track changes, you need to go through and decide whether to accept or reject each of the revisions. If you accept an insertion, the inserted text becomes part of the document. If you accept a deletion, the text is removed.

To Do: Accept and Reject Tracked Changes

Follow these steps to accept or reject the changes in a document:

1. Press Ctrl+Home to move to the top of the document.
2. Click the Next Change button in the Reviewing toolbar to find and select the next change.
3. Click the Accept Change or Reject Change toolbar button.
4. Click Next Change again, and continue accepting or rejecting changes until Word informs you that it found no tracked changes in the document.

You can also accept and reject changes in the Accept or Reject Changes dialog box. Choose Tools, Track Changes, Accept or Reject Changes, click the Find buttons to move from one change to the next, and click the Accept or Reject buttons to accept or reject them. One advantage of using this dialog box is that it lists the author and date of each change as you're reviewing the document. Another advantage is that it includes Accept All and Reject All buttons, which you can use to accept or reject all of the changes in a document without reviewing them one by one.

Protecting Documents from Being Revised

You might want to keep your document (or template) from being revised by other people. If you turn on this type of protection, other people can open and edit your document, but they can't overwrite the original document with their revised version. Instead, they are prompted to save the edited document under a different name and/or location.

To Do: Protect Your Document from Revisions

To protect your document from revisions, follow these steps:

1. With the document onscreen, choose File, Save As.

2. Click the Tools button at the top of the Save As dialog box, and click General Options.

3. In the Save dialog box (see Figure 21.12), type a password in the Password to Modify text box. Passwords can be up to 15 characters long, and they are case sensitive.

FIGURE 21.12

Type a password up to 15 characters long in the Password to Modify text box.

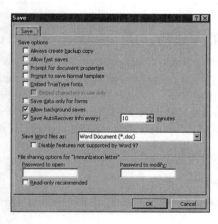

4. Click OK.

5. Retype the password in the Confirm Password dialog box, and click OK again to return to the Save As dialog box.

6. Finish saving the document.

The next time you open the document, the Password dialog box appears (see Figure 21.13). If you know the password to modify the document, you can enter it and click OK. Otherwise, you have to click the Read Only button to open the document.

FIGURE 21.13

Type the password and click OK if you want to modify the document.

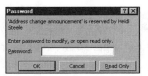

If you open the document as a read-only file, the label [Read-Only] appears in the title bar to remind you that if you revise the document, you will have to save the edited document under a new name.

> If you enter a password in the Password to Open text box (refer to Figure 21.12), the user can't even open the document without the password. The Read-Only Recommended check box is the lightest level of protection. If you mark it, Word suggests that the user open the document as a read-only file, but doesn't require him/her to do so. (You would most likely use this check box instead of requiring either type of password.)

Saving Different Versions of a Document

If you need to create several versions of the same document (several versions of your résumé, perhaps), you might want to keep them all in one place under the same filename instead of saving them as separate documents. Word's versioning feature lets you save multiple versions of a document under the same name. For each version, Word stores information about who created it, when it was created, and a brief description of it.

To Do: Save a Version of a Document

To save a version of a document, follow these steps:

1. Open the document, and revise it to create the version that you want to save.
2. Choose File, Save As.
3. Click the Tools button at the top of the Save As dialog box, and click Save Version.
4. In the Save Version dialog box, type a brief comment about the version that's onscreen (see Figure 21.14).

FIGURE 21.14

Describe the version of the document you're saving in the Save Version dialog box.

5. Click OK.

When you later want to open a particular version of a document, first open the document, and then choose File, Versions to display the Versions dialog box (see Figure 21.15). This dialog box lists any versions of the document that you have saved with the versioning feature. Select the one that you want to work with, and click the Open button.

FIGURE 21.15

Choose the version you want to open in the Versions dialog box.

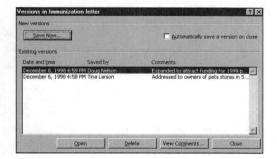

Making Your Word Documents Compatible with Earlier Versions of Word

Word 2000 saves files in the same format as Word 97, so someone who is using Word 97 can open your Word 2000 documents without converting them. By the same token, you can open Word 97 documents in Word 2000 with no conversion process. However, Word 2000 does have some features that are not supported by Word 97. If you want to be sure that your documents will look the same in Word 97 as they do in Word 2000 (perhaps most of the people in your office are still using Office 97), you can tell Word 2000 to disable all the features that Word 97 does not support.

21

To Do: Disable Word 2000 Features Not Supported by Word 97

1. Choose Tools, Options.
2. Click the Save tab (see Figure 21.16).

FIGURE 21.16

Use the Save tab to disable features not supported by Word 97.

3. Mark the Disable Features Not Supported by Word 97 check box.
4. Click OK.

Word 2000 does not save files in the same format as Word 6.0 or Word 95 (Word 7.0). If you want to give a document to someone who is using one of these versions of Word, you need to save it in the Word 6.0/95 format. To do so, choose Word 6.0/95 in the Save As Type list at the bottom of the Save As dialog box. When you open a Word 6.0 or Word 95 file in Word 2000, it automatically converts it to Word 2000 format for you.

Summary

Collaborating on documents with other people has plenty of rewards, but it can be frustrating if you lose track of who made what changes when. Word's collaboration features can bring some semblance of order to an essentially messy process. Now that you know what features Word has to offer, you'll be better able to decide whether and how you and your colleagues might work on Word documents as a team.

Q&A

Q **Can we use track changes and comments together?**

A Yes. It works just fine to insert comments when track changes is turned on. If you do, each person's comments appear in the comment pane in the color assigned to that person's revisions. When track changes is on, Word treats comments as inserted text, so you can easily remove them when you're accepting and rejecting changes by "rejecting" the associated insertions.

21

HOUR **22**

Using Data from Other Office 2000 Applications in Your Word Documents

Chances are, you acquired Word as a part of Office 2000. If Word is the only Office application you use, no problem—there's nothing wrong with ignoring Word's siblings. If, however, you do use other Office applications and want to use data from them in your Word documents, you'll learn some useful techniques in this hour. (Even if you bought Word 2000 as a standalone program, you may still want to skim this hour to learn general principles related to integrating Windows applications.) Keep in mind that you can integrate Office applications in many ways—this hour does not discuss all of them. Rather, it uses Excel and PowerPoint to introduce a few methods that you can use as a jump-off point for further exploration.

The highlights of this hour include

- Inserting linked data from an Excel worksheet in your Word document

- Embedding data from Excel in your Word document
- Exporting a PowerPoint presentation to a Word document
- Adding an individual PowerPoint slide to a Word document

Inserting Data from Excel Worksheets

If you want to insert data from an Excel worksheet, you can, of course, copy it into a Word document with the Copy and Paste commands. (Select the desired cells in Excel, issue the Copy command, switch to the Word document, click at the desired location, and issue the Paste command.)

When you use this method, Word puts the Excel data in a table, which you can format and modify with the techniques you learned in Hour 16, "Columns and Tables." In Figure 22.1, the data in the table was pasted from an Excel worksheet.

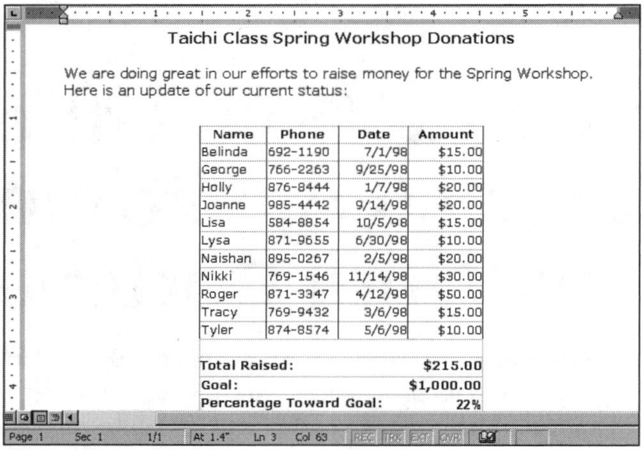

FIGURE 22.1

Excel data that you insert with the Copy and Paste commands appears in a Word table.

This method has two drawbacks. First, the Excel formulas are converted to plain numbers, so they won't update if you revise any of the numbers in the table. Second, no link exists between the pasted data in the Word document and the original data in the Excel worksheet, so revising the data in Excel does not update it in Word.

One way to avoid these shortcomings is to *link* the pasted data in Word to the original data in the Excel worksheet. Then whenever you update the data in Excel, it is automatically updated in the Word document.

To Do: Insert Linked Data from an Excel Worksheet

To Do

To insert linked data from Excel into your Word document, follow these steps:

1. In Excel, select the cells that you want to copy to Word and issue the Copy command.

2. Switch to the Word document, move the insertion point to the desired location, and choose Edit, Paste Special to display the Paste Special dialog box.

3. Mark the Paste Link option button, choose Microsoft Excel Worksheet Object in the list in the middle of the dialog box (see Figure 22.2), and click OK.

FIGURE 22.2

Choose Paste Link in the Paste Special dialog box to link the pasted data with the original data in Excel.

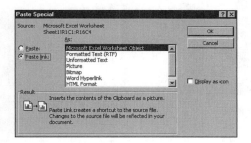

4. Switch back to Excel, press Escape to turn off the marquee around the copied data, and then close the workbook.

The data is pasted into Word as an object, as shown in Figure 22.3 (note the selection handles around the data). You can use techniques you learned in Hour 18, "Manipulating Graphics," for working with pictures, drawing objects, and WordArt to position the Excel object in your document and format its appearance.

FIGURE 22.3

Your Excel data appears as an object in Word.

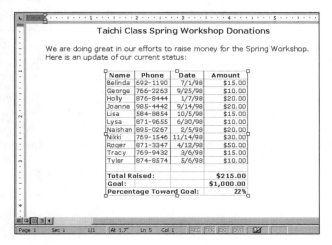

22

To edit the data in Excel, double-click the linked object in your Word document. In a moment, the associated worksheet opens in Excel with the linked cells selected (see Figure 22.4). When you revise the data in Excel, it is instantly updated in the Word document. (You can't edit the linked data in the Word document.)

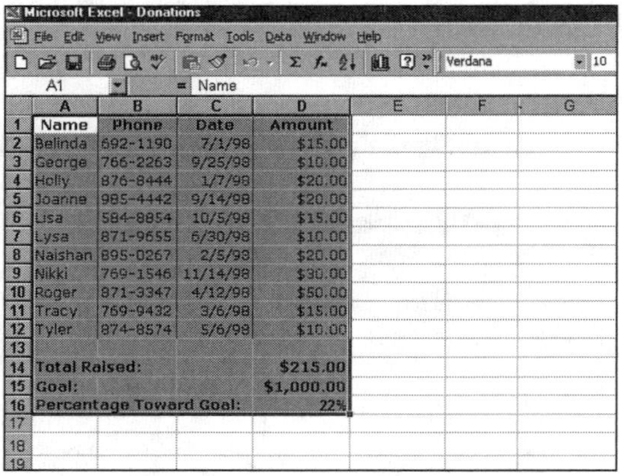

FIGURE 22.4

Any changes you make to the data in Excel are immediately reflected in your Word document.

If the Word document isn't open when you revise the data in Excel, it's updated the next time you open the document.

If you move the Excel workbook that contains the source data, you have to tell Word where to find it. To do so, select the linked object in Word, and choose Edit, Links to display the Links dialog box. Click the Change Source button, navigate to and select the workbook in the Change Source dialog box, click the Open button, and then click OK.

Another option is to *embed* the Excel data in your Word document. When you use this technique, double-clicking the embedded object displays the Excel interface—menus, toolbars, and so on—within the Word window, so you can use Excel controls to revise the data without ever leaving Word. When you embed data, the Excel data "lives" in the Word document and is not linked to original data in Excel. When you edit the data in the Word document, it does not get updated in the original Excel worksheet, and vice versa.

To Do: Embed Data from an Excel Worksheet

To embed Excel data in a Word document, follow these steps:

1. In Excel, select the cells that you want to copy to Word and issue the Copy command.

2. Switch to the Word document, move the insertion point to the desired location, and choose Edit, Paste Special to display the Paste Special dialog box.

3. Mark the Paste option button, choose Microsoft Excel Worksheet Object in the list in the middle of the dialog box (see Figure 22.5), and click OK.

FIGURE 22.5

Choose Paste in the Paste Special dialog box to embed the pasted data in the Word document.

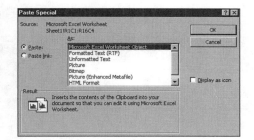

4. Switch back to Excel and press Escape to turn off the marquee around the copied data, and then close the workbook.

Just as when you link the data, embedded data is pasted into Word as an object. However, Word responds differently when you double-click an embedded object. Instead of displaying the source data in Excel, it displays the Excel interface in the Word window, as shown in Figure 22.6.

FIGURE 22.6

You can use Excel controls to edit the embedded data in your Word document.

Excel controls

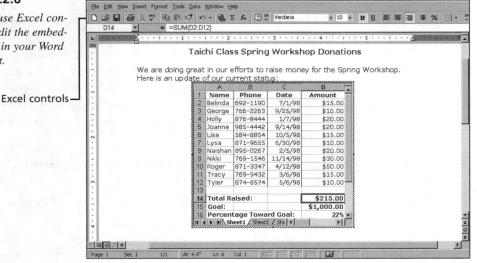

You can also start an embedded Excel worksheet from scratch in your Word document instead of beginning with data that you pasted from an existing Excel worksheet. To do so, click the Insert Microsoft Excel Worksheet toolbar button in the Standard toolbar, drag across the number of cells that you want to start out with in the drop-down grid (see Figure 22.7), and release the mouse button.

Insert Microsoft Excel Worksheet

FIGURE 22.7

To start an empty embedded Excel worksheet, use the Insert Microsoft Excel Worksheet button in the Standard toolbar.

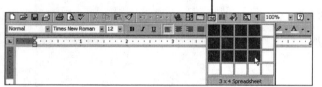

Inserting PowerPoint Presentations and Slides

You can, of course, use a no-frills approach to getting text and slides from a PowerPoint presentation into your Word documents. Simply use the standard Copy and Paste commands. If you go this route, your pasted data maintains no link to the source data in the PowerPoint presentation. If you want to get a little fancier, try one of the other options described here.

If you want to export a PowerPoint presentation to a Word document, you can issue a command in PowerPoint to create a *write-up* of the presentation in Word. When you do this, you can choose to paste the slides in the write-up as embedded or linked objects. If you embed the slides in the Word document, they are not linked with the original presentation. When you double-click one of the slides, the PowerPoint interface appears in the Word window. In contrast, if you link the slides, double-clicking one of them in the Word document opens the source slide in PowerPoint. If you edit the slide in PowerPoint, you can tell Word to update it in the write-up.

To Do: Export Your PowerPoint Presentation to a Word Document

Follow these steps to create a write-up of your presentation in a Word document:

1. Start PowerPoint and open the presentation (see Figure 22.8).

▼

FIGURE 22.8

Open the presentation that you want to export to a Word document.

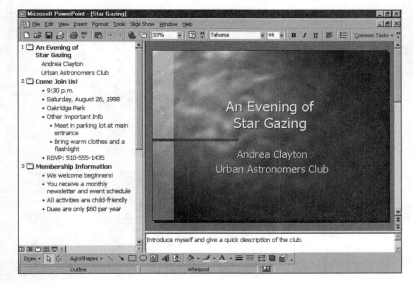

2. Choose File, Send To, Microsoft Word to display the Write-Up dialog box (see Figure 22.9).

FIGURE 22.9

The Write-Up dialog box lets you choose how you want the presentation to look in Word.

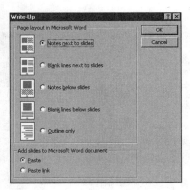

3. Mark the option button under Page Layout in Microsoft Word that most closely matches the layout you want to use.

4. Mark the Paste option button to embed the slides in the Word document, or mark the Paste Link option button to link them to the original slides in PowerPoint.

▲   5. Click OK.

In a moment, the presentation appears in a Word document (see Figure 22.10). Note that Word has placed it in a table, so you can modify its appearance with all the techniques you learned in Hour 16.

FIGURE 22.10

The PowerPoint presentation appears in a Word table.

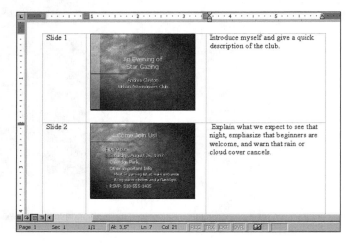

If you chose Paste in step 4, each slide in the Word document is an embedded object. When you double-click a slide, the PowerPoint controls appear in the Word window, as shown in Figure 22.11.

FIGURE 22.11

You can use PowerPoint controls to edit the embedded slides in your Word document.

PowerPoint controls

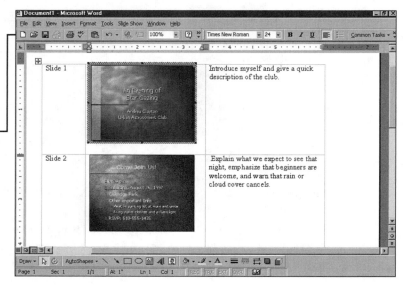

22

If you chose Paste Link in step 4, each slide in the Word document is an object that's linked to the original slide in PowerPoint. To edit the slide in PowerPoint, double-click it in the Word document. Unlike linked Excel data, linked PowerPoint slides don't update instantly when you modify them in PowerPoint. To update the slide object in Word, select it and press F9.

To ensure that the most current version of the slides always prints, choose File, Print in Word, click the Options button in the lower-left corner of the Print dialog box, mark the Update Links check box, and click OK. Back in the Print dialog box, click OK to print or Close to close the dialog box without printing.

If you don't have a color printer, your write-up will look better if you switch to view the presentation in black and white (choose View, Black and White) in PowerPoint before issuing the File, Send To, Microsoft Word command.

In addition to exporting an entire PowerPoint presentation to a Word document as a write-up, you can also insert individual slides, either as linked or embedded objects.

To Do: Insert a PowerPoint Slide

Follow these steps to insert an individual slide in your Word document:

1. In PowerPoint, choose View, Slide Sorter to switch to Slide Sorter view.

2. Right-click the slide that you want to copy to Word, and choose Copy.

3. Switch to the Word document, move the insertion point to the desired location, and choose Edit, Paste Special to display the Paste Special dialog box.

4. Mark the Paste or Paste Link option button, and choose Microsoft PowerPoint Slide Object in the list in the middle of the dialog box (see Figure 22.12), and click OK.

FIGURE 22.12

Choose Paste or Paste Link in the Paste Special dialog box to embed or link the pasted slide in the Word document.

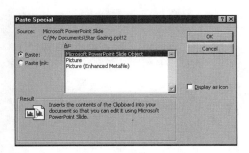

If you have linked PowerPoint slide objects (either in a write-up or individual slides) in a Word document, make sure to select the slides and press F9 to update them if you edit the source slides in PowerPoint. Also, you need to tell Word if you move the source presentation. Select all the slide objects in the Word document (see "Selecting Multiple Images" in Hour 18) and choose Edit, Links to display the Links dialog box. Select the objects in the Links dialog box (drag to select more than one), click the Change Source button, select the source presentation in the Change Source dialog box, click Open, and then click OK.

Summary

In this hour, you learned how to enhance your Word documents with material that you created in other Office applications. The general principles of linking and embedding are not limited to Office 2000—they apply to all Windows applications. Feel free to take ideas from this hour and experiment with bringing data from other applications into your Word documents, or bringing Word text into documents in other applications. In the next hour, you learn how to use Word for email.

Q&A

Q I have a lot of linked objects in my Word document, including PowerPoint slides, Excel data, and so on. Can I update them all at once?

A Yes. If you want to make sure that all linked objects in your document are current, select any one of them and choose Edit, Links. In the Links dialog box, drag over all of them to select them, click the Update Now button, and click OK. (You can also select all the objects and press F9.)

HOUR **23**

Using Word for Email

Word 2000 has powerful email capabilities that make it a snap to compose and send email from the Word window. One advantage of using Word for email is that you don't have to leave the Word window and launch your email program to send a message. Another advantage is that if you create email messages in Word, you can take advantage of Word features such as automatic spell and grammar checking, AutoCorrect, tables, and bulleted and numbered lists. In this hour, you learn three ways to use Word for email.

The highlights of this hour include

- Understanding the system requirements for sending email from Word
- Sending an email message from Word
- Sending a Word document as an email message
- Sending a Word document as an attachment to an email message
- Sending any document as an email attachment

What Programs Do You Need to Create Email in Word?

To create and send email messages from Word, you have to have Outlook 2000, which comes with most editions of Office 2000, or Outlook Express 5.0, which comes with Internet Explorer 5.0. And Outlook 2000 or Outlook Express 5.0 must be set as your default email editor. Outlook Express 5.0 was used for the examples in this hour.

To send Word documents as attachments to email messages, you aren't limited to Outlook 2000 and Outlook Express 5.0 for email. Most newer email programs work just fine.

Creating and Sending an Email Message from Word

It's just as easy to send an email message from Word as it is from an email program.

 Email messages that you create in Word are sent in HTML format, so your recipient has to have an email program that can read HTML-formatted messages. (Most newer email programs can.)

 ## To Do: Create and Send an Email Message from Word

To create and send an email message from Word, follow these steps:

1. Choose File, New to display the New dialog box, click the General tab, and double-click the Email Message icon (see Figure 23.1).

FIGURE 23.1

Double-click the Email Message icon in the New dialog box to start an email message in Word.

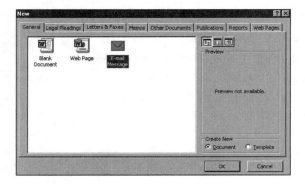

2. The new message opens in the Word window. You use the *email header* to address the message. Type the recipient's email address in the To text box, and optionally enter the email address of a person to whom you want to copy the message in the Cc text box. Then type a subject in the Subject text box, and type the email message itself in the blank area below the Subject line (see Figure 23.2).

FIGURE 23.2

Fill in the email header information and type your message.

Click to send the email message.

Email header

23

3. When you're finished, click the Send button to send the message.

If you're not currently online, you may see a message prompting you to go online or informing you that your computer is connecting. After you're online, the message is sent out. The Word window remains open so you can continue using it.

When your recipient receives the message, it will look something like the one shown in Figure 23.3.

FIGURE 23.3

This message was composed and sent from Word.

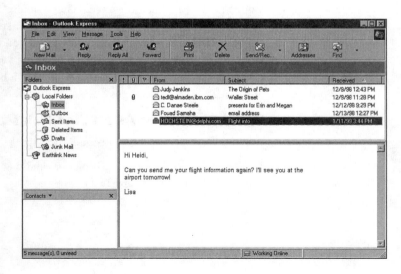

If you want to create a signature that Word automatically appends to all email messages that you send from Word, choose Tools, Options, click the General tab, and click the Email Options button. In the Email Signature tab of the Email Options dialog box, type a title for the signature at the top of the dialog box, type and format the signature itself in the bottom half of the dialog box, and click the Add button (see Figure 23.4). Then click OK.

FIGURE 23.4

Optionally create a signature that Word adds to all your email messages.

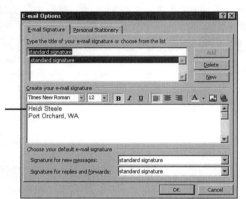

This signature will be appended to all messages you create in Word.

Sending a Word Document As Your Email Message

You can send a Word document as an email message. When you use this method, Word converts the document to HTML format before sending it out. Unlike the traditional plain-text email messages, HTML messages can contain graphics and other types of formatting, so your Word document retains much of its formatting when it is sent. The recipient does not have to have Word to read the message, although he or she does need an email program that can read HTML messages.

To Do: Send a Word Document As an Email Message

Follow these steps to send a Word document as an email message:

1. Create a new Word document or open an existing one, and then click the Email button in the Standard toolbar (see Figure 23.5).

▼ To Do

23

FIGURE 23.5

Click the Email button to send the active document as an email message.

Email

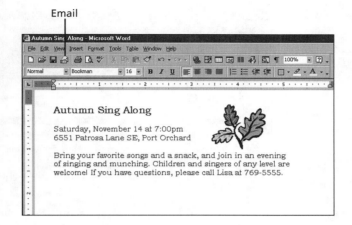

2. An email header appears at the top of the document. Fill in the header information. By default, Word uses the document name as the subject of the message, but you can change it to whatever you like.

3. Click the Send a Copy button to send a copy of the document as an email message (see Figure 23.6). (The original document remains in its current location on your computer system.)

FIGURE 23.6

Fill in the email header and send the message.

Click to send the Word document as an email message.

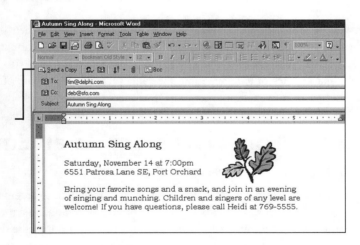

Your computer connects to the Internet if you aren't already online, and then Word sends the message. When the recipient receives it, it looks something like the message shown in Figure 23.7. Note that the graphic image in the document has shifted to the left margin. HTML can't duplicate Word formatting exactly, so you can expect the HTML-formatted message to differ somewhat from the original Word document.

FIGURE 23.7

This message is a Word document, now format-ted in HTML.

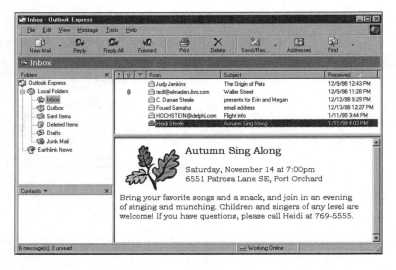

If you want to see what your document will look like on the receiving end, follow these steps, but send a test copy of the message to yourself (put your own email address in the To text box) before sending it to the recipient.

After you've sent a Word document once as an email message, when you open it in the future and click the Email toolbar button, all the email header information that you filled in the last time you sent the document is already inserted for you. This makes it easy to send regular updates of a document to the same recipient. (You can, of course, change the email header information to send the document to someone else if you need to.)

Sending a Word Document As an Email Attachment

Another option is to send a Word document as an attachment to an email message. The advantage of doing this is that the formatting of your Word document remains intact. However, the recipient must have Word 97 or Word 2000 to open the document.

To Do: Send a Word Document As an Email Attachment

Follow these steps to attach a Word document to an email message and send it:

1. Create or open the document that you want to send as an email attachment.
2. Choose File, Send To, Mail Recipient (As Attachment).

The Reviewing toolbar, discussed in the "Tracking Changes to a Document" section of Hour 21, "Collaborating on Documents," contains a Send to Mail Recipient (As Attachment) toolbar button. If this toolbar is displayed, you can click this button instead of using the File, Send To, Mail Recipient (As Attachment) command.

23

3. A message window in your default email program opens. Note that the attachment is listed in the Attach line in the Outlook Express 5.0 message shown in Figure 23.8 (your email program may use a slightly different label). Fill in the rest of the email header information, and type the email message itself. If your email program lets you send HTML messages, you can optionally modify the message formatting.

FIGURE 23.8

The Word document is attached to the email message.

Attached Word document

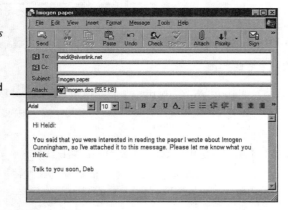

4. Click the Send button (or whatever button your email program provides for sending messages).

Your computer connects to the Internet if you aren't already online, and then Word sends the message and its attachment. Figure 23.9 shows a message with an attachment as it will appear on the receiving end. Most email programs use a paper clip icon to indicate that a message has an attachment. Use the command for saving an attachment in your email program (usually something like File, Save Attachments) to copy the attached Word document to a folder of your choosing on your computer or network. You can then open it in Word in the usual manner.

FIGURE 23.9

Most email programs use a paper clip to indicate that a message has an attachment.

The paper clip indicates an attached document.

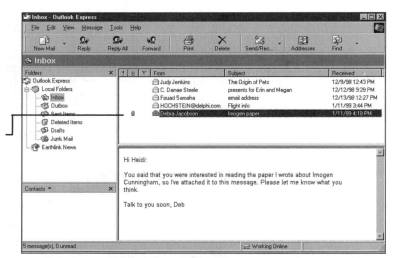

Sending Any Document As an Attachment to an Email Message

You aren't limited to attaching Word documents to email messages. If you create a message in Word, you can attach any document to the message, including Excel workbooks, PowerPoint presentations, or files created in other programs.

To Do: Attach a Document to an Email Message

Follow the steps in "Sending an Email Message from Word" or "Sending a Word Document As an Email Message" earlier in this hour, but in step 2, add this procedure:

1. Click the Attach File button in the email header (see Figure 23.10).

FIGURE 23.10

Click the Attach File button to attach any document to your email message.

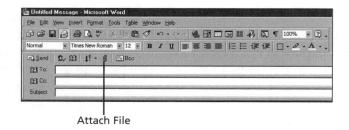

Attach File

2. In the Insert Attachment dialog box, navigate to and select the document that you want to attach. In Figure 23.11, the file is a PowerPoint presentation. Click the Attach button.

FIGURE 23.11

Select the file to attach in the Insert Attachment dialog box.

23

3. An Attach line now appears beneath the Subject line in the email header (see Figure 23.12). Attach any additional documents to the message if you like, and then finish the remaining steps in "Sending an Email Message from Word" or "Sending a Word Document As an Email Message" to complete and send the message.

FIGURE 23.12

The files you've attached to the message are listed in the Attach line.

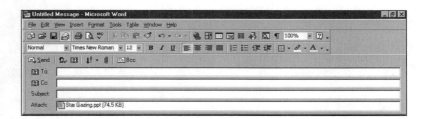

Summary

Word offers several convenient ways to create and send email without leaving the Word window. If you do a lot of email, at least one of the approaches explained in this hour will probably become an indispensable part of your repertoire. In the final hour of this book, you explore Word's Web page features.

Q&A

Q I want to send my message to more than one person. How do I do that?

A In the To box, type each person's email address, separated by commas.

Q I created a beautiful email message with fancy formatting, but when my friend received it, all the formatting had disappeared. What went wrong?

A The most likely problem is that your friend's email program can't handle HTML-formatted messages.

Q I added two signatures in the Email Options dialog box, one for business use and one for personal use. How can I switch between them?

A Word automatically inserts the signatures that are listed in the Signature for New Messages and Signature for Replies and Forwards lists at the bottom of the Email Options dialog box. To change the signature in a particular message you're composing, right-click it in the body of the message and choose the signature you want from the context menu that appears.

HOUR 24

Word and the Web

Word 2000 gives you a host of options for integrating Word and the Web. You can turn Word documents into Web pages, turn Web pages into Word documents, and create Web pages from scratch in Word. And if you are responsible for making Web pages accessible to other people on an intranet or Internet site, you can even handle this task from the Word window. In this last hour of the book, you get a sense of what you can accomplish when Word and the Web work as a team.

The highlights of this hour include

- Converting Word documents to Web pages
- Converting Web pages to Word documents
- Using Themes to create Web pages
- Making your Web pages available to others

Converting Word Documents to Web Pages

If you have information in a Word document that you want to let a large number of people read, you can convert the document to a Web page and then post the page on a Web site, the Internet, or your company intranet. Before you convert your document, however, check with your network administrator to see whether it's necessary. In some cases, you can put Word documents on company intranets without changing the document format at all.

To Do: Convert a Word Document to a Web Page

Follow these steps to save a Word document as a Web page:

1. Open the Word document that you want to convert or create a document now (see Figure 24.1).

FIGURE 24.1

Open the document that you want to convert to a Web page.

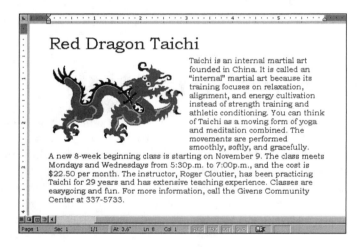

2. Choose File, Save As Web Page to display the Save As dialog box.

3. Optionally click the Change Title button to revise the title that will appear in the title bar for the page. Then specify a name and location for the page (see Figure 24.2), and click the Save button.

4. You may see a message such as the one shown in Figure 24.3 stating how Word will modify formatting that can't be rendered in a Web page. If you do, click the Continue button.

FIGURE 24.2

Choose a name and location for your Web page.

FIGURE 24.3

Word tells you it can't convert all the formatting in the Word document.

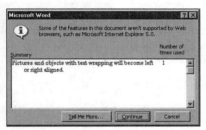

24

5. The newly converted Web page appears in the Word window (see Figure 24.4). Word automatically switches to Web Layout view (View, Web Layout) whenever it displays a Web page.

FIGURE 24.4

Word displays your Web page in Web Layout view.

Red Dragon Taichi

Taichi is an internal martial art founded in China. It is called an "internal" martial art because its training focuses on relaxation, alignment, and energy cultivation instead of strength training and athletic conditioning. You can think of Taichi as a moving form of yoga and meditation combined. The movements are performed smoothly, softly, and gracefully.

A new 8-week beginning class is starting on November 9. The class meets Mondays and Wednesdays from 5:30p.m. to 7:00p.m., and the cost is $22.50 per month. The instructor, Roger Cloutier, has been practicing Taichi for 29 years and has extensive teaching experience. Classes are easygoing and fun. For more information, call the Givens Community Center at 337-5733.

6. If you want to see what the page will look like when viewed in a browser, choose File, Web Page Preview.

7. Your browser opens and displays the Web page. In Figure 24.5, the Web page is displayed in Internet Explorer 5.0. Close your browser when you're finished viewing the page.

FIGURE 24.5

You can view your Web page in your browser to see how it will look to others.

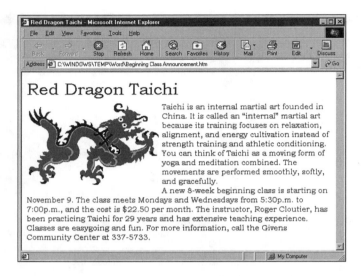

Converting Web Pages to Word Documents

Once in a while, you may want to save a Web page as a Word document. Perhaps you found a recipe on a Web site and want to edit the text in Word, or you discovered a Web page about woodworking and want to take advantage of Word's formatting and printing capabilities to spruce it up a bit. When you convert a Web page to a Word document, Word does its best to preserve the formatting in the page.

To Do: Convert a Web Page to a Word Document

Follow these steps to save a Web page as a Word document:

1. Display the Open dialog box, type the address for the Web page in the File Name text box, as shown in Figure 24.6, and click the Open button. (Make sure to include the `http://` at the beginning of the address in the File Name text box.)

2. Word prompts you to connect to the Internet if necessary, and then opens the Web page in the Word window (see Figure 24.7). Choose File, Save As to display the Save As dialog box.

3. Choose a location for the document, and type a name in the File Name text box.

▲ To Do

FIGURE 24.6

Type the complete address for the Web page in the File Name text box.

FIGURE 24.7

Word can display Web pages as well as Word documents.

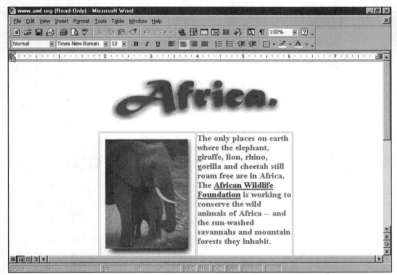

4. Display the Save As Type list and select Word Document (see Figure 24.8).

5. Click the Save button.

The Web page is saved as a Word document, and all the graphics are included in the document itself (see Hours 17, "Inserting Graphics, Drawing Shapes, and Creating Text Effects with WordArt," and 18, "Manipulating Graphics," if you need help working with them).

FIGURE 24.8

Choose Word Document in the Save As Type list to save the Web page as a Word document.

Step 1 in the previous steps describes how to open a Web page directly from the Internet. You could also use your browser to save the page to your hard disk, and then open it from your hard disk. If you use this latter method, make sure to select All Files in the Files of Type list in the Open dialog box so that the Web page will be visible. (By default, Word shows only Word documents in the Open dialog box.)

Creating Web Pages in Word

Word gives you a variety of ways to create Web pages—and you don't have to be a professional Web page designer to make them look good. In this section, you get a taste of creating a Web page from scratch. For practice, you'll create a "personal Web page" and use one of Word's many *themes* ("looks") to give the page some visual flair.

To Do: Create a Web Page Using a Theme

To create a Web page with a theme, follow these steps:

1. Choose File, New to display the New dialog box.

2. Click the Web Pages tab, click the Personal Web Page icon, and then click OK (see Figure 24.9).

3. The default Web page opens (see Figure 24.10). The hyperlinks under Contents (Work Information, Favorite Links, and so on) lead to locations in the same page. To make the page more visually appealing, choose Format, Theme.

▼

FIGURE 24.9

Select Personal Web Page to practice creating a Web page in Word.

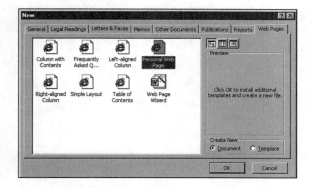

FIGURE 24.10

Word creates the Web page with plain formatting and placeholder text.

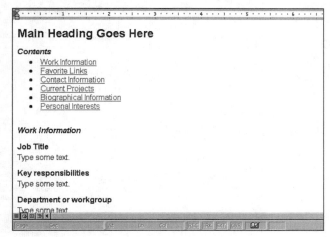

24

4. In the Theme dialog box, click a few themes in the Choose a Theme list. You can preview each theme in the Sample of Theme area. When you find one that you like, select it (see Figure 24.11) and click OK.

5. Word applies the theme to the Web page. Select all the placeholder text and replace it with your actual text (see Figure 24.12). Then save and close the page.

▲

> You can add hyperlinks to your Web page (or modify existing ones) in the same way that you do with Word documents. See "Inserting Hyperlinks" earlier in Hour 15, "Working with Long Documents."

FIGURE 24.11

Choose a theme that is visually appealing to you.

FIGURE 24.12

Replace the place-holder text with your content.

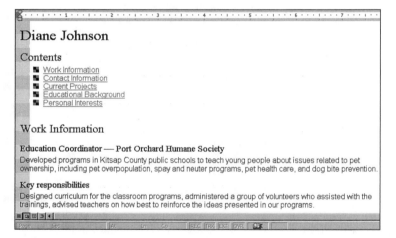

Making Your Web Pages Available to Others

To make your Web pages visible to others, you have to copy (*upload*) them to the Internet Web site or intranet site where they will "live." You can do this in the Save As dialog box. Choose File, Save As, and then click the Web Folders icon on the left side of the dialog box. If you see the location you want, select it and then click the Save button. If you don't see the right location here, you can specify the location yourself.

You typically upload pages to a Web or intranet site via a *protocol* called FTP, for File Transfer Protocol. So telling Word where you want to upload your Web pages involves defining an FTP location. You have to do this only once. From then on, you will be able to choose the FTP site in the Save As dialog box.

To Do: Define an FTP Location

Follow these steps to set up an FTP location for uploading your Web pages to a Web site on an intranet or the Internet:

1. Choose File, Save As, and then select Add/Modify FTP Locations in the Save In list (see Figure 24.13).

FIGURE 24.13

Use Add/Modify FTP Locations in the Save In list.

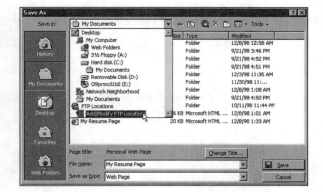

2. Word displays the Add/Modify FTP Locations dialog box. Type the name of the site in the Name of FTP Site text box. Most FTP sites begin with *ftp*. (If you aren't sure of the name, ask the system administrator at the site.)

3. If you don't have a personal account at the site, mark the Anonymous option button. If you do, mark the User option button, and enter your username and password. Then click the Add button to add the site to the list of FTP sites at the bottom of the dialog box (see Figure 24.14) and click OK.

FIGURE 24.14

Use the Add/Modify FTP Locations dialog box to tell Word about your FTP site.

> Many companies let people who don't have personal accounts log in to their FTP site as anonymous users. Anonymous users have access to only certain public areas of a site, and they may not be permitted to upload files at all.

4. The new FTP location now appears in the Save In list (and in the Look In list in the Open dialog box). Select it if necessary, and then click the Open button.

5. Word connects to the Internet (or your intranet) if you aren't already online, and displays the contents of the folders at the FTP site (see Figure 24.15).

FIGURE 24.15

The contents of the FTP site appear in the Save As dialog box.

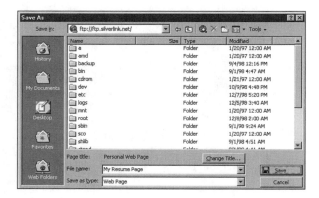

6. Navigate to the folder in which you want to save the Web page, type a name for it in the File Name text box (use all lowercase), and click the Save button.

Word saves your Web page at the FTP site. It is now in a location where other people can access it via their browsers. If you need help with this process, ask your network or system administrator.

Summary

In this last hour, you took a tour of Word's Web-related features. You now have the skills to create simple Web pages and make them available to your friends and coworkers.

Q&A

Q **I created a Web page in Word and put it on my Web site, and it looks really different in my friend's browser. What is going on?**

A Unfortunately, not all browsers interpret the underlying HTML code in Web pages the same way. You can expect some differences in how Web pages look in different browsers. Ideally, you should "test drive" your Web pages in several popular browsers before actually uploading them to a Web site.

Q **I'm creating my Web page in Word without using a theme, and I want to add a background color to the page. What command do I use?**

A Choose Format, Background, and click the desired color in the submenu that appears.

24

APPENDIX A

Modifying and Repairing Your Word Installation

Word, like other Office 2000 applications, has so many components that few people need to use *all* of them. For example, if you don't need to type mathematical equations in your Word documents, you will never need the Equation Editor, and if you don't have to read documents in an Asian language, you won't need Asian language support. For this reason, when you install Word using the default options, not all of it is automatically included. In this appendix, you learn how to install components when you need them, and remove ones you don't need. You also get some pointers on repairing Word if the installation starts behaving strangely.

Office 2000 comes in several different *editions*. Each edition contains a slightly different combination of Office applications. The examples in this appendix show the Premium Edition. You may have a different edition, such as the Standard Edition, Professional Edition, or Small Business Edition. The dialog boxes you see when you modify your installation will reflect this difference, but the steps remain the same.

Installing on First Use

If you perform the default installation of Word, the most widely used features are installed on your hard disk. Features that you are less likely to need are installed on "first-use" basis. (This is also referred to as *install on demand*.) The first time you issue a command to use the feature, you are prompted to insert the Office 2000 CD or provide access to the network location that contains your Office 2000 setup files. The necessary files are copied to your hard drive, and the feature becomes part of your installation.

Word informs you when a feature is set to install on first use. For example, in Figure A.1 the Contemporary Resume template is selected in the New dialog box, but instead of showing a preview of it in the Preview area, Word displays a message telling you to click OK to install it.

FIGURE A.1

You will see a message such as the one shown on the right side of the New dialog box when the feature you want to use is not yet installed.

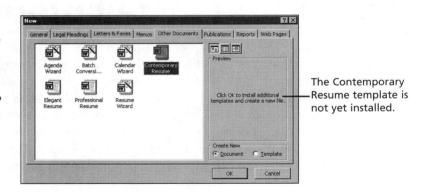

The Contemporary Resume template is not yet installed.

To show you another example, if you choose Format, Theme to display the Theme dialog box and select a theme that isn't yet installed, Word displays a message telling you to click the Install button to install it (see Figure A.2).

FIGURE A.2

The Theme dialog box lets you know when the selected theme is not yet installed.

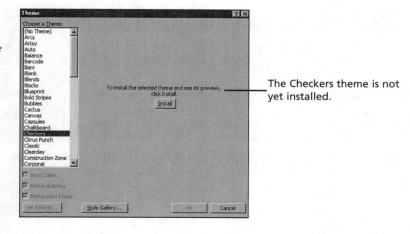

The Checkers theme is not yet installed.

When you see messages such as those shown in Figures A.1 and A.2 and click OK or Install, Office checks whether it can access the Office 2000 CD or the network location that contains your Office setup files. If it can, it automatically starts installing the feature. If it can't, it displays a message box such as the one shown in Figure A.3.

FIGURE A.3

If necessary, Word prompts you to provide access to your Office 2000 setup files.

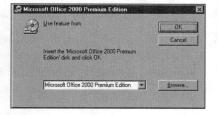

If you receive this type of prompt, put your CD in the CD-ROM drive (or use the Browse button to select the network location that contains your Office setup files), and click OK. Word begins copying the necessary files to your hard disk. During this process, it displays the message box shown in Figure A.4.

FIGURE A.4

A message box informs you of the status of the installation.

As soon as the installation is complete, the feature becomes available.

Modifying Your Word Installation

When you install Office 2000 with the default options, the setup program decides whether and how to install each Word component. As you learned in the preceding section, the most important components are installed on your disk. Others are installed on first use. Some even less frequently used components are not installed at all. You can change the installation option for any component to one of these four settings:

- Run from My Computer—The component is installed to your hard disk.
- Run from CD (or Run from Network)—Office finds the files required by the component on your Office 2000 CD or on the network each time you need it.
- Installed on First Use—The first time you use the component, Office installs it to your hard disk.
- Not Available—The component is not installed.

To change the installation option for a Word component, run the Office 2000 setup program. When the setup program detects that Office 2000 is already installed on your computer, it automatically runs in *maintenance mode* to let you modify your installation.

To Do: Modify Installation Options for Word Components

Follow these steps to modify the installation options for Word's various components:

1. Make sure Word is closed, use Windows Explorer or My Computer to display the contents of your Office 2000 CD (or navigate to the network location that contains your Office 2000 setup files), and double-click the file Setup.exe. In a few moments, the Microsoft Office 2000 Maintenance Mode dialog box appears (see Figure A.5).

2. Click the Add or Remove Features button to display the Microsoft Office: Update Features dialog box.

You can also get to the Microsoft Office 2000 Maintenance Mode dialog box by double-clicking the Add/Remove Programs icon in the Control Panel. In the Install/Uninstall tab of the Add/Remove Programs Properties dialog box, select Microsoft Office 2000, and click the Add/Remove button.

FIGURE A.5

The Microsoft Office 2000 Maintenance Mode dialog box appears if Office 2000 is already installed on your computer.

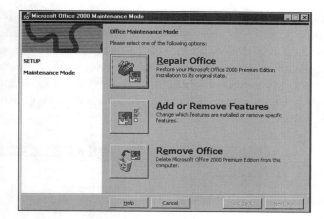

3. Click the plus sign next to Microsoft Word for Windows to expand its contents, as shown in Figure A.6. (The plus sign changes to a minus sign as soon as the item is expanded.) The icons on gray backgrounds indicate items that contain subcomponents; icons on white backgrounds represent components that don't contain any subcomponents. (In Figure A.6, for example, the Help and Wizards and Templates items contain subcomponents.) The specific icon for each component indicates the current installation option. In Figure A.6, the Office Tools component of Office 2000 is expanded in addition to Microsoft Word for Windows so that you can see examples of all the different icons.

The Microsoft Word for Windows item is expanded.

FIGURE A.6

Expand the Microsoft Word for Windows item to display the categories of Word components.

Installed on First Use

Run from CD

Run from My Computer

Not Available

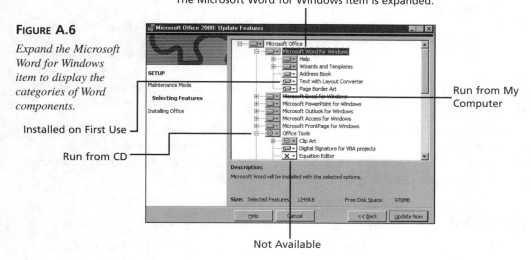

A

4. To change the installation option for a component, click its icon, and then click the desired option in the menu that appears. If you want to install the component to your hard disk, choose Run from My Computer. To run it from your CD (or network), choose Run from CD (or Run from Network). To remove it from your installation, choose Not Available. In Figure A.7, the installation option for résumé wizards and templates will be changed from Installed on First Use to Run from My Computer.

FIGURE A.7

Click the desired installation option in the menu that appears.

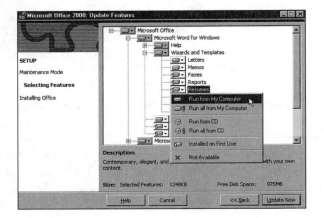

If the item that you're changing contains subcomponents, you can choose Run All from My Computer to install the item and all of its subcomponents to your hard disk. If you want to run the item and all of its subcomponents from your Office 2000 CD (or the setup location on your network), choose Run All from CD (or Run All from Network).

5. Change the installation options for any other components that you like, and then click the Update Now button to begin the maintenance setup process.

As Office is modifying your installation, it displays a progress bar to show its current status. When it's finished, it displays a message box informing you that setup was completed successfully. Click OK. Depending on how you modified your Office 2000 installation, you may be prompted to restart your computer.

Repairing Word

If Word seems to be misbehaving and you are not able to figure out what's going by looking in the help system or asking a knowledgeable friend, it could be that some of the files that Word requires to operate properly are either damaged or missing. All the Office 2000 applications come with a Detect and Repair feature, which can, in some cases, track down these types of problems and fix them. Keep in mind that Detect and Repair does not fix damaged Word documents or templates; it repairs only program files.

To Do: Detect and Repair Problems with Your Word Installation

Follow these steps to try to fix problems with your Word installation:

1. Close any other open applications, and choose Help, Detect and Repair in the Microsoft Word window.

2. The Detect and Repair dialog box appears to inform you that Office will fix any problems that it finds with your Word installation (see Figure A.8). Click the Start button to begin the process.

> Mark the Restore My Shortcuts While Repairing check box if your Word shortcut is missing from the Start menu and you want to restore it.

FIGURE A.8

Click the Start button to begin the detect and repair process.

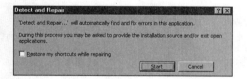

3. You may see a dialog box asking you to close Word and any other applications that are still open (see Figure A.9). If this happens, close the applications, and then click the Retry button.

FIGURE A.9

You may be prompted to close applications, including Word.

4. Office completes the detect and repair process. When it's finished, you are prompted to restart the computer. Click the Yes button.

▲

If you prefer, you can also repair your Word installation by running the Office 2000 maintenance setup program and clicking the Repair Office button (refer to Figure A.5).

INDEX

A

DEMCO